Hidden from the Holocaust

Hidden from the Holocaust

*Stories of Resilient Children
Who Survived and Thrived*

KERRY BLUGLASS

FOREWORD BY ANTHONY CLARE

PRAEGER

**Westport, Connecticut
London**

Library of Congress Cataloging-in-Publication Data

Bluglass, Kerry, 1935–
    Hidden from the Holocaust : stories of resilient children who survived and thrived / Kerry
Bluglass ; foreword by Anthony Clare.
        p. cm.
    Includes bibliographical references and index.
    ISBN 0–275–97486–3 (alk. paper)
        1. Jewish children in the Holocaust—Biography.   2. Holocaust Survivors—Biography.
3. Holocaust survivors—Psychology.   4. World War, 1939–1945—Jews—Rescue.
5. Holocaust, Jewish (1939–1945)—Personal narratives.   6. Righteous Gentiles in the
Holocaust.   I. Title.
D804.48.B55   2003
940.53'18'083—dc21   2003053556

British Library Cataloguing in Publication Data is available.

Library of Congress Catalog Card Number: 2003053556
ISBN: 0–275–97486–3

First published in 2003

Praeger Publishers, 88 Post Road West, Westport, CT 06881
An imprint of Greenwood Publishing Group, Inc.
www.praeger.com

Printed in the United States of America

The paper used in this book complies with the
Permanent Paper Standard issued by the National
Information Standards Organization (Z39.48–1984).

10 9 8 7 6 5 4 3 2 1

Copyright Acknowledgments

The author and publisher gratefully acknowledge permission for use of the following material:

"Speak, You Also," by Paul Celan. From *Poems of Paul Celan: Revised & Expended*, translated
by Michael Hamburger. Translation copyright © 1972, 1980, 1988, 2002. Reprinted by permission of Persea Books, Inc. (New York). Also published by Anvil Press Poetry in 1989.

Paul Celan, Von Schwelle zu Schwelle © 1955 Deutsche Verlags-Anstalt GmbH, Stuttgart.

John Rivkin for the photograph of Dr. Henry Birnbaum and Mrs. Charlotte Weber, previously published in the Jewish Chronicle.

Testimony from the archive of Bettine M*, Survivors of the Shoah Visual History Foundation. For information or to support: www.vhf.org.

For Bob, Charles, Mandy, Amanda, Luke, and Maya

Contents

Foreword

The destructive impact of particularly terrible traumatic events on the emotional health of those who have been exposed to them and have physically survived them has, over recent years, been the subject of intense study. Such events include war, serious accidents, sieges, kidnapping, violent assault and rape, major terrorist bombings, as well as massive and unexpected accidents of nature including earthquakes, firestorms, volcanic eruptions, and floods. Most of us have little difficulty grasping the notion that such stresses can cause catastrophic mental reactions. Indeed, when asked, the general public repeatedly endorses traumatic life events—violence, bereavement, loss, betrayal, man-made and so-called natural disasters—as a possible cause of psychiatric illness over all other causes. It has even been suggested that one of the better consequences of war has been the greater awareness of the role played by traumatic events in the origins of serious psychological disturbance. Not surprisingly, therefore, what was arguably the most catastrophic and traumatic horror of the last century—the Holocaust—is acknowledged as a most potent cause of terrible trauma and suffering for those at the center of its violence who survived it.

As they live out their lives, these survivors tell us much, not only about the terrible deeds human beings have done and do to each other but also what it is that enables the victims of such abuse to survive. This book contains the narratives of many such survivors. In their accounts there is an acute sense of the strength of the culture from which so many of them emerged. These are individuals who as children inhabited a world in which relationships were valued, education was valued, marital and family life was valued, being not only Jewish or Christian but German, Austrian,

French, or whatever was valued. These were not rootless, disconnected, fragmented individuals but members of an educated, spiritual, and integrated society. The irony of the twentieth century's most horrendous event is that Aryan supremacy identified as marginal, peripheral, and subhuman people who were so much part and parcel of their culture, locality, and society, so law abiding, so respectful, so trusting and believing in civilized and democratic values.

While these virtues ill-prepared them for the emergence of the malevolent perversion that was Nazism, it did provide them with the means to endure its consequences. In their recollections of and reflections on their experiences, few if any emerge as cynical or disillusioned. Psychiatrists are familiar with depression, demoralization, and despair in the face of abuse, betrayal, and exploitation. Most of these survivors, however, retain a belief in the essential goodness of mankind and a life-enhancing view of human existence. Most of them, when even quite young and vulnerable, displayed astonishing maturity. Indeed some made such good emotional attachments with foster and adoptive parents that reconnection after the war with their biological parents proved very painful and difficult.

It does seem likely that the long-term psychological impact of a particularly stressful event is in part at any rate determined by how the survivor coped during the course of it. Survivors of such diverse trauma as hostage sieges and bank raids often emerge enhanced by the knowledge that under such pressures they remained cool, showed clear judgment, did not panic, and even exhibited qualities of leadership. Many of the individuals interviewed by Dr. Bluglass did indeed handle themselves remarkably well in crisis. Discovering such resources undoubtedly served them well in the post-Holocaust world. Whether they were quite young children or adults at the time, isolated, separated from their families and in alien situations, they dug into their own psychological reserves, drew on the strength of their religious and cultural beliefs, and survived. Their accounts go a long way to justifying their own belief in the essential strength, goodness, and resilience of human beings, and this book serves as a testimony to their courage.

Anthony Clare, M.D.
Professor of Clinical Psychiatry, Trinity College Dublin
Medical Director, St. Patrick's Hospital, Dublin
Broadcaster, BBC radio series, "In the Psychiatrist's Chair"
Dublin 2003

Acknowledgments

My very grateful thanks to Professor Anthony Clare for so generously contributing a Foreword to this book. Without the inspiration of Irena Milewska, I would never have embarked on this work. Without Nicole David's remarkable networking abilities and enthusiasm, I would have been unable to meet and interview a substantial number of Hidden Children. The wise observations of her husband, Ernest David, have been an additional bonus.

Serendipity played a part; a chance conversation with my Dutch friend Professor Johannes Huber and Dr. Anat Schatz of Tel Aviv led me simultaneously to three Dutch Hidden Children. Johannes's mother, who had recently died at an advanced age, rescued and hid many Jews, among them Bert Woudstra (Chapter 5) and his mother. Another of Mrs. Huber's sons married a Hidden Child. Anat's mother and aunt were both hidden in Holland and her aunt, Anita Waisvisz (Chapter 5), now lives in Israel.

The staff at the Wiener Library, London, in particular, and at the British Library and Warwick University have been unfailingly helpful and patient. Rowenna Davis, Information Officer at the Royal College of Psychiatrists, London, was extremely quick and efficient. Advice from historians Sir Martin Gilbert, CBE; Bill Williams of the University of Manchester; and Rob Perks of the British Library has been encouraging and practical. Several early discussions with Dr. Susie van Marle about the project led me to George E. Vaillant's approach to "mature defenses" in relation to coping skills. I am indebted also to my friends Dr. Gaby Glassman, Dr. Henry Greenspan, and Dr. Sula Wolff; to the late Dr. Irene Bloomfield and Dr. Paul Valent for information, help, and constructive comments and for reading relevant portions of the typescript in draft, as did Bill

Williams. Professor Robert Krell most generously offered to read the whole typescript at a late stage and gave me invaluable advice. His transatlantic friendship and support have been a delight. Elise Tibber not only talked to me but also kindly lent me her master's dissertation, "Jewish Resistance Activities in Belgium 1940–45" (University College, London, 1990).

Dr. Wendy Whitworth, omniscient powerhouse at the center of the Remembering for the Future Holocaust Conference 2000, has been an untiring source of information and wisdom.

Dr. Maurice Vanderpol, a recent correspondent by the miracles of electronic communication, shares my interest in the importance of resilience.

Alina Jarvin in Australia and Dr. Mira Reym Binford have provided me with helpful information and friendship.

Bernice Krantz and others in the Visual History Foundation project "Survivors of the Shoah" have been generous with time, help, and encouragement. The Staff at Beth Shalom, Nottinghamshire, have been a source of sustained support.

I also owe an enormous debt of gratitude to all those who have so generously and patiently talked to me about their lives in hiding and their losses and achievements; they have taught me so much.

The advice of many survivors, scholars, friends, and specialists in other professional fields, which impinge on the content of this book, has been invaluable. In particular, historians, illustrators, photographic specialists, and professional colleagues who share my interest in the effects of trauma and loss, of attachment, childhood adaptation, and resilience have been kind enough to read drafts of the typescript and give helpful advice. My original London editor at GPG, Elisabetta Linton, was the first person who really understood and encouraged the project, and I would like to thank all the team at Greenwood who took over from her for their huge support and patience in answering my queries. Support and encouragement from friends and family have been constant. Lastly, but certainly not least, I thank my husband, Professor Robert Bluglass, CBE, who believed in the importance of this work from an early stage, and in its final ones, and who has been highly involved in helping me with the technical details of preparing the typescript. His tolerance of my long hours spent in preparation is matched only by his ability to unscramble a refractory computer when this has proved beyond me. I hope that he will not find life dull when the book is completed and that he will appreciate having more of my time and attention. No spouse could have been more encouraging and supportive (or cooked more restorative minestrone).

SPEAK, YOU ALSO

Speak, you also,
speak as the last,
have your say.

Speak—
But keep yes and no unsplit.
And give your say this meaning:
Give it the shade.

Give it shade enough,
give it as much
as you know has been dealt out between
midnight and midday and midnight.

Look around:
look how it all leaps alive——
where death is! Alive!
He speaks truly who speaks the shade.

But now shrinks the place where you stand:
where now, stripped by shade, will you go?
Upward. Grope your way up.
Thinner you grow, less knowable, finer.
Finer: a thread by which
it wants to be lowered, the star:
to float farther down, down below
where it sees itself gleam: in the swell
of wandering words.

Paul Celan (1920–1970) "Poet, Survivor, Jew"

Translation by Michael Hamburger, first published by Anvil Press Poetry, 1988. The original German version appears in Appendix A of this volume.

Introduction

Ten years before my work in this field began, I was privileged to meet a charming French woman in Brussels where I was presenting a paper at a conference on bereavement. Like me she was a professional in the field. There was nothing in her manner or in her perspective on life to distinguish her from other professional participants.

At that time my knowledge of the psychological effects of the Holocaust was like that of many professionals, a rather stereotyped perception of the courageous but often terribly traumatized individual. This was augmented by the clinical experience of a number of my older colleagues who had treated mentally ill survivors or their families. I had some limited experience of my own in treating the wife of an extremely damaged camp survivor whose wartime trauma had influenced his ability to form stable and lasting relationships.

So I learned with some surprise, in due course, that my friend, as she later became, was not really French but Polish and that her life story as it unfolded throughout our acquaintance seemed "stranger than fiction." As a psychiatrist, one learns to be astonished by very little in the narratives of troubled people suffering from personal and psychological pain. Events, whether of the magnitude of pebbles or boulders, have clearly contributed to persisting difficulties in their path through life, for which they seek insight and resolution. Here, however, was a person who, although as she freely acknowledged, had suffered greatly but was quite obviously now *bien dans sa peau* (a term that seems much more satisfactory and expressive than the English "well-adjusted") and certainly not someone in need of treatment. Indeed her own personal strengths had liberated her to attend to and sustain the needs of others in quite demanding professional settings, such as terminal/palliative care and bereavement, and to extend her skills to teaching and training others all over France.

For a time I urged her to document her own story of survival, but she was too modest to agree, feeling perhaps too close to the content to be completely objective.

A few years later, in 1993, by which time she had gradually recounted many more of her experiences, I heard a BBC Woman's Hour broadcast by Nicole David highlighting the stories of other "Hidden Children" now living in England, most of which had not been previously heard or published. By this time I was inspired to learn more, impressed by the achievements and adjustments of those whose lives were described in the broadcast. It seemed to me that, as professionals, we often pursue accounts of pathology or sickness following trauma at the expense of the recognition of resilience and comparative health, so we may fail to record and validate successful outcomes when "bad things happen to good people" (Kushner, 2001).

Through further enquiry I obtained the help of Nicole David and discovered that this small group in England was a part of a much larger one of successful child survivors of the Holocaust, many of whom had been hidden in one way or another, like my friend, in many of the countries of Europe. There were many reasons, explored in this book and discussed in Chapter 2, for the delay in recognition, let alone the documenting, of the experiences of young children emerging from their clandestine lives between 1939 and 1945, certainly a much later time than descriptions of the experiences of adult survivors (Krell, 2001).

Other stereotypes, myths, and assumptions were inaccurate and unhelpful. The general public in England, familiar with *The Diary of Anne Frank* (1989) and her fate (Gies, 1987), probably had little knowledge of the statistics of Jewish children in hiding, the proportions who survived, and other details of the various European countries under Nazi Occupation until the painstaking work of Gilbert (1987) and Gill (1988), and more recently the astonishing educational efforts of the Smith family at Beth Shalom Holocaust Center in Nottinghamshire, England, and the opening of the Holocaust Exhibition at the Imperial War Museum in London in 2000.

There is a remarkable contrast between the adaptation and day-to-day functioning of some of these psychologically robust, emotionally resilient people who had experienced such traumatic events and that of a clinic population, individuals with no traumatic wartime experience, but whose lives are sufficiently affected in one way or another as to require psychiatric help. It seemed worthwhile to draw attention and interest to these aspects of survival.

This led me to embark on a series of interviews in 1997. It was not very clear at the outset what form these would take nor whether they could or would be published. The more I listened to the men and women whose early lives are recorded in these pages, the more important it seemed to recognize their achievements and, indirectly, the achievements of others like them. I hoped that their narratives could be collected unadorned with little comment or interpretation, although it became clear that, for publication, some background and discussion would be necessary. The original raw, unedited accounts so often recounted—it is interesting that I used this word in an early proposal for this book some time before I was aware of the work of Henry Greenspan (1998)[1] and his own emphasis on that word—in such a matter-of-fact way were of such profoundly moving content that I wished to preserve them as unaltered as possible.

It may seem strange and incomplete to restrict these poignant accounts to such a relatively small number. A statistical study would require significant numbers and comparison groups. However, the aim was not to be in any way scientific or clinical but simply to try to capture a fraction, a fragment, of the wisps of personal responses to deprivation and adversity.

Publication inevitably constrains space and number. I would have liked to include much more material than was possible here, particularly about the lives of those Hidden Children who emigrated to Israel immediately after World War II when still very young. Their subsequent experiences as described to me seem necessarily different from those who remained to grow up in Europe. The opportunity to interview a large number of them arose after this work was well under way, but at least two such children, both Dutch in origin and now living in Israel, have contributed to the original series of interviews and conversations. Comments from and experiences of others I have met are woven into it.

Most of these Hidden Children now live in the United Kingdom; some live in France, Belgium, and the Netherlands, and two in Israel. Those of Polish origin now live in Western Europe. Most of our conversations were recorded in English, not, of course, their first or often even their second language. Some I interviewed in French (our only common language) and translated the transcripts.

I have learned much from my encounters with many more survivors than can be included here. In the past, interviews of this kind were sometimes conducted by journalists, historians, and sociologists, for example Studs Terkel, *Hard Times* (1970); Tony Parker, *Out of the Frying Pan* (1970), and *The People of Providence* (1983). Because I am neither journalist nor sociologist but a physician specializing in psychiatry, I am deeply grateful to those who have so generously contributed their time, expertise, and advice in helping me with background accuracy.

A physician, however, also has to be a historian, and those working in psychiatry learn the skills of listening and reflecting as they take the history, the narrative of their patients' life experiences. But the disciplined process, formally gathering in chronological order the life events of the person we encounter, also has to be balanced with qualifying, clarifying, and empathic statements and reflections; otherwise, they might as well be collected by means of an impersonal questionnaire or computer program.

EXPLORATION VERSUS "TESTIMONY"

Although I was interested in the historical, chronological settings of the early and later lives of these survivors, in order to put them into context, I hoped to explore their own perspectives on overcoming adversity. Frequently our meetings developed into dialogues, which deepened the level of the discourse, as Henry Greenspan has discussed.

Although the initial interviews were tape-recorded and transcribed, there were later conversations and meetings. Nearly all those Hidden Children who I have included here attended a day meeting in London for survivors,[2] where I talked with them again. Some, as well as others I had not met, also participated with me in a workshop on "Loyalty and Ambivalence" toward their rescuers, and I met and talked with others at the Oxford Scholars' Conference, Remembering for the Future 2000, which followed (Roth and Maxwell, 2001).

Henry Greenspan, who has worked with survivors for many years, has emphasized the importance of hearing and listening to what they say, as opposed to merely documenting testimonies, important as those are for other reasons. Before I encountered his work, I had already tentatively subtitled the material contained in this book *Conversations with Successful Child Survivors*, as opposed to "reflections" or "interviews." Greenspan also recounts how he used comments on their experiences in one-to-one conversations with others so as to introduce them to one another, so to speak, so that a form of virtual group experience occurred, reflecting shared experience and solidarity.

Although the world of the hidden Jewish child in Western Europe is a relatively small one, it is fortunately not nearly as small as it would have been if Hitler's plans for the Jews had been successful. Some of the people I have come to know already knew one another; many did not. Yet, as Sophie observed (Chapter 4), even when they first meet they feel more like siblings than strangers. At a recent meeting of the French Association of Enfants Cachés[3] in Paris in November 2001, I could see this for myself, an atmosphere of confident, relaxed familiarity (which, like siblingship, does not preclude squabbling at times). Unlike other groups and associations, their relationships resemble more those of brothers and sisters than colleagues and associates, summed up in the word *mishpoche* (family). For many, the other child survivors of the Holocaust are indeed their only family.

Although this work is not a clinical appraisal of those people who have contributed to it, as a clinician I hope that some of my skills and experience, particularly in working with traumatized and bereaved individuals, have helped me here. One of the aims of this book is to convey an informed perspective, from the viewpoint of my professional experience, on the positive attributes of these individuals who have lived through and surmounted such adversity. I hope too that my current professional focus on legal aspects of child protection will have helped to inform this work and may perhaps generate some ideas relevant to the care of children in potentially traumatizing situations today.

LIMITATIONS OF ADJUSTMENT

The personal achievements of the men and women whose lives appear in these pages have not been accomplished without difficulties or without significant suffering along the way. "Adjustment" and "surviving well" are relative concepts. Inevitably there are lacunae of pain, sadness, and loss in their accounts; yet there is much healthy adaptation to be discovered in them. Their own perception of their experiences differs significantly from those of others who have *not* experienced such disruption and disadvantage in childhood but who need help; and, of course, many survivors with similar wartime histories have required professional intervention to relieve enduring distress.

To begin to understand some of the life tasks of the child survivors described here, imagine, for example, the child who is told repeatedly after World War II (Robert Krell)[4] that his or her experience is not considered relevant or important compared with that of older survivors. Yet as the child grows up and starts to learn of the fate of parents and grandparents who were deported, humiliated, and annihilated, the details of the terror unfold and disclose their personal significance.

It is a difficult and agonizing period for any student of Holocaust history to absorb, but when the detail (Levi, 1979; Des Pres, 1976; Gill, ibid.; Gilbert, ibid.; Karski, 1944) concerns the fate of loved ones, then the reader can understand that survivors are not only dealing with losses and bereavement, they are also having to absorb the detail and the manner of those deaths. Irena[5] searched for years to find details of her father's last two years in France before deportation. As she had no recollection of him, she was trying to confirm his existence, which she ultimately found in Klarsfeld's *Memorial* (1983). It was only much later, when she had the opportunity to visit Israel, that she found his name in a list of deportees at Yad Vashem[6] and felt she could mourn for him. For a long time she found herself obsessively scanning group photographs of Jews deported from France, even films and photographs of concentration camps to see if she could find a glimpse of him.

It is likely that part of the success, in relative terms, of these Hidden Children is in their attribution,[7] in their general positive and life-affirming perspective. Robert Krell (2001), as a Hidden Child himself, emphasizes the appropriateness of expressing such emotions as anger, grief, and sadness while not being overwhelmed by them to the detriment of all other aspects of life.

The term "resilience" is frequently used here (Vaillant, 1993; Rutter, 1990; Krell, 1985, 2001; Valent, 1998; Cyrulnik, 1999, 2000) and will be discussed later (Chapter 9, Understanding Resilience), where I have endeavored to keep a balance between current research in a complex subject and what is accessible to the reader. For this reason I attempt to give an overview of current thought in this field, referring to some key sources for those who would like to pursue the subject further.

After many discussions and conversations with my French-Polish friend Irena, whose experiences led to my work in this field and whose "onion layers" of life unfolded to me over time, I read as widely as I could before I made contact with others like her. As students of this period are aware, it is never easy reading.

IMPACT OF EUROPEAN EVENTS IN BRITAIN

As a small child in Scotland, one of my earliest memories (my fourth birthday, so I can easily fix the date) is of my aunt telling me that Germany had that day invaded Poland and that war had been declared. This probably had more significance for her, as she had been traveling in Germany not long before and had been alarmed by what she had seen of fascist activities and military developments. For her contemporaries, unless they were involved in politics, Germany and Poland must have seemed very distant.

Radio bulletins announcing the end of the war also had an obvious, more joyful, impact in Britain. Soon films of the liberation were shown on British newsreels. Jubilant relief was clouded by a growing realization of what the Nazi regime had also accomplished in occupied Europe, over and above war, bombing, destruction, and hunger. Some time elapsed, nevertheless, before the general public was able to distinguish between the terms "*camps*," "prisoner of war and internment camps," and "concentration" camps. Possibly much of this naïveté lasted until the Nuremberg Trials.[8] The efforts of Jan Karski (ibid.) and the suicide of Zygelboym, as a desperate response to the news of the treatment and ultimate fate of Jews in Poland, were not generally known by the British public.

ORAL HISTORY ARCHIVES

One of the hardest tasks to accomplish in a work such as this is that of condensing and editing narratives, which represent the warp and weft of people's lives. At times it feels uncomfortably like cutting into a beautifully tailored garment and reshaping it, hoping that the essential design and quality of the fabric will survive. Most of these accounts and conversations were too long to include in their original unedited form but are nonetheless important to preserve. Tapes and transcriptions will be stored in the oral history archives of the relevant countries, with a master copy in The British Library, London.

Survivors frequently referred to the importance of educating the young about the events of World War II (now fortunately recognized in the national curriculum and in the establishment of a National Holocaust Memorial Day). This was especially highlighted for me when I assembled the first narratives and began to have them transcribed. Names, places, and events in Europe from the period before, during, and after the World War II were clearly completely unfamiliar to some readers, so that apart from the material that I myself transcribed, I was lucky to obtain the assistance of Brenda Hovey, a Jehovah's Witness, whose knowledge of the period, together with a familiarity with the history of religious prejudice and persecution of the time, added enormous understanding and empathy to the undertaking.

The number of illustrations is constrained by editorial considerations of space. Because of this, I have not been able to include all the material available to me, but I am enormously grateful to those who have provided precious photographic records and documents, often stimulating further useful discussion.

Some of the people I met had told their stories before, in one form or another; several had participated in television interviews or documentaries, or in the Survivors of the Shoah (Visual History Foundation)[9] project.

The extent to which exposure and repetition alters, distorts, stereotypes, or at least affects or influences the account is a serious matter for historians and is discussed later. Although I am naturally interested in the individual and his or her attributions, I have tried to be aware of this issue and make allowances for it, concentrating my focus more on the dialogue, the personality, and his or her reaction to significant life events. Some were clearly used to giving a clear chronological account of their lives in hiding and afterwards; others had to be encouraged or asked more open questions.[10] One had written her autobiographical account (Fischler-Martinho, 1998) but had never before been directly interviewed. Another, more recently, expressed surprise at the breadth and extent of her transcript when she came to read it, feeling that the process of dialogue had encouraged her to recount much more detail than she had hitherto volunteered.

Even for those with previous experience of recounting the story of their life, it is always a painful process, though frequently lightened by the humor that was characteristic of these courageous and uncomplaining people. Listening to the tapes conveys what the written word cannot: the catch in the voice, the tears, the restlessness, the distortion of sound in a calm account momentarily suspended as a man recalls his father, and the table microphone accidentally knocked over in his struggle to gain control of his emotions.

I knew that the process could be disruptive and disturbing, and how much trust was involved in meeting and talking to me, a stranger, a psychiatrist, a non-Jew. Throughout the time I have been meeting with my contributors, talking on the telephone, and corresponding, I have marveled at the generosity of spirit, time, information, and enthusiasm offered to me. Their own encouragement to pursue the project and their belief in it has enormously sustained my work.

All were curious to know what perspective and interpretation I would put on their personal achievement and resilience, on their "surviving well" when others in similar, or less traumatic, situations are in greater difficulty with their emotional adjustment. Although the interpretations found in these pages are my own, it may be that, ultimately, we cannot possibly answer all the questions raised here. As Claude Lévi-Strauss (1908–), the French philosopher, says: "The scientific mind does not so much provide the right answers as ask the right questions."

It is important to encourage thought and reflection about children's resistance to adversity in certain circumstances. Survivors share a wish to encourage information and education derived from their experience. We respect and honor the courage and suffering experienced by all Holocaust survivors during those terrible years, and many of us care deeply about efforts to reduce or eliminate prejudice and all forms of genocide.

It has become clear in the past few years that we do not give sufficient credit to the natural powers of recovery and adaptability of the human organism, what Vaillant (1993) calls "the Wisdom of the Ego." We should not ignore the more optimistic message: sometimes emotional resilience in the face of adversity *is* a real possibility, against all the odds.[11]

NOTES

1. Henry Greenspan, *On Listening to Holocaust Survivors: Recounting and Life History.* Connecticut: Praeger Publishers, 1998.

2. International Gathering of Child Survivors, opening the Conference Remembering for the Future 2000, Oxford and London.

3. France has two associations for child survivors: *Les Fils et Filles des Déportés Juifs,* and L'Association des Enfants Cachés, both based in Paris. A full account of the treatment of "foreign" and French Jews in France, how and why relatively more survived, can be found in Zucotti, *The Holocaust, the French and the Jews.* 1993.

The rather different situation affecting Jewish families in Italy is also well described in Zucotti, *The Italians and the Holocaust: Persecution, Rescue and Survival.* 1987.

Alexander Stille has also examined the contrasts inherent in the ways Jews were treated in Italy in an interesting study: *Benevolence and Betrayal: Five Italian Jewish Families Under Fascism.* 1991.

4. Robert Krell (2001) and others, and several Hidden Children in this work have explained how their experiences as child survivors were dismissed after the war as being of little consequence; people suggested that they were "too young to understand."

Krell and co-authors Chaim Dasberg, Martin Gilbert, Sarah Moskovitz, and Elie Wiesel have published their reflections on Child Survivors (see Krell 2001).

5. Irena Milewska, personal communication.

6. Yad Vashem, The Martyrs' and Heroes' Remembrance Authority, Jerusalem Holocaust Memorial Center, Jerusalem.

7. Attribution (see Vaillant). Attributional style means the way we regard our own responsibility for the good and bad events that happen to us.

8. Nuremberg Trials; The trial of German Major War Criminals, Nuremberg, Germany, 1946.

9. Survivors of the Shoah, the Visual History Foundation. Shoah Visual History Foundation (PO Box 3168, Los Angeles, CA 90078-3168, USA).

10. An open question is one that does not presuppose a yes or no answer but begins with words such as "how," "when," or "why." Closed questions anticipate one-word negative or positive answers or do not allow the possibility of expanding on an answer.

11. Maurice Vanderpol, "Resilience: The Missing Link in Our Understanding of Survival," *Harvard Review of Psychiatry* no 10. (2002): 302–6.

PART I

CHAPTER 1

⟁~⟁

The Effect of the Holocaust in Europe on Child Survivors

The physical care and emotional needs of children have not always received the same consideration and attention as that in developed countries today (de Mause, 1974). The evolution of childhood in Europe as a distinct developmental state has been a slow and gradual one. Well beyond the Middle Ages children were viewed as miniature adults, having no special needs of their own. Infant and childhood mortality was much higher, equivalent to that of many contemporary underdeveloped countries, so children were long considered expendable. Many were conceived in the hope that one or more would live (Montaigne, 1993) to earn his or her sustenance in working for the family. "Surplus" children who could not be supported, especially girls, were sent out to work, often into service like the servant girl who became the model for the artist Vermeer, touchingly described by Chevalier (2000), in *Girl with a Pearl Earring*. Boys were apprenticed—if they were lucky—and expected to earn their living and make their own way in the world.

The concept of the one cherished child, or cluster of little children around the family table (compare the novels of Charles Dickens) is therefore comparatively recent. In the early twentieth century, infant mortality in Northern Europe was declining, although by contemporary standards of illness and disease prevention children still died of many conditions, such as tuberculosis, diphtheria, and typhoid, diseases that are largely preventable or treatable today.

The luxury of a close and loving relationship with one's children, who were now so much more likely to survive, is also a relatively recent phenomenon. Although this was still less obvious both in the most burdened poor and more emotionally distant upper-class families, the middle classes were evolving toward late-nineteenth- and twentieth-century ideals of family life.

Even before the tragedies of the First and Second World Wars, children were increasingly valued, loved, and cherished. This was true as much in the prewar rural and often impoverished central European *shtetls* (Hoffman, 1999) as in the comfortable apartments of the prosperous immigrants in Berlin, Antwerp, Amsterdam, and Paris.[1] Emigration from the pogroms of Eastern Europe was not only an escape from religious persecution but also provided hope of a better life for the family.[2] Large families were still common (Wiesel, 1995; Hoffman, ibid.). In very religious communities, as is still the case today, parents married young and often had many children, obeying the injunction to "be fruitful and multiply." With declining disease and more manageable mortality, more children were likely to survive. Rural families of ten or more children were not unusual. It is likely that in towns and cities, smaller family size was an effect of assimilation (Glassman, 1984).

And so by the end of the 1920s and 1930s there were, as we shall see, increasing numbers of small, nuclear families in urban areas, with close, intimate, and deeply affectionate relationships between parents and their one or two precious young children. This trend seems to have been the case for the generation of children whose parents had emigrated to Western Europe from more traditional families in Poland and Germany.

In this setting the shadow of persecution spreading over Germany toward other countries led to increasing emigration of Jewish men and families westward (Berghahn, 1988) and later, in particular, to the huge and desperate efforts to organize the *Kindertransport.*[3]

At the risk of never seeing their children again, courageous parents parted with them "into the hands of strangers." The concept of saving children from impending danger was thus well established by the late 1930s. Many families hoped for escape, at the occupation of Poland and the outbreak of war, by fleeing to Holland, Belgium, or France. Many were too late and turned back, as did the families of Nicole and of Henry and Charlotte. Debórah Dwork, who has written the most comprehensive account of the lives of Jewish children in Nazi Europe (Dwork, 1991), also described the different means of rescuing and hiding them. As she explains, many families had difficulty in accepting that they and their children would have to hide and therefore delayed too long. In other circumstances persuasive Resistance workers, in situations of increasing urgency, convinced the reluctant parents to part with children.

CHILDREN IN HIDING

The story of Anne Frank and her family, as recounted in her own diaries and by Miep Gies (1987), the woman who helped to hide them, tells of their daily lives and those of their fellow tenants, *onderduijkers*, who lived behind the walls of the secret annex of the building in the Prinsengracht in Amsterdam.

The poignancy of the events described is heightened by the knowledge that Anne Frank nearly survived the war in Bergen-Belsen, only to succumb in its last few days to typhus. Like the Franks, many Dutch families in hiding were denounced, discovered, and deported to their deaths, like others throughout Europe, although some did survive.

As the war progressed, families became increasingly aware of the risks involved in hiding together, and many made efforts to conceal or save their children separately by various means. There are chilling descriptions (Dwork, 1991; Birnbaum, master's thesis) of desperate people begging total strangers in the street to shelter their children.

Unlike Poland, with the largest Jewish population in Europe, there were no closed ghettos in France, the Netherlands, or Belgium. Before their likely fate and the intentions of the Nazi regime were fully perceived—or believed—families sooner or later wrestled with the pain of sending their child or children away into safety. Awareness of the likely fate of children impelled Resistance groups to take positive action and approach parents directly. Inevitably some parents could not part with their children.

In Poland (Dwork, 1991), principally in Warsaw but also later in Kraków, and Lwow (now in Ukraine), there were relatively well organized groups, for example, Żegota and other organizations such as Centos, rescuing children who were already confined but at risk in the ghettos, as well as individual initiatives. The role of the various Catholic orders of nuns, for example, the Family of Mary and the Grey Ursulines, in saving children within their convents is described by Kurek-Lesik (1988, cited in Dwork). She suggests that two-thirds of female religious communities helped Jewish children and adults, saving an estimated 1,500 children.

The parents of Janek (Chapter 3) made their own provisional arrangements in advance while still in the ghetto of Kraków. When it became clear one day that they would be moved to the work/concentration camp at Płaszów, on the following day they embarked on their prearranged plan to save their seven-year-old son. Plans to hide a child could fail at any stage, as many did, dependent as they were on the most precarious of arrangements. Janek considers that his successful escape was due to a combination of lucky circumstances. Decisions to use one form of concealment or another depended on adults being able to make realistic judgments of the child's ability to cooperate with the plan: neither too young to follow instructions or to keep completely still or quiet in certain circumstances, but at the same time mature enough to have some awareness of the dangers and, if luck held, without the totally paralyzing fear that could increase the risk of detection.

In Janek's case, his parents bravely gambled on his cooperation, not only with the manner of his escape from the ghetto in a suitcase but also in the details of his subsequent concealment by others.

With little human contact and strict rules of concealment, he remained obedient and uncomplaining in a locked room, effectively in solitary confinement for two-and-a-half years, at an age when most little boys enjoy robust and noisy games out of doors. The consequences of his isolation and deprivation could have sown the seeds of later neurosis or depression. Today childcare professionals might be pessimistic about the emotional development of any child subjected to such experiences. Dismissing them as the cultural norm for wartime children cannot of course adequately explain the child's adaptation to and survival of such potential damage to achieve a state of psychological well-being.

It may be much easier for us today to sustain a comforting image of those children who were successfully hidden and survived; those who, like Ruth (Chapter 4) and Milly (Chapter 5), remained in reasonably stable and favorable placements throughout, but it is clear that many had a variety of experiences, hidden visibly and invisibly at different times. For some there were innumerable moves too. Dwork cites one child who had over thirty. Anita's account (Chapter 5) demonstrates constant moves and disruptions, forming and breaking attachments in a sequence of hiding families. Some of the treatment of Hidden Children, including one of her placements of which she has positive memories, was of a standard that today would barely qualify as "good enough" parenting.[4] Other children (Valent, 1994; Krell, 2001) were frequently harshly treated and emotionally, physically, and sometimes appallingly sexually abused. Even today, with well-planned and supervised foster placements, and here in the United Kingdom with the provisions of the Children Act 1989, there are still people who will take advantage of vulnerable children in their care and abuse them, despite the existing safeguards and controls. So it should not surprise us that not all rescuers acted entirely altruistically or benevolently, or that other members of a household exploited or maltreated a child. Mira[5] struggled for years to understand the behavior of the father of the household in which she was hidden. Hiding from the Nazis himself, he was concealed with her behind a wardrobe sometimes for long periods of time. Although he taught her to read and write, he also beat her irrationally, bizarrely insisting on laughter as a response. As a defenseless little child and even as an adult she had believed for years that this was somehow her fault. Much later she exorcised the guilt and confusion when, as a distinguished filmmaker, she returned to the Polish town of Będzin and, encountering one of this man's daughters, learned that he had behaved in similarly abusive ways with his own family.

The care of children taken in by religious foundations, convents, and orphanages varied enormously. Ostensibly benevolent, the setting was nevertheless inevitably institutional and was never ideal. Frequently poorly clothed, malnourished even by wartime standards, the children were often ill and emotionally deprived. In Eastern Europe individual priests and nuns of the Roman Catholic church did not necessarily insist upon conversion as such (David, 1981), but it was usually judged expedient for effective concealment of a child for it to be able to pass as a Catholic child (Reicher, 1996). Dwork highlights the distinctions between younger and older children, the impact of anti-Semitism, and the effect on later religious adherence. Some children were carefully instructed in, or quickly informed themselves of, the appropriate prayers and practices of the Christian Church, and many came to find the rituals comforting. For Sophie (Chapter 4), however, it was deemed too dangerous for her own safety and that of other children for her to remain openly in a Church school in Brussels and her rescuers were asked to remove her. Like other children in similar situations, she was not to return to education "outside" until liberation, but unlike others whose education was curtailed, she benefited in an unexpected and extraordinary way. Through Resistance connections of the family hiding her, a young teacher volunteered to give her clandestine lessons. With individual tuition of a high order and the strict insistence of her "foster father" on most meticulously kept exercise books over the ensuing three years, she returned after the war to open education with her peers, quickly achieving first place in her class.

The effect of her experience in hiding on her personality, despite the benefits to her education, could have been extremely damaging. Today she describes it with the insight of an adult looking back, understanding that her hiding family could no more help the gloomy atmosphere in the household than she could her own timidity and psychological withdrawal. Rapidly removed from her position as a cherished only child, "spoiled rotten" (*pourrie-gatée*) as she describes it with a wry smile, with little or no preparation or explanation other than a firm reminder of her false name and new identity, she was transferred to the care of a completely unfamiliar couple. They themselves were suffering from the recent deportation of their son to Germany. All were involved in work for the Resistance; all were at risk, and all the more so for hiding a Jewish child.

Little wonder that her recollection of her life in these circumstances is of the sad and oppressive passage of these months and years, only slightly reassured by her foster mother, who insisted that her own son and Sophie's parents would all come back one day. Of the three, only Sophie's father returned. Like many widowed survivors he soon began to try to recapture his prewar life, but with a new wife who rejected his little daughter.

Why was this not a recipe for psychological disaster? She too recalls having to be excessively obedient (Valent, 1998), or rather not so much having to be as imposing this upon herself for fear of being put out on the streets, knowing herself to be in extreme danger. Silence, sadness, and withdrawal were so much a part of daily life that the previously outgoing, capricious little girl became timidly over-compliant and unforthcoming: difficult to recognize now in the vivacious and assertive person she is to-day. Yet despite the excessively strict insistence of her foster father on per-fection in her written lessons, it was her hiding mother, her "aunt" to whom she turned for comfort and support when, later, she had her own child.

For some children, individuals in the Catholic Church were concerned and solicitous of a child's Jewish identity; Milly learned much later that, in her case, a foster "uncle" opposed hasty baptism, because there was no way to obtain her parents' permission; in Nicole's case, an elder daugh-ter of her foster family who became a nun, carried out the child's mother's request, reminding her daily never to forget to say her Jewish prayer (*Sh'ma Israel*). A local curate stopped plans to baptize Ruth as her par-ents were still alive.

Irena, who was too young to remember any family or life before her infancy in the Warsaw ghetto, describes unutterably bleak years in orphan-ages and children's homes all over Poland. Her perception of her life at the time and later, until she came to the West, was that this deprived ex-istence was the norm for such children in the care of religious institutions during the war. Many children, as is clear from Śliwowska (1993, 1998), were never reclaimed after the war, never learned of their Jewish identi-ties, and have lived out the rest of their lives as Catholics. Opinions are divided as to the extent to which baptism and conversion to Catholicism in Poland was simply a safeguard for concealed Jewish children or may have represented a more positive policy on the part of the Church. But as Dwork suggests,

> the onus of the acceptance of Christianity, the ultimate adaptation of the Jewish child to the gentile world, lies with the Nazis and their allies, and not the foster families and religious institutions which participated in pro-tecting and defending these young people's lives.

For those who learned later, painfully in Irena's case, of their true ori-gins, there was a period of gradual adaptation, often of great and bitter ambivalence. One woman, having judged it expedient to suppress her Jewish identity after the war, nevertheless pejoratively described[6] the off-spring she had had with her Gentile husband as "those Poles."

The institutionalized child at least shared his or her relatively impersonal life and hardships with peers. For some, the group may have provided a degree of support and affection (Clarke and Clarke, 2000). But a child hidden on his or her own, old enough to remember parents and siblings, nevertheless often pined for contact or news, even if hidden with supportive rescuers (Meed, 1987; Reicher, 1996).

Adaptation to new customs, culture, and religious practices were vital. Some children (Dwork, 1991) describe this process as a conscious one, deliberately acting out the new identity as if in a play, with some satisfaction, while not forgetting their real one (see letter from Marcel to his foster mother, Olga, for the experience in reverse, Chapter 6).

Some, conversely, have now forgotten, or perhaps have emotionally blocked, their assumed identity and name. Some, like Milly, have discovered late in life that they were actually baptized as infants to protect them and subsequently mused, half self-mockingly, "what am I, a Roman Catholic Jew? or a Jewish Roman Catholic?"

She describes the most touching and affectionate memento, a watercolor of Moses in the bulrushes given to her by her rescuers as a wedding present "in memory of the frightening times you spent with us."

But a child like Lea, hidden as a purely commercial transaction in the cellar of a laundry in Brussels, without fresh air, light, or education for two years, harshly treated as a virtual slave by a woman who, by any standards, should never have had the care of a child, suffered interminably.

Standards of childcare in wartime differed greatly from those of today, but it would not be surprising if, like many abused and deprived young people, she had suffered severe physical and psychological consequences. Yet she grew to seize every opportunity and regard every experience after the war as a bonus, becoming an enthusiastic and contented adult with a positive appreciation of her new circumstances and welcoming every new change and challenge.

Dwork and others have distinguished between children "in hiding and hidden" and those "in hiding and visible." Some were in both categories at different times.

Alina (personal communication, 2001, and described in Armstrong, 2001), separated from her mother at the point of deportation, was forced to travel alone through Greater Germany, to take refuge in the apartment of relations in Berlin, where she had to fend for herself. Later she had to make the return journey across Poland to Warsaw. To this day she has no recollection of how she managed all this unassisted. There is also a third group, as Dwork points out, of children who had to act independently, "scrambling to survive" by wandering in the Polish countryside, finding work on farms.

Janina was one such child who survived with neither prior planning or calculation, nor with help from underground Resistance workers, but through sheer necessity and her own abilities. After her elder brother had rushed her through a sewer in Kraków to emerge beyond the walls of the ghetto, she was suddenly on her own. She was a highly resourceful and confident little girl, used to moving around independently on essential errands for her family and others in the ghetto and to living by her wits, but nothing could have prepared this urban child for the physical and psychological isolation and dangers of surviving the rigors of the Polish countryside in winter. Hiring herself out as a farmhand she also ran the risk of the exposure of her assumed Aryan identity. Indeed, at one point, when she was living with a comparatively kind and compassionate family, she was denounced and had to move on.

The individual accounts recorded in Śliwowska's collection of autobiographies (1998) show that there were several children who managed to conceal themselves in this way. Kosinsky and Kuper (Dwork, 1991) were others in a similar plight. In a further collection of interviews in *The Children Accuse*, Hochberg-Mariańska (1996) documents the ingenuity displayed by quite young children. Janina candidly describes herself at this time as living "like a little animal." Children in the ghettos and those surviving alone in the countryside clearly had to develop skills of self-preservation and survival. These involved verbal and physical behaviors not usually associated with normally socialized children. It is interesting to consider how, or how soon, and by what influences most children became resocialized to conform with normal standards of behavior and perhaps what proportion did not. Ben Helfgott (personal communication, 2002) who, as a young adolescent survived forced labor in Poland and is himself a robust example of overcoming adversity, has strong views about this. He reflects on the qualities of the families from which these surviving children came—warm, affectionate beginnings in which a strong moral sense was nourished and in which "love, not hate and revenge" was fostered. He sees a clear difference between the perversion of normal values necessary for sheer survival and delinquent behavior learned as a maladaptive response (see Bok, 1998), perhaps in delinquent neighborhoods, to "normal" life. Thus behavior patterns adopted in order to find food, for example, were easily relinquished when food was no longer an issue, although (see Gilbert, 1997, and Gill, 1988) this could take time.

Generally, unsocialized criminal or delinquent acts occurring in peacetime should be distinguished from the effect that the learned survival strategy to find and retain as much as a crust of bread had upon the mealtimes at Windermere (see Gilbert 1997, and Moskovitz, 1988). Paul Valent (1998) cites the case of Richard, a child who survived in hiding with the partisans near Radom in Poland. The "most beautiful birthday present" he was given at this time was some bread, which he hid in his shirt. Restored to civilized life in Paris after the war, his attempt to conceal slices of roast meat under his shirt at the dinner table resulted in his being banished to an orphanage for the next four-and-one-half years. "But what they did not know was that, just as I had learned to be a savage, I could have learned not to steal food, and gone to school like a normal child."

Edward Reicher's account of his war years in hiding, translated by his daughter, Elisabeth Bizouart-Reicher (*Une vie de Juif: L'odyssée d'un médecin juif en Pologne*, 1939–45), tells of the apparently random theft of Elzbieta's favorite toy bear, snatched by a passing street child. But his family, a well-known criminal gang, had trained that child, a little Warsaw "Artful Dodger," in calculated theft. The theft was not so random since the bear contained jewelery and money hidden by Dr. Reicher for the eventual survival of his family in what he had hoped was a safe place. It was apparently stolen to order. He had to pay a substantial proportion of the value as ransom to recover it. Years later in Paris, he met the young thief's father, himself a survivor of the ghetto, now a nightclub proprietor. The thief had studied law and was a successful and popular advocate in Paris. In this case a child, reared in criminality and organized theft, quite independent of the survival motive, had overcome his early indoctrination.

SHORT- AND LONG-TERM CONSEQUENCES

Some children were able to maintain contact in some form or other with family members. Babies and infants, for example, rescued by the various Resistance movements, however, had no recollection of their parents and rarely retrieved mementoes or family photographs of them after the war. When the fate of the many populations deported and murdered in the camps became known, many rescuers doubted that anyone would return to claim their children. Such returns as did occur were often painful for all concerned if a child had settled well with the only family he or she knew. The arrival of surviving relatives, so obviously depleted physically, emotionally and materially, was often shocking to the rescuers. Children sometimes failed to recognize a returning parent.

Janek, who remained for a time with his hiding family after his own personal liberation from his solitary confinement, viewed the return of his mother from Bergen-Belsen with indifference and a lack of recognition. Surrounded by adults anticipating a joyful reunion, he told her that she seemed vaguely familiar to him and returned calmly to his room. This fact surprises him even today. They had, of course, been separated for two-and-one-half years, a significant and traumatic period for them both.

Richard, the boy who hid food in his shirt, describes a similar reaction when he was reunited with his mother.

My mother made a fuss about me. . . . I thought it was uncalled for. It was just another event when you live one day at a time. Yesterday I caught a rabbit. Today I am reunited with my mother. . . . After one-and-a-half years I was a tough partisan. I let her cry. And she worried that I did not have a clean handkerchief and that I would catch a cold. She thought I was a nine-and-a-half-year-old child.

Richard, who had "put a feather under one hundred noses" to confirm for the partisans that executed Germans soldiers were truly dead and who survived winters of minus forty degrees, thought his mother "lived in an unreal world" (Valent, 1994; Marks, 1994).

For those children who had become strongly attached to their new families, the prospect of yet another separation was distressing, potentially damaging, and for some elicited the "loyalty conflict" (Moskovitz, 1988). In the Netherlands, for example, different groups argued about the children's future, whether to rear them as Jews or Christians (Dwork, 1991) and to whom they should belong. Ways of managing this were sometimes resolved by a determined effort on one side or the other to form an alliance rather than a power struggle (Vegh, 1979). Claudine was not the only child whose parental figures resolved the conflict by allowing the child to return to the hiding family for holidays, as if to distant relatives. Even when the purpose was to save them, parents sometimes resented the affection that had developed between hidden child and hiding parents.

Basia, now living in Israel with her own family but retaining close links and strong loyalty to her hiding family in Holland, still battles with the enduring jealousy of her own mother toward them. Her mother sometimes talks reproachfully of the time "when you left us," as though such a small child could have acted independently. Basia does not overreact to such a rebuke; her mother is elderly now, but she notices and is a little hurt. Ruth, on the other hand, relates with amusement and mock horror the reaction of her rescuers when her surviving parents offered payment after the war.

RESCUERS

When children were hidden, their rescuers often had to be paid the cost of extra rations by Resistance workers or by their family if hidden in a private arrangement. Of course, no financial payment could actually compensate for the danger and risk to which they and their families were exposed. The fact that so many rescuers acted entirely altruistically has been explored in detail by many authors, notably Oliner (1988), Paldiel (1989), Bloch and Drucker (1992), and Gilbert (2003) and recognized in the Yad Vashem awards to the Righteous amongst the Nations.

Although much has been written about the selflessness of rescuers, and this text is primarily concerned with the outcome of the children they cared for, it is impossible to listen to their own accounts of the families who sheltered them in their various ways without being moved by the extraordinary bravery of these people.

For the most part, people who willingly sheltered children at such danger to themselves, unlike those with purely material motives, seem to have had altruistic personalities, were as child centered as circumstances and the times permitted, and frequently engendered enduring affection and loyalty in the children. These attachments (Fonagy, 1992) are likely to have been protective in the psychological as much as the physical sense. Shaping behavior and moral values, and demonstrating affection and other positive attributes by their own actions may have provided positive models of appropriate adult behavior, contributing to the stability of these children in adult life. Vaillant in *The Wisdom of the Ego* (1993) discusses in detail the way in which potentially vulnerable people were strengthened by their immediate social supports.

IDENTITY

Children like Irena, whose parents were presumed to have perished, were considered to be war orphans. They made their first Communion at the appropriate age in the Catholic orphanage or children's home. To discover as she did a little later that she actually belonged to a group still regarded with hatred and suspicion by many Polish people was shocking and confusing. Other surviving Jewish children returning from the East were poor, homeless, and stigmatized. She had been "adopted" postwar by a middle-class woman, and although this was an unhappy experience, she had been well provided for materially. She did not wish to identify herself with the "Jewish orphans from Russia," deprived and unpopular as they were. The confusion this caused lasted for some time and affected her adolescent behavior and, for a time, her educational progress.

ADJUSTMENT

Older children, exposed to the conditions of the Polish ghettos, became adept at forms of activity that in other circumstances would have been seen as totally unsocialized behavior. Smuggling, stealing, lying, deception, and risk-taking were skills developed by children who were often the only means of trade and barter between the ghetto and the outside Aryan world.

Janina, in Kraków (Fischler-Martinho, 1998, and interview with author, Chapter 3), learned to hand over with sophistication beyond her years a *pourboire* to the Polish policemen guarding the exits and entrances of the ghetto. When she did not always have the necessary cash or equivalent bribe, they would give credit and she could pay later.

For some children the necessity of deceptive behavior, bribery, and other forms of venality (Moskovitz's description of children at Windermere, 1988; Gilbert, 1997, in *The Boys*, for illustrations of unsocialized behavior, particularly in relation to food, which took time and loving care to "socialize" after the war) must have become a way of life that may not always have responded to resocialization. The author J. G. Ballard (1994) has described the effects on children of "running wild" with the total breakdown of social norms in Japanese prisoner of war camps in *The Empire of the Sun*.

POSTWAR RESPONSE

Gradually, as accounts from the liberated camps spread, the rest of Europe and America became aware of the extent of atrocities and extermination committed on huge numbers of Jews, Roma, Jehovah's Witnesses, homosexuals, and others, and the suffering of camp survivors. Anne Karpf (1996) describes the reaction of Anglo-Jewry. Anton Gill (1988) observes: "Often, where they had hoped to find sympathetic interest in their stories, which they were eager to tell . . . they found instead indifference or even hostility. Relatives who had left in time, or those who had long lived away from mainland Europe, adopted an attitude of 'don't tell me—it's too horrible—I don't want to hear it,' which deeply wounded the survivors and drove some into a silence that lasted decades." Even now, when so much more is known about the suffering endured and the fate of European Jews is much more widely discussed and understood, it is not unusual to encounter this response. It also occurred when describing the preparation for this book to people whose grandparents were immigrants to Britain at the end of the nineteenth century, who had little knowledge of what was happening in Occupied Europe between 1939 and 1945. Of course, such reactions are probably less dismissive than it would appear, almost certainly involving painful and guilty emotions.

To be sure, many survivors' own numbness from trauma and the sheer inability to talk of the unimaginable reinforced an absence of sympathetic questions, resulting in silence (Levi, 1979; Greenspan, 1998). When they were moved to speak, they often elicited the rejoinder, "but we were bombed during the war, and we too were short of food." Such responses naturally discouraged the survivor from talking of his or her experiences.

Most, glad to be alive, threw themselves as quickly as possible into the tasks of building new lives and families and finding work.

As we will see in Chapter 2, however, it seems that early descriptions of postwar, Holocaust-related trauma emerged initially from clinical accounts of suffering recorded by American psychiatrists, in particular, documenting the difficulties experienced by survivors in obtaining compensation under the German government legislation despite severe physical and emotional problems. Other psychiatrists (Eitinger, 1961; Eitinger and Krell, 1985), however, also began to describe the severe problems suffered by camp survivors as a consequence of malnutrition, starvation, and disease. Difficulties of emotional adjustment sometimes resulted in florid mental illnesses, burdens added to the suffering already endured (Gill, ibid., quoting Bastiaans, 1957). As time went on, new problems were identified. As Krell observes, the actual nature and number of emotionally robust, resilient survivors was not known, and the problems were revealed primarily by those who sought treatment.

Survivors (Gilbert, 1987), desperate to return to life and to create or re-create lost families, often rapidly formed new relationships with equally damaged partners. "After the war, the urge to marry, both as a flight from loneliness and the War from a desire to replace the people who had been lost, was very strong" (Gill, ibid., Chapter 5). These new relationships could not always replace or compensate for past losses. There were sometimes unsuitable liaisons and marital problems, and as their children were born and grew up, unresolved difficulties in one or both parents were sometimes associated with difficulties in the second generation (Gill, ibid.; Epstein, ibid.; and others, e.g., Karpf, ibid.). Glassman (unpublished master's thesis, 1984) however, warns against overgeneralization from some flawed earlier studies.

The outcome of a special group of young people, *The Boys* as described by Gilbert (1997) and others (Moskowitz, ibid., and Ben Helfgott in Gill, ibid.), appears to have been an exception, partly because particularly careful arrangements were made in Britain for their reception and rehabilitation. Developments during and after the war in the understanding of emotional as well as the physical needs of children accelerated due to the work of Bowlby (1960). Anna Freud (the child therapist and daughter of Sigmund Freud) was one of those involved in the care and rehabilitation of these young people.

UNDERSTANDING TRAUMA

The literature of recognized psychological trauma has grown steadily larger. It has also increased understanding of what we now call post-traumatic stress disorder, which had its origins in recognition of battle stress. In World War I, lack of understanding of this condition resulted in young soldiers, paralyzed by fear, being shot as deserters or court-martialed and executed. Improved awareness in World War II led to better management of military battle fatigue pioneered by the Cassell Hospital in London. So the scene was set for a developing professional interest and understanding of the scars of war. Consequently, clinical accounts of the sequelae were more likely to reach other interested professionals (Gill, 1988; Davidson, 1972; Eitinger, 1961; Bastiaans, 1957).

Clinicians document illness in good faith but do not always explore sufficiently the other side of the coin, namely relative health or immunity to its breakdown. This is because they are trained to prevent primary or secondary illness and try to understand it by documenting or recording it first. This focus on pathology (Vanderpol, 2002) has often led to lack of interest in more robust, resilient, or resistant individuals (see section on understanding resilience, Chapter 9).

CHILD SURVIVORS

As far as the psychological impact on survivors is concerned, there were even greater difficulties for children than for those of their parents' generation, not only in validating their experiences but also in finding a way to express their experiences to those who would listen and hear what they had to say. Culturally and historically, it was a "pre-Spock" era, when children were expected to be seen and not heard. These problems were to be compounded by their difficulty in obtaining restitution.

Compensation for their experiences was as difficult, complex, and daunting to obtain—and often virtually impossible—as it was for adults. Initially, it was not even recognized for child survivors "since their minds were not considered to have been sufficiently developed to be affected" (Gill, ibid.), although subsequently this situation improved. One of the Hidden Children interviewed here has only recently received compensation for the loss of her father deported from France sixty years ago (Irena, personal communication). It was even more difficult to obtain compensation for those who remained in Eastern Europe behind the Iron Curtain.

TO WHAT EXTENT WERE THESE CHILDREN AT RISK EMOTIONALLY?

Although our views of what constitutes adequate childcare at the end of the twentieth century and the beginning of this century have undoubtedly changed, there is no doubt that most of these children were significantly at risk. Not only their lives, but also their emotional and psychological health were threatened, even if they survived the physical effects of severe malnutrition and disease, especially tuberculosis. Any risk assessment of potential damage to the personality and of later difficulties in life would probably forecast a poor outcome, although one important study illustrates how some child survivors overcame a very poor prognosis (Hemmendinger and Krell, 2000).

SOURCES OF HARM TO CHILDREN

The list of losses and hardships is formidable. Children lost their homes and familiar surroundings and often their parents, temporarily or permanently. They witnessed traumatic events, including beatings or deaths of relatives and strangers. They were often expected to function in ways that were inappropriate for their years, smuggling, lying, working like adults, or living like partisans in the forests. Fostered by more or less welcoming or caring adults, they experienced disruption of bonds when moved and yet again if parents returned to claim them. They were in constant fear of impending danger, beyond the degree of apprehension felt by other children during raids and bombardments. They were required to change identity, religion, and sometimes to conceal gender.

Many recall the extent to which they had to learn to lie (Janina, Janek, Irena). It is surprising that habits of deceit for personal gain did not persist. Fear was ever present and not only of discovery or deportation. Children such as Ruth felt helpless and vulnerable, lacking the support or comfort of prayer available to other children. She believed that "Jesus does not listen to an unbaptized child" and that if she died she would go straight to hell.

Many experienced pervasive feelings of guilt in many dimensions of their lives, for example, for pretending to accept or for accepting a Catholic identity while knowing that they were Jewish; for surviving at all; for feelings of resentment and bitterness at what they perceived as abandonment by parents who had sent them into hiding (Irena). It took time before they could accept that hiding a child (Dwork, 1991) was an act of heroic self-sacrifice. Many later described their inability to express distress after the war. Sophie (Chapter 4), has told me of her relief at finding it possible (at the New York Conference in 1991) to reclaim "the status of victim" (of the Holocaust) to which, like many, she had not felt entitled. This should be distinguished from the reaction of a person who feels victimized, which is quite different.

Children who were concealed or lost opportunities for development through play, education, and social relationships were, like Janek, frequently undernourished and undersized on release. Their verbal ability was initially affected through their isolation. Many, like Bert (Chapter 5), lost educational opportunities. Sophie's accelerated "special tuition" was unusual. Physical and sexual development was often delayed due to concealment and malnutrition. Janina considers herself lucky in this regard: As a childlike twelve-year-old, she was spared unwelcome advances while traveling in the Polish countryside.

Given such a negative substrate, once the world in general and professionals in particular realized that children's feelings and development did matter, that it was wrong to believe that they were too young to feel and understand (Krell, 2001), that they were thus oblivious and impervious to suffering, it is little wonder that we have often assumed that the child survivor was invariably damaged.

Of course, everything is relative. Listening now to those who endured those terrible childhood experiences, we should not minimize the cost of present achievements.

Those who now regard themselves as functioning well are not super-individuals nor are they unaffected or unmarked. Sometimes the difficult events in life seem to have steeled these children who have been strengthened as a result (Rutter's "bad tasting medicine" analogy).[7]

NOTES

1. Lively images of this life are captured in an outstanding collection of photographs of Polish Jews entitled, "And I still see their faces," Fondacia Shalom, Warsaw.

2. Although much emigration also reflected fear of compulsory conscription into the army.

3. *Kindertransport* was the evacuation of Jewish children from Germany, Austria, and Czechoslovakia to safety in 1938.

4. Anita (Chapter 5) cheerfully described to me how her hiding mother used to treat her exactly as she would her own children for some misdemeanor, leading her across the yard "by the ear." Yet what she describes is a warm and loving home in which she felt entirely safe and protected.

5. Mira, personal communication, 2001.

6. Wlodka, personal communication.

7. Sir Michael Rutter, the distinguished British child psychiatrist, who considered mechanisms that can protect children from psychological insult, uses the analogy of protective processes with nasty "medicine"; medicines that work are often those that have the most unpleasant taste.

CHAPTER 2

‍‍‍‍‍‍‍

Surviving Well

As a psychiatrist talking to resilient Hidden Children and exploring their lives in hiding during World War II, I realized that there has been insufficient recognition of good, as well as bad, consequences resulting from severe deprivation and dislocation. This can lead to pervasive and negative cultural and professional stereotypes (Bluglass, 2001). Yet those who feel that they have overcome adversity hope to record an optimistic message about the strength and infinite variety of the human organism for the benefit of future generations. They do not wish the world to view them as helpless victims. While the protagonists' memories are still vivid, the later chapters of this book explore their reflections on their experiences, enabling us to challenge the perception that the effect of Holocaust experiences inevitably resulted in poor outcomes for all child survivors (Bergman and Jucovy, 1982; Wolffheim, 1966; Freud and Dann, 1951; Wangh, 1971; Wijsenbeek, 1977).

Many writers and scholarly studies have considered the consequences to survivors primarily in terms of their physical dimensions: deportation, imprisonment, starvation, and every manifestation of loss. Although many studying or working in this field personally know survivors who have not been totally crushed, the stereotype of the damaged individual lingers and understandably permeates popular consciousness. Robinson (1979) found that the sequelae of trauma in concentration camp victims were not much different from those found in the group that survived through hiding, for example, "Harry R" hidden in Slovakia or "Joseph S" hidden at the age of eight (Bergman and Jucovy, 1982). Although people hidden as children have endured potentially damaging experiences, many have gradually adapted and now consider themselves to be well-adjusted and functioning effectively.

BACKGROUND

Recognition of the profound emotional effects of World War II on survivors took time to establish (Fogelman and Savran, 1980; Fogelman, 1988; Porter, 1979; Kestenberg and Brenner, 1996). Once professionals, psychiatrists, and psychologists began to pay attention to these experiences, the natural focus moved to the extremely severe nature and wide range of problems arising from the experience of deportation and incarceration and later to the children, the "second generation" born to these survivors (Krystal, 1968). This recognition was important for damaged individuals and for the education of professionals who could begin to work with the survivors' broken minds and bodies: "Perhaps temporal and emotional distance was necessary before the survivors were able to remember and before mental health professionals themselves were ready to deal with the problem" (Bergman and Jucovy, 1981).

Fogelman and Savran (1980) and Kestenberg (1982) reviewed the process by which the German government approached the question of reparation, *Wiedergutmachung*, the convoluted and bureaucratic assessments that led those seeking reparation "to feel terribly wronged" by the injustices of the process (Fogelman and Savran, 1980; Kestenberg, 1982).

"When Germany introduced the indemnification program to compensate the Nazi victims, the good intentions of its originators were from the beginning marred by inconsistencies and pitfalls which eventually led to a virtual continuation of the persecution via 'legal' channels, and the increasing difficulty in obtaining reparation for physical, let alone for emotional damage, indeed initially the extent of psychological damage was probably under-reported" (Kestenberg, 1982).

According to Kestenberg, The Federal Indemnification Law of 1953 (*Bundesentschädigungsgesetz* or BEG) and the resulting restitution process fell far short of its ideals. He suggests that the injustices involved in the too easy refusal of reparations had two parallel explanations: first, that mounting costs of the proposed restitution, worked for by Chancellor Konrad Adenauer, alarmed the German government. This led to changes in the application of regulations and to discriminatory practices; and second, that as psychological damage became apparent, it was hard to convince younger German physicians and psychiatrists of the acts of their predecessors. This led to frequent refusal of psychological injury as grounds for obtaining compensation for survivors (ibid.).

Psychiatric conditions caused by persecution were recognized only in 1965, when German psychiatrist Karl Kisker (1961) challenged the then prevailing German view of all trauma as transient, any enduring condition being considered as necessarily genetic and therefore not *verfolgungsbedingt*, that is, unrelated to persecution. Consequently, in the face of such obvious injustices, American psychiatrists through their efforts and skills were required to document and support the survivors' applications.

Such cases were predominantly described in psychoanalytical terms and were perhaps relatively inaccessible to a newer generation of psychiatrists trained in Britain. After the creation of the National Health Service in 1947,[1] the emphasis was more eclectic and based on "acute" services rather than on longer term psychotherapies or psychoanalyses, rarely available as "free" treatment. The work of psychiatrists Eitinger (1961) and Davidson (1972) in Israel, however, demonstrated that the overwhelming impression was of pervasive posttraumatic damage, often requiring many years of painstaking psychoanalytical psychotherapy, sometimes with periods of hospitalization, before improvement was possible. Some very damaged individuals never truly regained their health. Robert Krell has written (Krell and Sherman, 1997) that "in general the psychiatric literature has reflected critically on the survivor with preconceived notions held by many health professionals. . . . [T]he exploration of victims' psychopathology obscured the remarkable adaptation made by some survivors and possible approaches to treatment were entirely absent from mainstream psychiatric textbooks throughout the nineteen sixties and the nineteen seventies."

It was some time before the effect on child survivors was fully considered. Anna Freud, however, pointed out, referring to the effects on children rescued from Theresienstadt, "It never crossed my mind that anyone could doubt the harm created by such adverse circumstances" (Freud quoted by Kestenberg, 1982, and Bergman and Jucovy, 1982).

Other authors, Sarah Moskovitz (1988) and Martin Gilbert (1997), described the experiences, recollections, and subsequent lives of rescued children and young people brought to Britain after World War II. The consequences of adult Holocaust survivors' experiences were suggested by studies of "second generation" phenomena, which attracted professional attention through psychoanalytical studies of some families and their children who manifested relationship and other problems (Rakoff, 1969; Sigal, 1971, 1973; Trossman, 1968; Krystal, 1968; Fogelman and Savran, 1980). Glassman (1984), however, has discussed some of the problems inherent in these studies.

Bergman and Jucovy (1982) qualified the relevance of these findings to the wider population, distinguishing correctly between a "clinic" population, individuals who seek help, and those who have not done so.

It was not surprising that the nature of the whole range of deprivation and other adverse experiences on children who had been in hiding were not immediately apparent, not least because of the difficulty in identifying a sizeable group for structured study.

Moskowitz (1989) surveyed a group of Hidden Children who responded to a questionnaire and, although small, it is unlikely that their experiences were in any way particularly untypical of children hidden in Europe as a whole (Vegh, 1984; Dwork, 1991; Bloch and Drucker, 1992; David, 1992; Marks, 1994; Valent, 1994; Fischler-Martinho, 1998; Śliwowska, 1981). From a developmental point of view, it took years before those who were children at the time were old enough to "reflect on their own situation and bear witness" (Dwork, 1991).

The experiences of Hidden Children were not initially seen as particularly relevant or important compared with those of the adult survivors of hiding, camps, or slave labor until the late 1980s or 1990s.[2] This also reflects a general prevailing view of children immediately after the war. Children who had survived by being hidden were considered fortunate to be alive at all, compared with the other children who had perished in the ghettos and in selections in the camps. They did not merit special consideration. Certainly this is a recurring theme mentioned by Hidden Children themselves. Robert Krell, now a distinguished Canadian physician and psychiatrist, who was himself a Hidden Child, comments that adult survivors, who remembered family life and endured concentration camps and unspeakable atrocities, considered the children to have been "lucky not to have known what happened. They were wrong" (Krell, 1985, 1998, 1999).

After meeting survivors at the First International Gathering of Children Hidden During World War II in 1991, the author Jane Marks wrote: "Many former hidden children still minimize their experiences because they were repeatedly told 'You were safe, you were lucky,' but every hidden child suffered in unimaginable ways, during the war, afterward, or both" (Marks, 1994).

An unknown number of children did survive, in Poland, for example, passing and reared as Catholics or adopted by Catholic families, unaware for years, if ever, of their identity, and their numbers are probably impossible to estimate. Hence, those who we are discussing are only those who were always aware of or later learned of their identity. As several of my interviewees have described, postwar and later adjustment were by no means straightforward. Even when a parent or family member did return to claim the child, there was sometimes a tug of war for care and possession of the child (Ribière, 1998) quite apart from the phenomenon that occurred during hiding and termed the "loyalty conflict," which was commonly experienced (Keilson, 1979).

There were of course many adult survivors who did, and still do, suffer in silence, unrelieved and traumatized for lack of available understanding and help or simply unable to seek that help spontaneously. "Survivor guilt" (Krystal, 1968) no doubt sometimes inhibited some, but there are many other reasons. For those who received appropriate help, growing professional understanding improved their lot. The outcome was not universally poor in terms of personal adjustment. The term "recovery," whether used for the bereaved or for survivors of any traumatic experience, is not particularly helpful. "Adaptation" or "adjustment" may be more appropriate and acceptable words. The variations and degrees of such adjustment are, of course, endless. For example, there are those who have adapted at one level to postwar life and work but are unable to discuss fully their experiences with their children. There are others who appear to function in most dimensions but who are, in fact, wholly preoccupied and consumed by their past, and whose children feel overburdened by their parents' inability to live in the present.

Professionally we should be cautious about premature assumptions of adjustment. Some individuals appeared to function well for years, as though blinkered or denying past traumas, but have relapsed in later years. Aging and other personal losses can rekindle unresolved memories and experiences, inevitably put "on hold" while the most immediate postwar survival tasks took priority.[3] Others, applying traumatic experiences to creativity, education, and literature, writers like Primo Levi (1979), Bruno Bettelheim[4] (1943), and poet Paul Celan (1996), appeared to have overcome their experiences but in the end were apparently defeated.

Levi's unexplained fall from the staircase of his apartment was thought to be suicidal and believed by some to indicate ultimate and unresolved despair (although Myriam Anissimov has minutely reexamined his life and death in a recent biography, 1999).

But at the same time accounts of more positive outcomes by the Hidden Children described here minimize the difficulties of large numbers of survivors and their families. They continue to merit all our understanding, support, and encouragement to live to testify to the havoc and damage wrought by the Nazi regime and its consequences. It also seems important to describe a group of individuals who seem to have been able to overcome the most potentially damaging experiences inflicted on them at a critically formative period of their lives. Valent's book (1994) makes the point well, namely, that it is possible to live with childhood trauma and overcome adversity. A very healthy, well-adjusted Dutch Hidden Child told me "not a day goes by but I think of those times." To be able to make a satisfactory adjustment also merits description as an important aspect of post-Holocaust study. Individual narratives and testimonies (Fischler-Martinho, 1998; Śliwowska, 1993; David, 1992), recordings for the Imperial War Museum archive, interviews with the Hidden Children participating in my study, and the video testimonies of the Shoah compiled

by the Visual History Foundation[5] demonstrate the inhumanities suffered
by many children in Europe between 1938 and 1945, many of whom are
no longer alive to describe them. They are witnesses to their own and
others' experience. No detail is insignificant or unimportant if we are to
teach current and future generations the historical lessons and implications of this period. It seems worthwhile to find a balance between the
documentation of the horror and trauma, and the surprising ability of
some to survive and overcome them. In some circumstances the capacity
of individuals for personal, psychological growth is remarkable. Psychiatrists listen every day to tragic and traumatic experiences of patients, trying to make sense of them and to help their narrators find meaning
(Frankl, 1989) and hope in their current and future lives, and resolution
of past difficulties. The experience of eliciting, encouraging, and recording the narrative history of another group of people, namely healthy Hidden Children of the Holocaust, is a moving, humbling, and altogether
different experience. It is difficult to exaggerate the impact of listening
to a Hidden Child.

In this particular group of successful Hidden Children, the past is recounted in a measured, reflective, and balanced manner; not, however,
without appropriate emotion or feeling. Of course, there is no hierarchy
of suffering. No individual who was subject to Holocaust trauma but
functions in a healthy way today is braver or more courageous than others
who do not; nor can they be compared with patients whose own perceptions of early problems and losses may require professional help. Each
individual is unique, with different strengths and vulnerabilities. Some,
however, do seem to be more resilient than others.

Viewed by contemporary standards for child protection and applying
the English law criteria of "significant harm" (The Children Act 1989)
and the gloomy and pessimistic prognoses that professionals forecast for
such children, it is perhaps surprising that these successful Hidden Children function so well. Even if there are many unexplained factors involved,
such resilience is worthy of note.

The following chapters highlight the experiences of some Hidden
Children in Poland and Western Europe during Nazi occupation. These
men and women do not qualify as pathological, either by their own sub-
jective criteria or that of the professional observer. They are neither in a
state of total denial, nor are they totally unmarked or unaffected by those
early life events. They are warm, confident, often assertive, self-aware,
frequently humorous, and joyful human beings. Compared with a group
of patients who attribute their current difficulties to childhood and upbringing, one is tempted to use the analogy of the "Princess and the Pea"
in Hans Christian Andersen's tale. This story describes the discomfort
complained of by the indulged and petulant little princess. She was so

exquisitely sensitive to the tiny irritant under the pile of mattresses that she was unable to sleep. There is no doubt that patients seeking help are sensitive to real or perceived injuries or injustices in their families of origin. They attribute to these events their past or present problems or relationship difficulties. Some of these, seen objectively, appear to be as minute but also as acutely irritating, as the pea under the pile of mattresses. Intervention from psychiatrists, psychotherapists, and clinicians involves helping such individuals to move on and live more comfortably and at ease. People who have suffered major injury, disaster, or damage, physical or psychological or both, often experience readily understandable difficulties. With appropriate intervention, some improve their adjustment.

Without trying to "overnormalize" the experience of survivors, we should now be able to recognize the positive attributes (Hassan, 1989) of those who have been able to overcome significant early adversity while applying our skills and understanding to the needs of those whose profound suffering continues.

In western countries occupied by the German Nazi regime between 1939 and 1945, cultural, geographical, environmental, and historical factors determined the range of hiding experiences, of which the most widely known is of course described in *The Diary of Anne Frank* (1989). Contrary to general belief, not all such children perished, hence the powerful educational impact made by survivors.

THE EFFECTS OF SEPARATION AND LOSS

Early work (for example, Bowlby, 1960; Spitz, 1965) based on observation of the effects of infant/mother separation suggested that early disrupted bonds increased the risk of delinquency and maladjustment.

Donald Winnicott (1965), the distinguished British child psychiatrist, described the "good enough mother," that is, not perfect but adequate for the child's needs.

Kolvin, Miller, Fleeting, and Kolvin (1988) have drawn attention to factors that protected children in criminal and deprived environments either from disturbance or from becoming delinquent, criminal, or both. Much of this work related to the conditions of postwar Britain and specifically addressed vulnerability to delinquency in particular, rather than protection from the later development of neuroses, depression, and other psychological problems. Other studies in the 1970s and 1980s focused on the antecedents of depression in unresolved losses (Parkes, 1972; Brown, Harris, and Copeland, 1977). Recently, however, Harrington and Harrison (1999), discussing children's resilience to adversity, challenged the necessity for a "counseling for all" culture, questioning in this context the notion that all bereaved children will need structured counseling.

"Various factors seem to protect against adverse effects . . . factors in the child include temperament, scholastic competence, high self-esteem and the capacity to form supportive relationships. Developmental stage is also important." The work of fostering and adoption agencies and the development of child protection agencies has become increasingly sophisticated in the United Kingdom, culminating in England with The Children Act 1989, so that we now have a quite precise yardstick by which to measure the "good enough" care of children.

Kestenberg (1982) speculated that "there must be healthy survivors" but "as therapists we did not have direct access to such cases," and "The testimony of researchers using interviews at the 1983 conference on the Holocaust at Yale University convinced us that a way has been found for survivors to report their Holocaust experience without suffering psychological injury . . . this may be due to the fact that the survivor . . . is not seeking personal help; he is called upon to bear witness. By being interviewed he is entering history. He is doing his share in remembering."

This is certainly my own experience when listening to these successful, well-adjusted Hidden Children. As clinicians, we focus so much on illness that we often ignore the study of health. The counterintuitive idea demonstrates that there are healthy positive factors that endure and reemerge in the face of what most would consider overwhelming psychological insult. Educationally, this is important, not only in the discrimination of important messages, but also in prioritizing resources for those in need.

The personal experiences of these Hidden Children recounted in the following chapters were of a nature to which many with less moving life histories might attribute current difficulties and dysfunction. As can be seen from their accounts, however, their perspective is optimistic, forward-looking, determined, and unvictimized.

Each is but one of a larger group of people who celebrate their healthy adult survival over childhood adversity. Many children were subjected to appalling events. Some did not survive. Of those who did, their subsequent lives could have been emotionally blighted. Śliwowska (1998), in a large collection of autobiographical accounts recently translated into English, documents the survival of children hidden in Poland. Viewed overall, it is remarkable how many describe effective lives in teaching, public service, and the caring professions. The role of altruism as one coping mechanism in survivors will be considered later.

CAN WE IDENTIFY PROTECTIVE FACTORS?

The second part of this book discusses how and why some survivors are resilient. The field of psychological adaptation and resilience now attracts serious academic attention. Any explanation for the fact that, following real adversity, some suffer lifelong disability, some do moderately well for a time or at different periods of their lives but decompensate under stress, and some do rather well psychologically, exceeding expectation, is extremely complex. To disentangle such a tangled skein of threads rigorously and scientifically is still very difficult. We do not know and could not study in any meaningful way the true numbers of those with significant difficulty, compared with those who feel they are functioning "well enough" or better.

It is important, however, to explore the capacity of the human organism and psyche for adaptation. While we document damage and disability in a very large number of survivors, allocating blame to the source, the Nazi regime and the resulting Holocaust, we can perhaps also record more robust adjustment of others who consider themselves as surviving well. There are surely messages to be extrapolated, lessons to be learned, in the fields of contemporary fostering and adoption, particularly as aid agencies seek to restore the equilibrium and provide and plan for the care and the futures of children subject to other contemporary genocides.

THE CONTRIBUTION OF RESCUERS
AND HIDING FAMILIES

What part did the characteristics of the rescuers play in the ultimate adaptation and adjustment of their charges?

The subject of rescuers, their characteristics (Oliner and Oliner, 1988; Paldiel, 1989; Bloch and Drucker, 1992) and motivations, is as complex as the study of those who survived. One could speculate about the extent to which adjustment was influenced not only by being hidden, sheltered, and protected, but also by aspects of the rescuers' behaviors, identifying with attitudes and values. Of course the experiences of children in hiding were enormously varied, some more positive than others and some frankly abusive in nature.

Standards of childcare in Occupied Europe cannot necessarily be equated with contemporary standards in the 2000s. For example, one child, hidden in Holland, now well-adjusted to life, having overcome not only her war years with dignity and strength but also her own illness and the death of her only daughter in childbirth a few years ago, told me of her feelings on being presented at the door of a simple farm in the countryside after removal from an orphanage where she had been placed.

"She was very large and strong," she said of the farmer's wife who opened the door to her, and "I instantly felt, 'Here I will be safe.'" However, she was also able to describe with some wry humor how the same motherly woman who absorbed her with ease into a simple rural household was also capable of treating her exactly as she would one of her own, by hauling her by the ear across the farmyard after some misdemeanor. Overall, however, her enduring experience in this hiding family was of warm affection and love, as well as of somewhat rough discipline. This enabled her to overcome the abrupt separation from her family and some bleak experiences after the war. Being well parented early on gave her the capacity to make appropriate affectional bonds (Bowlby, 1960) and to establish her own family relationships satisfactorily.

How important in the later development of some of these resilient survivors was the survival and return of one or more parent or sibling, which at first sight seems an attractive theory in the search for possible protective factors for the developing child? As we know, hopes and fantasies about the future after the war with the return of one or both parents were not often met. If they were, the reality often turned out to be disappointing. A parent who had survived a camp or slave labor was often in a poor physical and psychological state. Some children had bonded so closely to their rescuers that they were reluctant to be reclaimed and often protested. Although the range of variables makes it hard to quantify, within my group a number found at least one close family member surviving. Is this the only explanation for their healthy adaptation? Because the postwar years were often difficult (some judged them worse than their experience in hiding), and adjustment was often slow and painful, this is hard to confirm. A positive and protective effect on the developing personality, as has been described in group work with Kindertransport children, may well have been the security of their early attachments formed before being hidden. Children who have secure attachments in infancy and a warm, emotionally healthy family origin usually tolerate separation better than those from dysfunctional backgrounds with insecure attachments. However, this cannot be the whole explanation. There are exceptions, for example, the infant who was removed from the ghetto and consigned to a succession of orphanages and children's homes (perhaps she received some very effective mothering from her first foster mother) or in another case, the two little brothers who lost their mentally ill mother very shortly after the deportation of their father.

Personality and inherited characteristics must surely also play major parts. One person recalls that she was impressed by the strength of character of a surviving maternal aunt and later learned that her own mother had been unusually independent and assertive.

With the exception of the "hidden infants" in my group, with no conscious recollection of their family characteristics, one possibility may be that most of these children were in the latency period, that is, between the ages of five and ten. This period of childhood is characterized by relatively carefree attitudes, developing independence, but also a degree of compliance and obedience usually lost at adolescence. This is exemplified by the accounts of several of the children, notably Janek, described in Chapter 3, who was concealed in solitary confinement and who feels that he was young enough to view his experiences (of being smuggled out of the ghetto in a suitcase) as something of an adventure and was also sufficiently mature to comply with instructions and understand the dangers.

RELIGION, FAITH, AND IDENTITY

Did religious or spiritual adherence play a part in strengthening or protecting the child? Fogelman (1988) referred to the wide range of backgrounds, from deeply observant religious to highly assimilated, from which her sample of Hidden Children was drawn. While many found difficulty after the war in expressing or finding a Jewish identity after hiding in a Catholic milieu, it has been suggested that, for example, in parts of France, Protestants, being a minority, were less likely to try to convert their charges. So much, however, depended on the individual. Nicole remembers with affection the daughter of her Catholic rescuers who reminded her daily never to forget her Jewish prayer, the *Sh'ma*, as requested by her mother. In other locations, for example, in Poland, children had little chance of survival unless they were able to suppress their religious practices in order to pass convincingly as Catholics.

For some, like Irena, dawning recognition of a Jewish identity was uncomfortable and confusing. For others, circumstances or the remarriage of a surviving parent led to a return to religious orthodoxy and has provided a strong bulwark of faith that has sustained them and to which they would partially or wholly ascribe their current stable adjustment. Others have retained their identity but not their practice. However, some protective factors involve the attribution of the events by the individual and, perhaps, therefore, to innately positive qualities of the personality.

CONCLUSIONS

In summary, we have seen that there were understandable historical reasons for overwhelmingly negative assumptions about the outcome of survivors. Most of the early published work concerned adult survivors, and time was required for the surviving Hidden Children to reach an age and a listening audience for their experiences to be heard. Since then they have become vocal in their own right, recovered their own voices, and are insistent that the positive as well as the damaging aspects of their existence be recorded and validated. By presenting their experiences in a variety of ways, they help us to confront for the future the lessons of the past and to avoid cultural and professional stereotyping of the child survivor as a helpless victim.

NOTES

1. In England the creation of the National Health Service in 1947 "free at the point of delivery" and the development of newer ways of treating psychiatric and psychological disorders suggested that shorter and more effective methods were available. Consequently long-term psychoanalytical treatment was not accessible except to a very few, largely those able to pay for it; there was thus a difference in therapeutic philosophy and emphasis between the professional literature in the United Kingdom and other countries such as the United States, Israel, and initially to a great extent other European countries.

2. In May 1991, a group of Hidden Children launched the First International Gathering of Children Hidden during World War II in New York City. Jane Marks had drawn attention to this group in a New York magazine several months earlier.

3. What appeared to be a moderately healthy and adaptive way of dealing with the Holocaust could be achieved only with massive denial and repression of the traumatic period. It is not surprising that, eventually, the intolerable memories of the past returned to haunt the survivor (Bergman and Jucovy, 1982).

4. Bettelheim's camp experiences, however, were prewar and politically determined. Not only were they not comparable with Levi's, but his criticism of concentration camp survivors later attracted much opprobrium.

5. Shoah Visual History Foundation (PO Box 3168, Los Angeles, CA 90078-3168, USA).

CHAPTER 3

Poland

WLODKA ROBERTSON

Wlodka is one of a pair of Polish twins who were hidden separately. Her mother was a teacher active in the Polish (Socialist) Bund movement involved in setting up soup kitchens in the Warsaw ghetto. It was considered too dangerous to hide the twins together. She describes the very different life she led, hidden in the countryside by superstitious and often anti-Semitic farmers, while her sister remained hidden by a Polish Gentile family in the city, occasionally visiting her and bringing news. It was too dangerous for her to make reciprocal visits. She was usually frightened and isolated with little contact, and feared for the fate of her mother.

Eventually after the war, she and her twin followed very different paths. Wlodka moved to Britain and trained as a health professional. Rather than ascribe difficulties in her life to the misery and fear of her childhood, she tends to feel that they have on the whole strengthened her.

I was born on October 12, 1931. My family was very politically engaged. My father was one of the leaders of the Bund[1] and my mother, Fela Blit, belonged to the *Poalecjon* (*The Workers of Zion*, a leftist Zionist party). My mother was headmistress of a Yiddish school, and my father edited a Yiddish newspaper and was active as a youth leader for the Bund. I have a twin sister, Nelly. I remember people from Spain visiting our small apartment in quite a poor part of Warsaw in the Jewish district. My mother's family lived nearby in the same block; my grandfather was religious, and he had a small metal factory. Because both of my parents worked, which was rather unusual, we had a young Polish woman from the countryside living with us. She looked after us and we spent a lot of time with our grandparents. My other grandparents lived in another part of Warsaw. There was quite a lot of Yiddish spoken.

There is not much I can remember from before the war. I was eight when war broke out. We were on holiday that summer and had to come home very quickly because it was obvious the war was going to start. Then both my parents left because the younger people were at some point told to evacuate Warsaw because it was not going to be defended, and the army would be formed on the East Side. My parents told me where my sister and I and the Polish girl, Hela, would go to. We were taken to my aunt and uncle and told that my parents had to leave. We could see lots of people leaving Warsaw. But then there was some change of plan and the Polish government decided to defend Warsaw after all. So we all moved and lived in a block of flats that had courtyards like they have in Paris. There were soldiers in the courtyard and some bombing and fires. That's how I remember the beginning of the war.

Then the Germans came in; I don't think I saw them. My sister and I were taken to my other grandparents, and about six weeks later my mother came back. She had smuggled herself through the Russian frontier because the Russians occupied that part of Poland. Anyhow, she succeeded

Nelly (*left*) and Wlodka Blit (*right*) with their mother Fela Hertzlich Blit, Aunt Pola, and Grandparents. Warsaw 1940. Courtesy of Wlodka Robertson.

Nelly (*left*) and Wlodka before hiding.
Courtesy of Wlodka Robertson.

Nelly Dunkel (*left*) and Wlodka Robertson (*right*) celebrating their seventieth birthday in New York. Courtesy of Wlodka Robertson.

in coming back. I remember that it was a very cold winter and there was very little food. It was a smart apartment where my grandparents lived, but we just lived in one room and managed to heat it with a small fire in an iron stove. I remember talks about a ghetto being made, gangs of organized hooligans chasing Jews and beating them up in the streets. By that time everyone except children in Warsaw had to wear a band with a star, and I remember coming home by taxi, jumping out, and being surrounded by hooligans with sticks and my mother shouting at them: "They are not Jews!" So by the time we had to move into the ghetto, we were almost glad because it would be quiet, and we would be protected. We moved to my other grandparents with my mother who was running a kitchen at the school where she had been headmistress. It became a soup kitchen, mainly for the children who used to go to the school, but also for poor children as well. Emmanuel Ringelblum, the historian, writes about my mother in his book *Notes from the Warsaw Ghetto* (1974), about how she ran the kitchen. Looking back on it, it was obvious that things were getting worse and worse all the time, but we were somewhat protected, my sister and I, from the worst. We did see children who we knew dying of hunger with swollen stomachs and also people being drawn in from surrounding villages with nowhere to stay. But we had some food and my grandparents had some connections. They were still selling some metal things, crosses and crucifixes, so there was some money. Warsaw was not so isolated, and I think that food was being smuggled in from outside.

At first we went to some kind of private classes but not for very long. There were rumors that Jews were being shot and that it was going to be difficult to survive the war. Then I remember placards in German and Polish being plastered over Warsaw that said there would be evacuation. Some people who had special permission, who were perhaps working for the Germans or who had special documents, could stay. At first my mother, my sister, and I had these cards. I remember the Germans coming to this block of flats and not being able to find my card. It was very frightening—even now if I cannot find something, I remember this. But very quickly it became obvious that these cards would not help. So my uncle and my grandfather built hiding places in the cellars. We had a cellar in the block of flats with a false opening to it. When we heard the Germans coming we, with some other family, would run to this place. We would hear the shouting and the shooting. Before this, when I had come out with my card, I had seen people being divided to go to the right or the left. These were people that I knew.

These *Aktions* (roundups) would suddenly stop and life would seem to be almost normal. But every time this happened there were less and less people left in the ghetto. My other grandparents were taken away earlier in the war. Also most of the children were gone, and we knew that there were gassings. I remember listening to someone who had managed to get away from Treblinka, who came back to the ghetto because he had nowhere else to go. My mother asked him what was happening, and she was told that if we were called there was no point in taking any clothes or anything. My grandparents, uncles, and aunts, because of the metal factory, managed to arrange to work for an industrialist called Toebbens who opened a factory, a bit like Schindler. There were quite a few of them and that was supposed to protect them from being taken away. We had just heard that we had to move because this factory was in another part of the ghetto. We had a secret place in the bathroom, and we used to hide there and listen to the Germans shout and scream, but we were never found. About two months before the final liquidation of the ghetto my mother went somewhere with us. I don't know why. To find somewhere else to live? In the night we heard some shooting and then a friend—somebody from her political party— came in, and he had a gun. He tried to take us to a bunker, and I remember how exciting it seemed to see someone with a gun. He led us to a hiding place and we stayed there for three days, my mother, my twin sister, Nelly, and me.

After that we went back to my grandparents' place and then there was another call for everybody, all the people who were not working in the factories, to go to the Umschlagplatz. Again there would be some sort of selection, and so the younger people who worked in the factory and my grandfather went to the Umschlagplatz[2] hoping they would be allowed to come back.

Then we went to some terrible cellar or bunker. I don't know how the rest of the family knew of it, but there were more than one hundred people there of different families. Some of my friends were there. We were there for maybe two days and then my family was allowed to come back. We heard these terrible stories of people trying to smuggle their children out in coffins. Other people we knew committed suicide.

So then my mother made up her mind that the only way to survive was to get out of the ghetto. It was then February 1943, and she knew some close friends of my uncle who would possibly look after my sister and me. Strangely it was still possible to telephone in the ghetto. They said it was out of the question, but she knew Mikhal Klepfisz who was a Bundist and an engineer. He had been living outside, making some sort of bottle bombs, and he came to the ghetto to say that he could take my sister and me because the Bund was trying to find places with Polish families outside the ghetto. We were not asked if we wanted to go, we were just told to put our things, dresses and clothes, together and take them to the wall of the ghetto in the evening.

I know my grandfather was worried that I should become a Christian and I said, "No, no, no, that is such a silly story, it is impossible!" But he said, "Oh, cleverer people than you believe it!" I don't know why he said that; maybe he thought it was the worst thing that could happen, I don't know. He was very worried. We went to some point that was obviously used for smuggling, and the Germans were bribed. There was a ladder and we were told to climb it, and there would be another on the other side. Mikhal Klepfisz told us to go with him wherever he went. We jumped on a tram—there were still trams outside the ghetto—and then some people began to look at us, so he told us to jump off quickly and onto another tram and then another.

For the first time I realized that I had to be afraid of not just the Germans but of the Poles also. He took us, Nelly and me, to a tiny apartment where he lived with a Catholic family who owned a factory where he was caretaker before the war. So they were friendly toward him and helped him. He was making his bombs—Molotov Cocktails—helping people get out of the ghetto and smuggling arms. It was an exciting time because he was quite happy to talk to my sister and me, I remember that. He was in his mid-thirties. There was also someone called Vladka (Feigele Peltel), a courier who came there. But then the Dubiels, the family we came to, moved to a bigger apartment. They knew some other Jewish family who were going to come to them as well and give them money to buy this bigger apartment just opposite the ghetto wall. We moved there but Mikhal didn't come with us. My mother used to come to the other side of the wall, and we would look through the window on the third floor and wave. So my mother knew we were safe. But very soon after that, because we were so close to the wall, we saw the ghetto surrounded and shooting and so on. We saw German soldiers pouring petrol on some of the houses and setting them alight. There were lots of people jumping out and being shot.

Mrs. Dubiel was afraid to have two children because of the things she saw. So she said that she couldn't have both of us, and I would have to go somewhere else. By that time Mikhal Klepfisz had smuggled himself into the ghetto on an assignment and was shot. Vladka,[3] the courier, had found some other family outside Warsaw, and she took me by train, just me. The Dubiel family was prepared to keep Nelly; maybe she looked less Jewish or seemed more cheerful or something.

I think I was a bit numb by that time. It was just one other thing that happened. What I remember was being continuously unsupported—perhaps not a good enough word. The father of this other family was very nice to me but the wife was terrible, and she clearly didn't want me there. The girl was my age, and at the start I was hoping to be quite friendly but she was so cruel, laughing at me and telling me I should not be alive. It was a surprise; I didn't expect it. But I didn't stay there for long. It was near the railway and some of their chickens got run over, and they thought that this was an omen that they shouldn't keep me. This Polish family lived near the railway line, where the father was a railway man on a small station. The dead chickens were "my fault," so I was then taken to another family back in Warsaw. This was a young couple with a small child. He was an alcoholic, but he was only about twenty-three. He wasn't nice. Although he never harmed me, I was afraid of him. He used to beat his wife.

Wlodka remained with this family for some time.

I was with them really until the Russians came, so it must have been almost two years. If anything like a toothbrush was brought in for me by Vladka it always disappeared.

Communication with her mother was impossible.

Once the ghetto was burned we assumed that everyone was dead, so I just didn't think about it. I was not allowed to go to visit my sister because some neighbors had seen me before, and there was a story invented as to why I wasn't there. Anyhow, I wasn't even told her address but she knew where I was, and she came from time to time. She was still with the same family and was all right. She seemed quite cheerful. I used to go out and play with some of the children in the old town of Warsaw, but often I would be called a Jewess, and I would be afraid. Then the Warsaw Uprising started, the Polish Uprising. And that seemed quite exciting because of where I was; that part of Warsaw was, of course, completely flattened. All the houses were bombed but, even so, the uprising was one of my better memories. I remember people in the cellar saying that some men, Jews from Greece, were liberated by the Polish fighters from the prison in Warsaw. They didn't speak Polish but, somehow, they were helping in this uprising. They were carrying water but then, when the Germans came, they were begging for clothes because they were still wearing their striped prison things. I don't know what happened to most of them.

I went to the cellar with the family I was with, and we were selected and taken to some big church near Warsaw after the capitulation of that part of the city. The younger people without children were taken on to Germany as forced laborers. Suddenly it was as if all these people were afraid and wanted to have a child with them—even me—to avoid being sent. The train stopped somewhere, and we jumped out of it, and we walked for what seemed like miles and miles until we reached a village. Again, it was just as when I came out of the ghetto, I was surprised to see normal life going on although the people were very poor because it was a very primitive village.

There was no electricity, and the water had to come from wells. It was winter, and there was not much more to do than tell stories to the children, and the men would listen as well. But again I have this memory of me dropping or letting a baby fall from a bed—I thought that no one knew that I was Jewish. I had a Polish name, Irena Szabaska, and did my best to pretend and thought that I had fooled everybody. But they began to shout that I was a Jewess and would call the Germans. They didn't call them, but it was just the shock of it, of being very friendly and thinking that they didn't know, then to realize that they did. But they didn't really know who I was, and they didn't know my name!

The Serafin family who were hiding Wlodka might well have left her behind.

But I think that they were rather hoping that, after the war, they would be rewarded. I think that they did get used to me anyway, and they were getting money before the Warsaw Uprising through the underground. It was a sort of job they were doing, although it was dangerous. They knew who I was and that there was some organization connected to me. So I think that partly they were hoping that they would get something out of it at the end. But though the people in the village didn't know who I was, they guessed I was Jewish and still kept me. I didn't remember all these good things until later—but when I started looking back I remember things like the food. There was so little food, and all their children were begging for food. I was there, but I ate what there was, what was given to me.

Suddenly in the winter it became obvious that the war was nearly over. We saw the Russians appear in the village. I had some contact with Vladka at one point, just by chance. During the worst of the Polish Uprising, she brought some of her family to the same building because they thought it would be safer there.

But, by chance, the Serafin family who were hiding me were at the market selling some of the stuff they had smuggled out of Warsaw and met Vladka who had come to see what had happened to the rest of her family. So when the Russians came, I just waited for her to come and fetch me. She did not come. We just waited and waited and then went by cart to Warsaw. It was completely ruined but we found some part of the house still standing. Someone from the Bund came looking for me, first to the village and then to the room in Warsaw, and she told me that my father was alive. I was glad that I still had a father and that I wasn't completely alone. That was a great relief because when I was sent to a children's home, I knew that eventually I would go to my father, that I had a father to go to. I was thirteen or fourteen years old. Later Nelly and I stayed in Łódź with a friend of my father. One day one of my cousins (he and his brother survived) knocked on the door where we were staying. I remember my sister opening the door to him, and I remember being very excited to see him. But I couldn't bear to think about my mother. In fact, up until recently, I felt guilty about my mother. I had some sleepless nights, thinking it over.

Quite soon Wlodka was reunited with her twin, Nelly.

I can't remember when exactly. I remember that she originally put up some resistance because she didn't want to leave the family, and she had some young boy who she liked. But not for long, and then she came. I can't remember really how Nelly seemed. We used to alternate—one of us would be more confident and one would depend on the other. Yes, she certainly seemed more confident, would take more initiative, and she made friends more easily.

Then my father got in touch. He was in London working as a journalist. He wrote to the Polish government in exile (he had connections with them) to arrange for me and my sister to come to London. The people we stayed with, although not Communist, were making their lives in Communist Poland and said how bad the West was, and we would do better to stay in Poland. So I had slightly mixed feelings. Someone from the Bund was coming from America (on behalf of the Jewish workers' committee), and he took us by train to Sweden and then on to London.

I remember meeting my father at Croydon Airport and then we went by coach to London. I remember calling him *Pan* (Mister) and feeling very strange with him. By that time he had a woman friend so there were complications.

We went to a small grammar school, as we were too old at fourteen to go to secondary school. We also had some private lessons with a Polish woman. It was surprising how there was just nothing special in those days for immigrant children, just nothing at all. But I did well at school quite quickly and stayed on until the sixth form. And I was praised because I made quick progress, whereas my sister was more socially adept. I used to think that I could have probably gone to university but Father may not have had the money. I eventually went into Radiography. I was accepted at the Royal Free Hospital, in a very inappropriate job for me. I quite enjoyed it, but it wasn't a very natural kind of job for me. I enjoyed working with the people; I enjoyed some of it but not necessarily the machinery.

*At first Wlodka's father lived in Finsbury Park, while the girls were at school,
but then he married and they moved to Muswell Hill.*

I think he found it quite hard, working as a journalist. First he wrote for
a Polish socialist paper, then for a paper in Austria, and for a Yiddish paper
in the United States.

Then he lectured at the London School of Slavonic Studies, part-time.
That was just for the last few years and he was very happy. My sister in
the meanwhile tried to do nursing but did not pass. She went to a Bundist
youth camp in Belgium where she met a young man who she went to
live with. She was nineteen, still at school, and then she got pregnant and
she got married. I spent some time truanting from my studies to baby-
sit for them.

Then I met Bruce, who is now my husband. He has a very Scottish
name, but he cannot trace the Scottishness so we think that the name was
just a coincidence.

By then my stepmother thought that I had been in her house long
enough (I was almost twenty-one). So I moved out and found a room
somewhere, and by then I knew Bruce. I have friends here, some who
have been through the Holocaust who came in 1945, so that made it
easier. Then my sister went to America with her husband and baby, and
I remember feeling very upset about that. But I trained and got a job
very easily in Walthamstow. All those hospitals I worked at are now closed.
We went to live in a little house in Crawley and later my husband got a
job in Paris. He was an economist but is retired now.

Living in Paris was certainly different from living in Crawley New
Town. It was a perpetual holiday for four years. We had two small children at that time, so in that way I did find it quite hard, not knowing
any French. I was pregnant so our son was born there. But even so it
was very different, and Bruce decided that he didn't want to be an émigré
and stay in France. So we came back to London. I began to work when
my youngest child was five. I found it quite easy to get jobs, and I worked
part-time or full-time as I wished.

Wlodka's eldest daughter in particular is interested in her history.

I am surprised at how many books she has about the ghetto. My husband, who is not Jewish, has been organizing for us to place a plaque for
our family in the Warsaw Jewish Cemetery. He has been doing this together with my cousins in Paris. So we went to Warsaw, and my eldest
daughter came with us. This was about three years ago. My cousin was
going to come but then decided not to.

My son has been asking about Yiddish records. I think that it has made
some impact on them, the fact that I have been through all this. My

daughter had some problems recently and, though she usually copes very well, she had to be off work. So we talked about this, but she didn't think that it was the obvious reason, but that it could be one, perhaps. The war was not one of the things we would talk about when she was little.

I have met some child survivors who had problems, right at the end of the war or a little later. They seemed to resent their parents. My children possibly think that when they have big problems that I can't take it, and they don't tell me their troubles.

Wlodka seems to be relatively relaxed and functioning well. Did she consider this her own perception or is it a front?

Well, I don't function very well in a crisis. I function all right otherwise.

What happens in a crisis?

I don't move. When my husband had a stroke I coped very well for two days, I seem to remember. Then after that I just couldn't get out of the chair. I am all right until something dramatic happens, until I have to make a decision, then I get paralyzed.

How does she view concealment of identity?

Some people have said that they became very adept at lying. Others said that they were very relieved not to have to do that anymore.

I remember that the people we stayed with in Łódź had a Polish name, and we had forged papers in their name, so it wasn't obvious we were Jewish. I remember not being surprised; I was so used to it even from the people who hid me and the people who fed me in the village. I was used to them thinking I was some kind of monster.

Even here I am quite conscious. I make an effort, because my husband is not Jewish and I am not obviously Jewish, to remind myself that it is not only Jews whom people say things about. I am very conscious of that and find it difficult to assert myself.

I was particularly struck by a woman who was hidden somewhere in a village, married a local boy, and nobody knew she was Jewish. She had children then suddenly made contact with some Jews and identified herself. She was so estranged from everyone in the village. I think that her husband had perhaps died, but she spoke of her own children as "these Poles."

Wlodka reflected on the continuing anti-Semitism in Poland.

From my experience I think the Church has a lot to do with it. Though I now know that there was a church very near to the Warsaw ghetto, and the priests were very helpful. But I was trying to hide myself. I was terrified of nuns, and I was told not to go near the priests by the Poles, "because it will be easy for them to find out that you are a Jew and not a Catholic." There was just that feeling that the Jews had murdered Christ and so that is what they deserve.

She also mentioned the railway family who thought that she represented a bad omen. These were very poor superstitious country people, very different from Wlodka's own family, who were involved in literature and politics and action. They had a wider vision of the world and a strong sense of social justice.

They were very, very active. That's why when I compare myself, I feel . . . inactive.

When I think about these experiences, I never thought that I was unique. I mean I thought it was happening to everybody. The time when I completely lost touch with the Jewish underground and my family, I was very desolate. I thought myself completely lost, never to be found again. But even when I was in that village, some of the time I made friendships with some of the children of my age.

Wlodka was separated from her parents, she had lost her mother and had no idea where her father was, yet other people who had similar experiences have coped less well as adults and have become quite seriously depressed.

I am surprised when so many people whom I meet seem to have become so energetic after the war and have managed very well. I suppose luck has something to do with it and whom one marries.

We speculate on the contribution of personality—and heredity. I remind Wlodka that her mother was a very strong woman.

Yes, I remember the stories of how it was she who smuggled her brother out after World War I. She got him out of Poland and into France. Both my parents were very active.

Thinking of my cousin I find it so amazing. He must have some problems, but I remember that he had such a terrible childhood even with his parents, because it was at the beginning of the war, he was a baby, and he was in the way. He was beaten by his parents. He doesn't remember them, and he had those terrible experiences afterward. In 1945, in the children's home, he could hardly speak, he was so disturbed. And he couldn't stand still in one place. I don't know how it happened that he became such a successful astronomer.

Wlodka's cousin now lives in Paris.

I know that he suddenly became very interested in and wanted to talk about his childhood. My name was Irka (Irena) when I was hidden. My Polish surname was Szabaska. I never had to use it, which was a good thing because I couldn't get my tongue round it. My parents were not religious Jews at all, in fact the opposite, very anti-establishment.

Some people who lost a parent in the war had a burning desire later to have a child of their own. Others became passionately opposed to having children. How did Wlodka perceive this?

I have to admit that I became pregnant very quickly but without much conscious thought. I know that some decided not to have children.

Sometimes the pain of having lost someone is so great that the fear of further ruptured attachment to another living person is too much. Wlodka clearly had a strong constitution to enable her to survive when similar things were happening to others who did not emerge with such intact emotional strength. How has the experience affected her twin, Nelly?

To my mind she seems strong when we are together. I think her life is much cozier. They live in New York in one of those big co-operative buildings that the Jewish Unions have built so that they are in an environment of very similar people. And I think that's very cozy. I think New York is very much the place where she wants to be. I see her once a year now. In fact she is coming over in three weeks time.

NOTES

1. Bund is the Jewish Socialist party.
2. Umschlagplatz is the collecting center where German soldiers assembled Jews for deportation.
3. Vladka was the pseudonym of Feigele Peltel-Miedkowska, a courier for the Bund.

IRENA MILEWSKA

Irena's early life had been deprived and harsh, but the postwar years were even more difficult. She had to live with a confusion of religion, identity, and constant deception. Concealment was a constant struggle. Yet she has become a lively, open, trustworthy person, capable of giving and accepting affection and understanding the vicissitudes of the past without bitterness. Reading the bare facts of her deprived early life, with the many years of hiding her identity and enforced dishonesty, it is all the more impressive to see that now she is no longer squeezed between the pressures of anti-Semitism and the Communist regime that she has blossomed into the delightful, dependable person she is today.

I was born in Paris and my false papers give my birth date as June 2, 1938, at Częstochowa, a Polish town, a holy place (like Lourdes in France) where I was supposed to have been born. My *nom de guerre*, my hiding name, is Irena Milewska.

My parents, Polish Jews from Warsaw, Anna Minkowska and Norbert Grasberg, had been studying in Paris and they married there.

My mother had come to France to do her sociology doctorate at the Sorbonne and my father studied agronomy, qualifying in 1939. So my parents had planned to live in France. I suppose they emigrated for their studies, partly because of the *numerus clausus*[1] in Poland, to study peacefully without the racial and anti-Semitic persecution of that time.

My father's cousins have said that he would have had a Jewish education, but I don't know whether he was very observant. My mother was from a family of intellectuals, rather left-wing, less well-off than my father's family and probably somewhat assimilated. They had a civil marriage in the *Mairie* of the fifth *arrondissement* of Paris.

I have found various places where they lived, especially in the Latin Quarter, as students did. A student friend of my mother who studied in Poland with her and then came with her to the Sorbonne, Nina Assorodobraj-Kula, who became a sociology professor in Warsaw, told me about their life.

In June 1939, during the summer vacation, Irena later learned that her mother had taken her back to Warsaw to visit grandparents. Her father, newly qualified, stayed behind in France to start his first post in Toulouse. He was later to be interned at Drancy. His subsequent deportation to Auschwitz is recorded in Klarsfeld's Memorial *(1983).*

At the outbreak of war in September 1939, Irena's mother was unable to leave Poland to rejoin her husband in France. She remained with her infant daughter and her own parents. Eventually they had to move into the

54

Irena Milewska, aged about thirteen. Courtesy
of Irena Milewska.

Irena today. Courtesy of Irena Milewska.

Warsaw ghetto. Irena has no idea how long she was there, but apparently her mother or grandparents arranged for some Polish Catholic neighbors, Halina and Tadeusz Paszkowski, to rescue her from the ghetto and care for her.

The wife was a librarian in the University of Warsaw, a neighbor of my grandparents. She told me that my mother handed me over the very high wall of the ghetto and that they collected me from the other side. I was not with them long because it was too dangerous, and I think I was pretty identifiably Jewish. So they put me in an orphanage.

I was in a series of children's homes throughout the war. I had no further contact with my mother; I don't even know how she disappeared. I don't know what happened to her and my grandparents, whether she was killed, whether she committed suicide. None of them left the ghetto alive.

So there I was on the Aryan side. I had a whole series of moves and many years in various orphanages but still in contact with the neighbors who were very, very kind to me. Whenever they came to see me, they brought me clothes, the little things that you would bring to a child when you visit. After the war, I went to see them from time to time, for Christmas and other holidays.

They managed to obtain a false birth certificate for me with the name Irena Milewska. I was supposed to have been born at Częstochowa, about the most Catholic town you can possibly imagine, so my identity was disguised.

I have vague memories of the first orphanages, but everything is a bit muddled up. I do have some little "flashes," fleeting memories, of a sort of transit camp near Warsaw, at Pruszków, in a sort of huge hangar. There were families with bundles. We were all sitting on the ground on blankets, I don't know if it was with my mother or with my rescuers. I just know that it was terribly cold and there were little insects marching along. I don't know if they were ants or what—I remember tracing them with my finger. I know we were hungry, it was dark; I couldn't sleep and I was crying.

I know that I was very ill in one orphanage and someone looked after me. In another, I had scabies, which they treated with disgusting smelling ointment; I had lice and abscesses everywhere. Of course we were all malnourished, and the hygiene was pretty rudimentary. I was rather anemic, a puny, miserable little child, like many of us then. It probably affected my growth. I remember the last orphanage, in a very pretty place with a very healthy climate on the outskirts of Warsaw. It was a prewar resort, with sanatoriums and convalescent homes, particularly recommended for people with tuberculosis. I suppose that our orphanage must have occupied one of these during the war. It was run by Catholic sisters (nuns) and there were lay teachers; the question of Jewish identity never arose. We were all little Catholics, with our papers all with correct baptismal certificates, all *comme il faut.*

I made my first Holy Communion in the church where I had my catechism lessons. We had a big celebration immediately after the ceremony. My rescuers, the friends of my parents, made me a little dress, bought me pretty shoes, white socks and a little coronet. The jasmine was in flower, and my teacher made me a little crown of fresh jasmine flowers. So for all of us it was a great event. Because it was such a long way to the church, the director of this orphanage specially organized a cart and horse to take us, I remember. It must have been May or perhaps June 1948. During the war itself, as I said, I was very young. I do remember a little, perhaps even the first orphanage in Warsaw: a big dormitory with lots of little beds, probably twenty or thirty. One night we were woken up by the noise of bombs. The sky was all red with flames. They dressed us quickly and put us in lorries in the middle of the night, and they took us to safety, probably to another orphanage or children's home. I also have vague memories of bombings, of lots of noise, of shouting in German, of the sound of hobnail boots clattering, running down cobbled streets. But now I couldn't tell you whether these are my own memories or whether they are things that I have read or seen in films. Everything is melded together because it's so long ago, but I remember this red sky, sirens, and the noise of bombs falling. Obviously these were very close because it was terribly loud.

After that there were other orphanages, all over the place. It was a really poverty-stricken existence. We had the same food all the time and it was pretty disgusting. There was . . . I don't even know the name in French . . . a kind of celery or something similar, a puree that they gave us called *broukiev.*[2] It was horrible. I have never eaten it since, even as an adult. I have never seen it in Poland, this horrible vegetable, but they gave it to us there. These days bran flakes are very fashionable, but then they gave us this awful "soup" with bran flakes every morning. It was probably rich in vitamins, but as children we didn't like it very much.

There was no butter, no meat, and no bread; food like that was just a dream. We didn't eat very well and we were often ill. I have lots of scars from those abscesses that I had in my childhood, in my infancy; it was really a dreadful, dreadful period.

It is only now, looking back, that it seems hard, but then I was among other children and we were all the same. We couldn't imagine anything different. You considered it as completely normal because you hadn't experienced anything else. So we were all in the same boat. We were like all children, sometimes happy, sometimes sad, but on the whole we played and passed the time as children do. Sometimes we had to be careful because there were bombing raids nearby or events that we didn't understand but which the teachers knew about. They took care of us as best they could, so we didn't feel unhappy. I can't say that I had an unhappy childhood, it's only when you look at it objectively that you say: "She didn't have any parents, she lacked affection." But in one way it was a normal childhood because it was the same for all of my school friends then.

My mother's university friend Nina had come back to Warsaw, too, to see her parents. The war had also prevented her from returning to study in Paris. The difference was that she wasn't forced into the ghetto; she was hidden with her family on the Aryan side.

She discovered from my rescuers that I was alive and that I was "hidden" as a Polish Catholic. She came to visit me in this orphanage and, of course, I didn't remember her at all. She had seen me only in Paris when I was a baby. Eventually she made an effort to find somebody who might be interested in adopting me.

Irena sometimes feels bitter about the well-intentioned but often clumsy attempts to "replace" lost families of bereaved survivors with orphaned children.

The person who adopted me was a Jewish woman, a doctor called Saloméa Mins, who had lost her children at Treblinka and her husband in the war. She had been deported and had been in several concentration camps: Mauthausen, Buchenwald, and Auschwitz. She never told me much about it. As she was a doctor and spoke several languages, she had worked as an interpreter at Auschwitz, which was how she had survived. Of course, she had a number tattooed on her arm and she was terribly, terribly traumatized by the war.

This adoption, which took place in October 1948 when I was ten, was an unhappy experience for me. With hindsight, her psychological war wounds had never healed, so she was incapable of giving me the affection I needed. She was terribly affected by her experiences. She had the most dreadful nightmares; she used to scream out in her sleep, and every night her cries woke me up.

In the daytime she was very busy at work. She was the head of a hospital department and was also very involved politically in the Polish Worker's Party. So I was alone throughout the day. When I came back from school, there was only a very anti-Semitic cleaning lady.

That time was the most difficult part of my sufferings. Of course in all those orphanages and children's homes, I had no idea that I was Jewish. I was completely integrated with the Catholic children and religion, but at the time of my adoption by Dr. Saloméa Mins I learned I was Jewish. I don't remember exactly if it was she who told me or my mother's neighbors or my mother's student friend.

You know, after the war, many couples in Poland wanted to adopt children because they had lost their own during the war; there were so many orphaned children, there was a major adoption campaign. For us children, I remember we all dreamed of being adopted, of course. Various people came to look at the children, and they used to bring us sweets or treats. So it was rather nice. I remember when this person had already decided to adopt me; she took me home to Warsaw for a weekend. To me it seemed extraordinary, really wonderful. She had a very beautiful apartment and she was very caring, very nice to me. So I am certain that she really, really wanted to rebuild her family and to give some affection to another child. But she was probably much too damaged by the war. And I was possibly too old to adapt to the situation. For me she was a strange person whom I never called "Aunt" or by her first name. I always addressed her formally, in the third person;[3] I didn't know her very well because she was away for whole days at a time. Then sometimes she would take me out to the theater. She would make very pretty plaits in my hair, woven with ribbons. I always had very beautiful hair. So, suddenly, I was a beautifully dressed child living in relatively affluent conditions compared with other children in my class, but all the time I was alone, always alone or with this very antipathetic maid.

When I discovered that I was Jewish, I was very uncomfortable. The older I became the more I hated it and felt I had to hide it. Of course, I had this totally Polish name and a plausible Catholic birthplace with false parents.

From time to time I could visit my mother's friend Nina and her family. The person who adopted me lived quite near them, in the same part of Warsaw, and I would go to this kind of surrogate family. That's where I really discovered what family life could be like; it became my family ideal. There was a father and a mother, real parents. I really loved going there. But there was never any religious observance there either. In any case, in Warsaw at that time there were no synagogues, *nobody* was Jewish, no one discussed it. Even in this family, the adults never spoke of their origins in front of the children. So, while I knew that I was Jewish, I knew that it was a taboo subject.

My adoption didn't go well. I was becoming adolescent; I was probably difficult, a bit rebellious and disobedient. This didn't go down very well with my adoptive mother. I never considered her as my mother anyway, or as my aunt or anyone close. So I went back to the orphanage, both of us having had a little bit too much. She was really taken aback, unsure how to make a good relationship with me. I don't know how to explain this, but actually I was very happy to go back to an orphanage. Unfortunately there was no room in Warsaw because the children's homes and orphanages were absolutely overflowing with so many children like me. So

I went to another town, Wrocław, in the winter, January 1951. I was not quite thirteen. She took me to this orphanage where I went into a mixed school. There were children there who had come from a Jewish orphanage. I absolutely detested these Jewish children; I distrusted them *because* they were Jewish. I considered myself better than them because I had been in a secular orphanage, because in Poland there were no Catholic orphanages after the war. The state ran all the orphanages and there was no religion. Because of that, my friends and I actively became Catholics; that was our background. There was a church not far away, so we used to run away to go there. There was a Franciscan monastery where the priests were delighted to see us because we were so enthusiastic. They gave us lots of reading material, little pictures, and so on. We were quite devout and we went a lot to church at that time. The classmates from the Jewish orphanage, for me, they were a sort of subrace, a little like children of an inferior race; I always distrusted them. Following the Yalta Agreement, Communists who had transferred back to Poland from annexed areas moved into Wrocław, the ancient town (previously Breslau in German) where I lived. Many of them were Jewish families. So there I was alongside these Jewish children in a new class where half of us were Catholics. I really wanted to integrate myself totally into the Polish Catholic community.

I don't remember it as being particularly anti-Semitic. Perhaps we were too young, but I just didn't want to be Jewish at any price. I did everything to conceal it. Obviously there was a basis of anti-Semitism behind it all, but I was unaware of it. I didn't know the word; it was an unspoken anti-Semitism for children, adolescents of my age.

Then began the next phase of Irena's life. Orphanages and children's homes encouraged vocational training for the older children, and eventually Irena began nursing training.

From this moment on I was in the middle of a group of girls where the question of religion never arose; it was assumed that we were all the same, all Catholics. But in any case, we didn't speak of religion or our origins, except that I had one friend who was closest to me. We were the youngest pupils accepted at this nursing school with special dispensation because we were below the official entry age. She was an even better student than I, two or three months younger, and she was from a very anti-Semitic family, actively anti-Semitic, without even understanding what it meant.

Despite being one of the youngest in her group Irena was also extremely bright academically and, along with her suspicious anti-Semitic friend, obtained very good examination results. They were rewarded with prestigious posts in a military hospital in Wrocław, in 1955.

Polish army medicine under the Communist regime was very privileged by comparison with other professions. As few nurses were state registered, the girls were immediately given responsible posts before they were eighteen.

I don't know how or why my friend got it into her head that I was Jewish, but she was suspicious and became more so with time. I was posted to orthopedics. The surgical department was just being launched. I had responsibilities that were quite beyond me, especially as I didn't have the authority to run a team, but my boss, a wonderful woman, really helped me in my profession. Throughout our nursing studies I was still attached to the orphanage, which helped me a little with expenses, but I was really very handicapped financially, unlike my friend whose parents were reasonably well off.

I was still in contact with my mother's friend Nina when I was in nursing school. I used to go to her family for Catholic festivals like Christmas and Easter, and after I started working I would sometimes take leave to stay with them during their summer vacation from their university posts. I also spent some winter holidays with the person who adopted me, possibly twice after I started work. Then suddenly there was an enormous rise of anti-Semitism, particularly in Warsaw, and she decided to emigrate to Israel in 1957.

She was not only Jewish, but also officially a member of the Communist Party, which protected her but at the same time gave her unpopular privileges. Actually I intended to go to Israel at this time myself. She began to write to me, encouraging me to leave Poland. Although I had my contacts with the friends of my mother, that was all. I had no family; I was alone. I was beginning to work, sharing an apartment with this anti-Semitic friend from nursing school and receiving these letters from Israel, which ultimately confirmed her suspicions about my origins. I began to take steps with the consulate of Israel to emigrate, to obtain a visa to depart for Israel.

In order to try to emigrate Irena had to resort to various subterfuges.

The most difficult thing was to obtain a passport because in Poland one only had an identity card. Only the police issued passports. I didn't want anyone where I worked to know that I was planning to emigrate to Israel. So I told work colleagues, and my flatmate, that the person who had adopted me had emigrated to the United States where I was going to join her. When I was receiving airmail letters, my friend didn't see the postmark at first, so my story of the United States was just plausible. Then one day she found a letter and understood that this person had emigrated not to the United States but to Israel, which confirmed her suspicions.

At this point Irena met a young man who had been injured in the Warsaw Ghetto Uprising. They fell in love and planned to marry, and he was the first person to whom she could confide her secret origins.

I was eighteen, perhaps a little more. He was a little older than me and lived in Warsaw and I was living in Wrocław, 500 kilometers away. So I abandoned the idea of emigrating to Israel, although at that time I had already bought my case, which had a prominent place in my studio apartment because I was already preparing to leave.

She had planned to get herself transferred to a military hospital in Warsaw to be near her fiancé. However, she had misgivings about coping with his physical disabilities and broke off the engagement. It finished sadly and, subsequently, she has regretted it because he was a fine young man.

But she changed course, abandoned the idea of emigrating and, while still nursing, took up her education again, intending to study medicine.

In Poland there is stiff competition to get into the Faculty of Medicine. I tried two years running. On the first occasion I was successful but was turned down because, as a registered nurse, I was already employed. My boss was appalled by my rejection and told me, "I will support you because you are a bright girl and you will make a very good doctor." So I applied again and passed the entrance exam, but I didn't get enough points overall. I couldn't get into the Faculty. Then I met another young man, and this time I got married and abandoned the idea of doing medicine.

Irena married in 1970. Her husband was from a Catholic family. Neither before nor during their marriage was she ever able to talk about her background.

Again she had to resort to complicated subterfuge, even traveling to her false birthplace, Częstochowa, to obtain papers for the wedding.

The church where my false birth certificate was issued had been destroyed during the war; that was probably why so many false certificates had been issued from this nonexistent parish. In any case, it all seemed completely plausible to him, he never doubted my identity, so I never told him who I really was. My parents-in-law were observant Catholics and very anti-Semitic. They were unhappy that their son didn't want a religious ceremony but did not insist. His parents were completely opposed to our marriage because they didn't want him to marry a "bastard." They actually said that!

But eventually, although I was hardly what they had hoped for, they accepted me and took me into their family. My father-in-law became seriously ill. As I was a nurse, I was involved in helping to nurse him, which reinforced our bond right up until his death; I became his favorite, his little darling.

I got on very well with all my in-laws. I had a child, a year more or less after our marriage, quite quickly. To please my parents-in-law and conform, I gave our child a Catholic upbringing.

My child, like all children of her age, went to catechism, and she made her first Communion, as I had done. This wasn't because her father insisted on it, it was to be the same as the others. As I wanted so much to be like everyone else, I behaved as if I was just like everybody else.

At about this time Irena's mother's old friend came across someone with the same name as her father (Grasberg). This led them to search for family connections for her, which ultimately led to a contact with the French branch of her father's family living in Paris, and so the next phase of her life opened up.

I received a letter from my second cousin in Paris, also called Irène. It was a family custom to call all the firstborn girls Irène/Irena. When she wrote to me in 1958 that she was happy to have discovered me and that I was part of their family, I was absolutely ecstatic to discover that I belonged somewhere.

When I met my husband I had hidden all this. He knew that I had family in the United States and family in Paris who had a French name (Binois), so that too was credible.

I was invited to Paris to come and meet her and her mother, the aunt in question. But in Poland at the time it was very difficult to obtain a passport, and I was turned down by the military police. That was a very black mark for me. There was an enquiry at work, and so my boss became aware of my plans.

At that time Irena was threatened with revelation of her Jewish identity. About 1957 or 1958, there was a collection in Poland for the French Dockers' strike. She was reluctant to contribute out of her meager salary.

I was with my boss in the theater block, big operating theaters with sliding doors. He shut himself in with me in one of these and said to me, "I'm begging you, do it for me, join in, otherwise I shall be obliged to tell them what I know." He blackmailed me in a way: "What I know about you can have very difficult consequences for you." So I subscribed, partly because I was really shocked and also because I didn't know what on earth to do. It was a threat to reveal my origins, although really it couldn't have had any consequences because I was just a little nurse, even though I was in charge of a theater block. It wasn't such an important post, after all, but I was terrified that things would come out. I was concerned for him too, as head of department. I did it partly for him, because he was really a good man, and partly because I was frightened. It was the first time in my life that I was faced with such a threatening, frightening situation.

After Irena was married, she again applied for a passport when her French cousin sent her a ticket and guarantee of accommodation. She was refused again. Only when she could leave her husband and child as hostages did she get permission to go to France. Coming from the deprivation of postwar Communist Poland, life in the West was a complete revelation.

I came to France for the first time in 1962. I was completely bowled over. Poland was in a very economically precarious situation. My cousin and her husband were both doctors, living comfortably in Paris in a very beautiful apartment. At first I was really terrified that they would be in debt for life after entertaining me. I realized that people in France could live better, they could travel, have cars, and holidays.

But, you know, I was young; I was so happy because finally I had my own family, my child, my husband. And I had my new family that I had found in France, which gave me some roots, some sense of identity.

Through my aunt I learned about my father studying in Paris, that he had met and married my mother there. My mother's friend in Warsaw, Nina, completed the story. She remembered going to visit my mother when I was born and remembered me as a very small baby. My life was like a puzzle with lots of gaps in it. There are still plenty of gaps, things that I don't know and that I shall probably never know.

After a further visit of two months to Paris in 1970, when her little daughter was eight, Irena began to tell her about France.

I had begun to understand French conversations better. I began to see the friends of my family, in other words the Jewish community and non-Jewish people. I realized that life could be led differently, that people could connect with their origins. I began to ask myself, "Who am I? Why am I living with this false identity?"

Irena returned to France in 1972 thinking about her origins. Living with a false identity began to weigh heavily on her and at about this time there were difficulties in her marriage.

She continued her education, began to teach psychology and technical subjects in the nursing school, and prepared to get her master's degree.

My husband had met somebody else and this decided it for me. But separating wasn't very easy in Poland. There were economic reasons that I gave as arguments for my husband to give me permission to leave on holiday with my daughter for several months. For myself I had decided to leave for good. My husband agreed because he was occupied elsewhere, which meant that I could leave with my little daughter. It was a good opportunity for her to learn French. So I arrived in France where the friends of my cousin had prepared the ground a little. Before, I hadn't really noticed the anti-Semitic environment in Poland, but these successive holidays had opened my eyes a bit.

It was such a weighty decision, so difficult to begin to turn the page like that. I had not quite committed myself to applying for political asylum, seeking refugee status, until suddenly I was called up by the Prefecture with threat of expulsion from France within twenty-four hours because my visa had expired. This pushed me into making an emergency application for political asylum in November 1976 with the help of my cousin's friends. So effectively the door of return was closed to me.

I knew that I would get refugee status but it was difficult because, although I had Jewish origins, I hadn't been persecuted. It wasn't enough to have Jewish origins in order to leave Poland, although anti-Semitism was increasing all the time and has never actually stopped. But my decision was determined as much by the desire to live comfortably with my Jewish identity as by the breakdown of my marriage. After two or three years I began my studies again here in Paris, took up the study of Social Psychology at the University of Paris in Nanterre, and obtained a teaching qualification.

So now, if you like, I am much more serene and tranquil because the circle is almost complete. It's extraordinary how events can change positively from one generation to another. I've told you a story that wasn't very beautiful at the beginning but that promises to end well.

So Irena's life passed through several phases: separation from her loving mother, a deprived and rudimentary existence in wartime children's homes and orphanages, a well-intentioned but failed adoption, and a confused identity. For years she kept this secret, hidden from the world but contained within her throughout marriage, professional work, and motherhood.

Even though she was able to reclaim her Jewish identity, she feels that she was unable to handle it for some time, not until she learned to live comfortably with it in France. Initially, establishing herself professionally as an immigrant single mother was hard. Irena was probably over-qualified and exploited in some of her early nursing posts. With further academic study, however, she eventually attained important professional status as a senior nurse educator for the Croix Rouge Française.[4] Her psychosocial training also enabled her to help the Enfants Cachés Association to run groups for former Hidden Children, whose need to talk and share their experiences had never been met.

Her life is full and busy with friends, volunteer work, and enjoyment of all the cultural opportunities in Paris.

Her daughter, Małgorzata (Małgosia), also uprooted, adapted remarkably to her new life and language, becoming an academic with a doctorate in Slavonic literature and teaching at the Sorbonne, where Irena has found her mother's publications from before the war. So the academic circle from the Polish sociologist Anna Minkowska is now complete and assuages a little the sadness of the past.

And the family continues too; her daughter and son-in-law and their three little children are her delight.

NOTES

1. *Numerus clausus* limited the quota of entry for various studies, effectively restricting access to Jewish students.

2. *Broukiev* was probably a type of coarse root vegetable, similar to swede, which was normally used as cattle fodder.

3. Formal address in Polish, the equivalent of the *vous* form in French, uses the third person.

4. The Croix Rouge Française (French Red Cross) has a prominent role in postgraduate medical as well as nursing education. Irena played a significant part in palliative care and bereavement education all over France.

JANEK WEBER

Janek only began to acknowledge his story in 1991, when he and his wife, also a Hidden Child, attended almost by chance the first Child Survivor Gathering in New York. He was amazed to discover people like himself, although many were engaged in or in need of long-term psychiatric care or psychotherapy. Neither Janek nor his wife, Charlotte (see Chapter 4), had ever considered professional help. His psychological stability is evident in all dimensions of his life. He is a successful businessman, loving husband and father, valued colleague and friend, and all of this is the more remarkable when one considers the strange facts of his concealment in what was effectively solitary confinement for two-and-a-half years of his early childhood in a small house behind the German barracks on the outskirts of Kraków. He had reached the family after his parents arranged for him to be smuggled out of the ghetto in a suitcase, on the eve of their move to the Płaszów concentration camp. Janek tells his often painful story, not because he is obsessed by it, but modestly, because he knows that it is an important segment of oral history that needs to be saved. Despite having lived in England for many years, his courteous manner, soft voice, and his attractive accent have echoes of middle Europe.

I was born in Kraków in 1934, an only child, and my parents lived in a town not far from Kraków called Kalvaria, where my father's family originated, and we were there when the war started in 1939. My father, like many others, decided to go east.

We went to Kraków to my grandparents' apartment, and my father returned a little later. He had had four sisters, and I had grandparents on both sides.

At the beginning of September 1939, when I was about five years old, the Germans entered one of the main streets of Kraków, and I remember the German army entering the city. There were lorries full of soldiers, armored vehicles, and machine guns, and it was quite exciting. My father came back two or three weeks after the war started, and we all lived together with my grandparents. The Germans were obviously not friendly to Jews, and there was a kind of general fear in the household about the Germans. One heard about people being insulted, people being beaten up. I remember for instance that there were instructions that Jews had to give up their jewelry first. One day I remember our apartment being checked by police who turned out the beds to see if anything was hidden there. I think that in 1940 I was going to a kindergarten, and so life was fairly normal. I come from quite a well-to-do family on both sides, and, clearly, money or jewelry was helpful even in those early days.

In March 1941 the ghetto was established in Kraków, which really meant that the town itself was going to become *Judenfrei*—free of Jews, who had to move into a specific area allocated for them. All the non-Jewish population was moved out from the area, walls were built around it, and Jews had to move into it.

From March 1941 on, it was illegal for Jews to live outside the ghetto. It was difficult to get accommodation in the ghetto because it was small, and so it was almost a privilege to get into the ghetto (for example see the following section on Janina Fischler-Martinho). Otherwise people had to move out of Kraków.

Some people moved into provincial towns where it was still legal for Jews to live. We managed to get into a small apartment in the ghetto, which accommodated almost ten people. It consisted of two rooms and a kitchen for my parents and me. A cousin of my grandfather with his three children lived in another room, and my grandparents lived in the kitchen.

Jews had to wear an armband[1] to identify them; it was not unusual to remove this to go shopping for food.

There were occasions when people were arrested, deported, or even shot, but the conditions in the ghetto in Kraków were far better than in places like Warsaw, where people were starving and dying on the streets.

Both my parents left the ghetto to go to work and in the evening they came back. I don't know what work they did. My grandfather was an importer/wholesaler of wood products. At the beginning of the war all businesses were confiscated, and the Germans put in their own administrators. But the Jews continued to run them, as employees, because the Germans lacked the knowledge to do so. I do not know if my grandfather continued to go to work. Thousands of people were allocated work, not necessarily in their profession, and it was believed that if you were working you were useful; you were less likely to be in trouble. But for the Jews things went from bad to worse.

At the beginning of 1942, when America entered the war, the Germans had no compunction about doing to the Jews whatever they wanted because they had no international consideration. In the ghetto we had the so-called deportations. The Germans decided that now you needed a piece of paper that would enable you to stay in the ghetto. It was usually based on your connections or the type of work that you were doing. Invariably the elderly and the children were targeted because they could not secure the right documents.

So the first major *Aktion* (roundup) in Kraków was sometime in May 1942 when I was seven. What was needed, if I recall rightly, was something called a *Blauschein*.[2] If you had one you were all right, if you didn't you were in trouble. So a large part of the population who didn't have a *Blauschein* was deported. I was very lucky because my parents had connections on the Aryan side of the ghetto, the small apartment of a

Janek Weber in about 1939, aged 4. Courtesy of
Janek Weber.

Janek Weber today. Courtesy of Janek Weber.

caretaker, Mrs. Nowakowa, who was very friendly toward us. She is still alive today, and she saved my life many times. What happened was that when there was danger or when there was a rumor about an *Aktion*, I was usually taken out of the ghetto.

It wasn't too difficult because there were gates with mainly Jewish policemen, and if they looked away you could sneak out. There were children going out all the time, you know, smuggling things, buying food, it was not a very tight control. I was out during that *Aktion* and came back after a week or so.

My problem was not only being out of the ghetto, but the apartment where I stayed with the caretaker had been confiscated by the Germans and made into a dental clinic. The German officers who lived and worked there knew me, so it was very tricky because, strictly, it was illegal for a Jew to be outside. In a few days I came back to the ghetto where it was safer because it was legal to be there. In the summer of 1942, because of the deportations, there was spare accommodation, so they cut off part of the ghetto, made it smaller and put up new boards.

Then there was another *Aktion* in the ghetto in Kraków in October 1942. It was a similar situation; you needed some more documentation, though a few people were shot on the spot. A few thousand people were taken away, and the ghetto became really small in terms of population. Again it was a matter of luck, and again I was outside. I think that at the beginning of 1943, I was out several times and when nothing happened for a few days, I was brought back.

In the second *Aktion* in October 1942, my parents had the right documents, but my grandparents didn't and they were hidden in a kind of warehouse. The Germans were, of course, checking the houses. My grandfather realized there was a ladder going up to the first floor, so he went up the ladder. But although my grandmother was only sixty, she was unable to do it; I think her hand was partly paralyzed or something. So she was taken away.

My grandfather suffered very much, but he survived. So now at the end of 1942 the situation is going from bad to worse. When we had to move again we were living in a place, just a kitchen, where there were my parents, me, my mother's unmarried brother, and my grandfather. The ghetto was divided into two, sections A and B. We were in Ghetto A with people who had work permits and their families. Ghetto B was for people who were not working.

In the beginning of 1943 my grandfather became ill. He was operated on in the ghetto hospital. My parents arranged for a gentile professor to come from outside to operate on him. This was possible with connections and money. I think he had cancer of the liver and he died in about February 1943. In hindsight it was a blessing.

At the beginning of 1943 the outlook was very bleak. It was only a matter of time. There was a concentration camp being built outside Kraków called Płaszów, and people speculated that eventually the ghetto would be liquidated; whoever was able to go would stay in Płaszów. Certainly the outlook for children was very bleak. I was eight years old at the time, and I knew there was all sorts of ingenuity by Jews to save themselves. My father struck up an acquaintance with a Polish family. This gentleman's name was Wirzbicki, and he was the head of the planning department in Kraków and, because my father was building an apartment house before the war, there was a connection. This family lived in a little villa just outside Kraków and in principle they agreed to take me, to look after me. But it was a question of timing. On one hand it was good to be in the ghetto, but my parents thought that if things got a bit difficult then I'd go to that family. Well, due to all the roundups in March 1943, when the ghetto was surrounded by police and the gates were heavily armed by Gestapo, there was no way of sneaking out. People with work permits were leaving as usual, but they would be going to the concentration camp. Everybody else had to stay behind and that meant death or deportation.

Arrangements were made by the German and Jewish authorities for people who were going to Płaszów to take some of their belongings, a suitcase or so. There were horse-driven carriages provided, so you put your belongings in a suitcase with your name on it, ready for a journey, then collected it at the other side. The problem was what to do. Lots of people tried to escape through the sewers, but only a few survived.

Janek remembers his father taking him to a nearby sewer manhole, contemplating it, and then changing his mind.

First of all you didn't know the way, then the Germans were waiting on the other side, and if you had spent a few hours in a sewer you obviously didn't look like the average person walking the street. My father decided to put me in a suitcase and put me on a cart that was going from the ghetto to Płaszów. I was eight-and-a-half and I was on the smallish side, and it was a large suitcase. I can remember him making holes in the suitcase to allow me to breathe.

I felt, surprisingly enough, that it was an adventure, and I don't recall being frightened. My luck, there is luck in such circumstances, is that I was sufficiently adult and grown up, mature enough to cope with the situation but unable to grasp the tragedy of it all. I don't remember them saying goodbye to me, but it must have been more difficult for them than for me. I remember being carried in that suitcase and it banging against his legs. I didn't know what happened from the moment I was put in the suitcase. My mother told me that there was a choice of carriages, so they were looking for somebody with a kind face. They put me in one of the carts and there were two people, one who was running the horses, probably the owner, and there was a Jewish policeman to look and see that no one was stealing.

They told him that in this suitcase was a child and would he please let me out between the ghetto and the concentration camp. The concentration camp was maybe six to seven kilometers away. So that is what happened. I remember feeling the cart starting to move so I knew that I was on the way. I remember looking through the holes and seeing the gates of the ghetto, so I knew I was out. Then at one stage the cart stopped, the suitcase was opened, and I was let out. I remember the face of that Jewish policeman smiling at me. I went to the caretaker as I had been told, and I stayed with her for a few days because I didn't know beyond that. I knew that there was somewhere that I could go eventually, but these things were always from day to day. I heard after the war that when my parents got to the concentration camp in the evening, they found the policeman and asked what had happened to me. He told them that when he opened the suitcase I jumped out, put my hands in my pockets, and started to whistle a Polish song and off I went. So I was obviously aware that it was important not to look different or look frightened but to look just like any other Polish child and completely merge with the crowd. I don't remember whistling.

So I went to our old house in Kraków and spent a few days with this Mrs. Nowakowa. What had happened was that the people who went to work went to Płaszów and the rest were deported the following day. Several hundred people were found in hiding and shot. My parents continued to work; they both had jobs outside the camp. Mrs. Nowakowa told me that she had a message from my father and after two or three days to meet him. He wanted to know what had happened to me—I was fine—but she told me this only recently when I was in Poland.

My father had been set to work to bury those people who were shot, and he was looking at each face to see whether it was me or not. Anyhow, they somehow contacted this Polish family who had agreed in principle to look after me, and one evening—a week or ten days or so later—a lady came and took me from Mrs. Nowakowa's to their place just outside Kraków. They had three children, two daughters a little older than me and a son, Marek, who was a year younger than me. I was put in a room. Marek was told that, as their grandmother had died a few months earlier, her room was to be closed up and no one was to enter it. The two daughters knew about me being there. It was perceived as dangerous for children to know because they went to school and they could say "we have someone staying with us." All the Jewish kids who were hidden had the same story, which was clearly suspicious that the father was an officer in the army who was taken prisoner during the war and their mother was taken for labor. "So we look after this little Polish child who has no one."

I stayed in that room for almost two years until the Liberation. I left only two or three times. The room is still there, you know. I had a night pot and the mother used to bring me food, usually in the evening but sometimes while I was asleep, and I found it in the morning. I had two or three books, which I knew by heart, but I was able to read because I had had private lessons in the ghetto, and I was able to write and count. But I never went to school until after the war.

Janek believes that he used to escape into fantasy. He missed his parents. He remembers crying, but he thinks he just became used to the boredom and inactivity.

In the summer of 1944 he had one lucky escape. The Polish underground was broadcasting from a secret radio station and the whole area was surrounded as the Germans checked each house. When they arrived, Janek was taken out through the back to the garden by one of the sisters. He had some documents, knew some of the basic Christian prayers, but had never been challenged. He recalled that he stayed in some bushes for a few hours, but the sister later told him that he had been hidden up a tree. He was nearly discovered when one of the Germans' dogs barked up at him. The German looked up, cursed the dog, and walked away. Janek did not recall this episode, which seems to have been so terrifying that, either subconsciously or deliberately, he blocked it out.

With hindsight, I find it incredible that a child of eight can spend two years in a room alone. I remember missing my parents; I think I was hoping that it would be all right at the end.

I think I am quite a disciplined person; I mean, I did not shout, I did not cry out. I wasn't allowed to get to the windows so I didn't, except on one occasion. They were quite strict with me, you know, very severe, but of course they were risking their lives and those of their families.

Janek does not remember any words of affection or comfort.

In January 1945, the Russians liberated Kraków. The word "liberation" is not very popular in Poland, but I still consider myself liberated. I remember it very well; I had a moment of enormous relief. The place was just outside Kraków and there was a barracks just behind it with soldiers. I knew that the war was over. I didn't know what had happened to my family. I don't really know why, but I stayed where I was for a while. Although there was a Jewish committee in Kraków, and they could have quite easily got rid of me, they kept me. I now lived openly with the family. Marek (the little boy downstairs) could hardly believe his eyes when he saw me—he had no idea I was there in the same house.

I learned after the war that my father had been killed and my mother survived in Bergen-Belsen. She was in Płaszów for some time and was one of the last people to be evacuated about a week or so before the war ended and a week before the Russians entered. She had been lucky because there were all sorts of jobs in the concentration camp. She was a servant, a maid to one of the German officers, so she had things relatively easy. There was no shortage of food. She had to look after his household, cleaning and looking after his dogs, and she was treated well. She was evacuated from Kraków to Auschwitz in the last few days, and she finally ended up in Belsen. The British liberated her in April 1945. After the war she was sick with typhus like thousands of people and many died.

She wanted to go back to Poland to see what had happened to me and to her husband, as many people did. She knew where she had left me, but she didn't know whether or not I had survived. She came back to Kraków some time in June 1945, two or three months after her liberation, and she found me exactly where she had left me, at the same address. I didn't recognize her, which I find quite amazing really because it had only been about two years or less. I would have expected a child of eight, even after two years, to have recognized his mother, but I didn't. I told her, "You look familiar to me, but I don't know who you are." We stayed in Kraków for a while, and, amazingly, life became normal very quickly.

We didn't have definite information because thousands of people were killed, but when my father didn't come back it, became clear that he had not survived. We heard that he was in a camp called Gross Rosen in East Germany. There were American and British airplanes flying over and dropping leaflets, and he was caught reading one of them and shot just weeks before the Liberation, about February 1945. Of my family only my uncle survived, my mother's brother. He also came back to Kraków to look for his family. Only one of my father's sisters and a niece survived.

The political situation was bad and my mother did not want to stay in Poland. In November 1945, I was taken by some acquaintances from Kraków to the Displaced Persons (DP) camp in Bergen-Belsen, Germany. My mother stayed behind because I think my uncle was still very sick. I had an aunt who lived in Bergen-Belsen so I went to stay with her. In the DP camp life was quite exciting, and "normal." Conditions were not very good but, compared to before, it was fine; we were not hungry, we had food.

After the war they burned down the concentration camp at Belsen because it was infested, and all the survivors were put into the army officer's camp next to it—about 10,000 to 15,000 people.

Then my mother came for me and we returned to Poland. In 1947 my mother met and married a Jewish man who also came originally from

Kraków and had lost his wife during the war. He had a son still alive in Hungary. The Americans had liberated my stepfather in Germany, and he decided to go to the West, having met a group of Belgian prisoners of war, and ending up in Belgium.

So this is where we settled. I was thirteen when we went to Belgium in 1947, and I lived there for seven years. This was the beginning of a fairly normal life.

There was discipline at home; I went to school and went home for the holidays. My mother and my stepfather wanted to emigrate to the United States but it was the time of the Cold War, there was the Korean War, and then there was the blockade of Berlin. We had some family in the States who said, "You are crazy to stay in Europe; you have survived the war, and you don't need another." But you had to wait to get a visa, so in the meantime they sent me to England to study English in anticipation of us going to America. I guess by then they were reasonably comfortable, as they could afford to send me to London.

I stayed with a family and went to English classes for a year. Meanwhile my parents decided to stay in Belgium because the war in Korea had finished. I wanted to stay in England, so I started to study food technology. I graduated a couple of years later and started work in 1956. In 1960 I got married and, well, that's it.

When I graduated I got a job as an analyst in a pickle factory in the East End of London.

After an early venture into business on his own in 1960, Janek joined a company dealing in East/West trade where his Polish background and ability to speak German were useful. Later he joined another British company, major importers of Russian watches into Britain. Some further work with an American company in East/West trade followed; he was earning well and was quite happy. The company eventually dealt in pharmaceutical chemicals, all related to East/West trade.

About twenty-one years ago I decided to branch out on my own. I started a little business dealing in plant protection chemicals, pesticides, that sort of thing, originally also orientated toward East/West. We were trading with countries behind the Iron Curtain. Now we are mainly importers and distributors of agrochemicals in the United Kingdom, and I am still working.

My mother died six years ago and my stepfather three years ago. The people that I lived with, the parents, the Wirzbickis, died quite a while ago. One of the daughters also died, but the younger daughter, with whom I was friendlier, is alive. We had arranged for a medal to be given to the family as "Righteous Gentiles." It is not an easy procedure, but we got all the evidence together. The daughter, Wanda, and Mrs. Nowakowa were there to receive it.

Mrs. Nowakowa still lives in the same room, although she has retired as a caretaker. I returned to Poland to see her, and she is fine; we spent several hours together and she told me stories from before the war, things that I didn't know.

So there was the ceremony in Kraków. They give about ten awards each time, and they do it quite well. The Israeli Ambassador in Warsaw spoke, and the deputy mayor of Kraków welcomed them. So it was quite a dignified ceremony. I spoke too.

I think that I am quite a controlled person; I am quite disciplined and I can do what I need to do. I met another lady who survived the war in Belgium, a wonderful person, and I am picking up bits of information. Sophie (see Chapter 4) was also hidden and with a non-Jewish family. You know we were taught to lie. I can lie without the slightest compunction, and I can tell you stories and look you straight in the eyes, and I have no problems that way. My wife cannot lie, but I can.

What I wonder is whether the war years made me the way I am or is it because I was the way I was that I survived?

I don't have guilt feelings, such as why should I have been saved and others not. I simply thought that I was extremely lucky. It was a set of circumstances that could have easily turned out the other way, not just once or twice, but hundreds of times. The people that I stayed with could have decided not to keep me. And who could criticize them? In my case it worked out but it worked out in very few cases. It is estimated that there were 5,000 Jewish kids in Poland after the war. Five thousand out of one million maybe. And, of course, far more girls than boys survived.

I don't know, but I think that I was sufficiently mature to know what was going on and to play the game. Had I been challenged I would have said: "Oh, no, I am Polish, my name is so and so," and I would have lied. How successfully I don't know, but I certainly would have tried.

Sophie Rechtman (see Chapter 4), who was a little older than me, told me that when she was living with a Belgian family, unlike me she was going to school, she was not always "hidden" in the physical sense. One day she was approached by another child who said, "You are Jewish." She didn't answer "No, I am not Jewish." She said instead, "Qu'est que c'est, 'Juive?'" (What's "Jewish?"). I found this fascinating that in that split second between life and death she said the right thing.

Janek feels that he was mature enough to play the part without fully understanding the tragedy, although he clearly sensed the danger. He was told to do things, so he did. He didn't rebel, protest, or scream but complied because he knew the alternatives.

People were so much more shattered after the war, because of what happened, than I was. I just thought that I was very lucky. I am quite a docile person I think. I knew that otherwise I would be found out and probably killed.

Even children were aware of the implications. It didn't come overnight, but over a period of two to three years you knew if you were in the street and you saw a German officer you would just cross over, away from him.

Janek does not know to what extent his qualities of discipline and docility, which he feels were contributory in his coping well, were inherited from his parents. He also seems to be thoughtful and philosophical in his reflections on the events of his childhood.

What I found quite amazing was how quickly life became normal after the war.

What about religion?

We came originally from an Orthodox home. I think most Jews from little towns were. I had some Jewish tuition before the war and I forgot it completely. I didn't even remember the Hebrew alphabet after the war. I spoke good Polish, incidentally, which was a very important factor. You know, very often the Polish Jews didn't speak good Polish, and they made typically "Jewish" mistakes that were instantly recognizable.

My stepfather also came from an Orthodox family, and he stayed Orthodox after the war, so once my mother remarried, we had a very Orthodox household. Whether this was helpful or not I don't know, but it was not an influence during the time that I was hidden.

Janek's wife (see Charlotte, Chapter 4) was born in Belgium and hidden during the war with her mother, her brother, and other members of the family.
They met through her brother, Henry (see Chapter 4), who was also studying at Chelsea Polytechnic. So Janek has also married another Hidden Child.

We married in 1960 and we have three children. My eldest daughter lives in Manchester and has four children. My son lives in Israel and he has three children. My youngest daughter is a doctor, who studied at the Royal Free Hospital in Hampstead, London.

So I am very proud of my wife and my family. I have spoken very little about the war years to my friends and family, but what triggered it off was our friendship with Nicole (see Chapter 4). There was a conference of Hidden Children in New York in 1991. We happened to be in New York for a family wedding, and we decided to go, and it was a real eye-opener. I had never realized that, forty years after the war, there were so many people walking around with open wounds. There were workshops and we were asked to tell our stories. You may think that my story is pretty bad, but it just pales compared with some of the stories I heard there. And this kind of triggered it off. The workshop was being run by a psychologist or psychiatrist with whom I chatted afterward and said that I was amazed by the stories. I told her that I had spent two years a virtual prisoner and asked her if there was anything wrong with me! She said, if you don't have problems, that's fine; don't look for any. Don't make trouble for yourself.

I think this clearly shaped my character, my future. But how different would I have been if it had not been for the war? What sort of person would I have been today if, instead of spending the war under the Nazi regime, my family had emigrated to America? I have no idea. Whether I would have been a nicer person or a worse person, surer of myself, less decisive . . . but I feel reasonably normal.

There were a lot of problems after the war when people remarried and there were stepchildren.

I heard the story of a woman, younger than me, who survived the war. She was handed as a baby to a Belgian family and knew nothing of her background at all. She was very happy with them until, in 1946, a strange man turned up and said, "I am your father." He took her back from that very friendly house and, on top of that, he was exceedingly Orthodox. So she was taken away from a Christian milieu, which was extremely traumatic. She said to me that her problems did not start until after the war. During the war she didn't know that she was Jewish, and she was very well looked after. She had love and affection and was very happy.

In defense of the situation, I think that one should say that people were aware of problems. But I think that there is a difference between therapeutic treatment in Europe and the United States. In the States every second person has an analyst. We cope with our problems ourselves, or at least we try to.

We were back to normal. But as I say, very little was said about the war years. In fact, very little was said about my father, or my stepfather's first wife. It was almost a taboo subject. These days we have friends and acquaintances that have remarried; one was a widow, but she talks about her first husband quite freely. I find it upsetting now fifty years later.

I think it is true that the psychological damage was never quite appreciated. If you were in a concentration camp this was bad, but if you were hidden and you didn't go out for two years, that was that. It was not perceived as a tragedy of equal size. And what I find quite unbelievable these days is the way people go to therapy if, say, they have been hijacked or held prisoner for a couple of days.

I remember that back in Bergen-Belsen, soon after 1946, there was a theater and people were now performing who a year or two earlier were escaping selection. It is only with hindsight that I appreciate just how quickly life, almost overnight, became normal. On the other hand, it is also true that, during the war, life in the ghetto was . . . well, men were playing cards and men had mistresses. And I was having private lessons, yet, as most of the families were going to the gas chambers anyway, what was the point of being taught multiplication tables?

Janek was given a false Polish identity, a name he cannot now recall, and forged documents, which were never used because he was concealed.

In the last few years, after the conference in New York, he has told his children more about his early life so now they know most of it.

My grandchildren know that Grandpa was in a suitcase. I remember that the nearest I got to death was probably escaping from that suitcase, and I took it as a bit of an adventure, you know.

NOTES

1. In the "General Government" (occupied Poland), Jews had to wear a white armband with a blue star, rather than the yellow star imposed elsewhere, including "Greater Germany."

2. *Blauschein* (blue document) was a work card in the Kraków ghetto.

JANINA FISCHLER-MARTINHO

Janina was one of three children living with her parents in a close and loving family circle in Kraków.

Their family circumstances became increasingly difficult and reduced in the early years of the war. When eventually the family moved into the ghetto, initially regarded as safer than "transport to the East," she ultimately witnessed the rounding up of her parents, aunt, and little brother.

Her elder brother pushed her into a sewer, enabling her to escape the Kraków ghetto. Throughout the harsh winter of 1943, she had to hide herself, wandering the countryside. Although still a young child she managed, with great difficulty, to survive by living by her wits and by offering casual work on farms and small holdings. It was a loveless, lonely, and highly dangerous existence. It is remarkable that she succumbed neither to illness, living for several months at one point with a farmer's wife with "open" tuberculosis, nor to permanent damage to her emotional adjustment.

As a neglected, uncared for, and parentless child she was deprived of appropriate nurturing and education for years. She could well have become a highly unsocialized individual, perpetuating in peacetime her wartime survival strategies. Instead she struggled to complete her education, and today she is a cultivated, charming, and elegant woman whose personality is undamaged by her privations.

I am now in my seventieth year; I was born in April 1930 in Kraków, Poland, the second of three children. My elder brother, Joseph, was born in 1923, and my little brother, Bartus, was born in 1933. My parents' circumstances were extremely modest, almost verging on poverty. I have since discovered that poverty is relative. My father was a footballer by profession but, of course, in those days, the 1920s and 1930s, it was a very unstable, insecure profession. By the time I was born he was in his late thirties and "the job" had petered out. He was approaching forty and we really lived from hand to mouth. Mamma was a very accomplished, fine needlewoman with an innate, natural gift. So she started sewing; that was how we made ends meet. As far as I remember she was really the bread winner. She was twenty-six when she married, and I think that she must have been well into her thirties by the time my father's job fizzled out. But we were a civilized family. She was fairly ambitious socially and she was a pretty woman, very attractive and fashion conscious. She was always beautifully turned out. I think that perhaps it was she who injected a fair dose of vanity into me. As a family, she kept us very clean, and our home, modest as it was, was very clean. She was a good cook and our food was very simple, very homey, and I think we ate quite well. There was never any money to spare and, once I had learned to read, she took me to join the public library. She already belonged to it because she was

Janina, aged about 13, Krakow 1943, during a brief respite from being on the run, photographed by Madame Wiktor, a kind Gentile friend. Janina's legs show marks of the abscesses from which she suffered. Courtesy of Janina Fischler-Martinho.

Janina Fischler-Martinho today. Courtesy of Janina Fischler-Martinho.

Application for admission to the ghetto showing her parents'
photographs and signatures: her father Henryk Fischler's form.
Courtesy of Janina Fischler-Martinho.

an avid reader; she had an excellent memory and knew a great deal of
Polish poetry by heart; our native tongue was Polish. My parents were
absolutely bilingual, because they went to school at the turn of the century when Poland was part of the Austro-Hungarian Empire and the official language was German. Ironic as it may appear, that became very
useful toward the end of their lives. I also remember that when my parents spoke to each other intimately, they always spoke in German if they
didn't want us to understand.

St. 16720

...en

...uftragten des Distriktschefs für die Stadt Krakau

Krakau

Ich bitte um Ausstellung einer Kennkarte für Juden und um Einweisung in den Judenwohnbezirk Krakau

Name: *Fischler*

(bei Ehefrauen Geburtsname): *Weinreb*

Vorname: *Ewa*

Geboren am: *28. Februar 1896* in: *Zasta Kei Thar*

Staatsbürgerschaft: *polnische*

Erlernter Beruf: *Schneiderin*

Derzeit ausgeübter Beruf: *r††o*

selbständig — unselbständig*)

Ledig — verheiratet — verwitwet — geschieden*)

Wohnhaft in: *Krakau*

Strasse: *Gdyńska* Nr. *39.*

Kinder unter 14 Jahren (nur vom Haushaltsvorstand auszufüllen)

Name	Vorname	Geboren am

Ewa Fischler
(Eigenhändige Unterschrift)

*) Nichtzutreffendes durchstreichen.
Druck: ZKW, Krakau, VIII, 1941, 280, 10.000

Ewa Fischler, née Weinreb, Janina's mother's application form for entry to the Kraków ghetto. Courtesy of Janina Fischler-Martinho.

When I started school I was nearly seven-and-a-half. I received two years of primary education, from 1937 to 1939, but, of course, when war broke out, my education came to an abrupt halt. I could read then but I couldn't write well. My letters were awkward and very clumsy. So in 1945, when the war ended, although I hadn't read for about six years, I found that I could still read. But my writing was totally nonexistent; I couldn't really sign my name, so I had to learn.

When the war broke out in 1939 Joseph was sixteen, I was nine, and Bartus was six. Life became extremely harsh. Mamma's income more or less disappeared, as people were not having frocks made, and my father was not earning at all. Joseph was not employed. But we continued in a very modest way, perhaps a little bit of buying and selling, the odd job here and there. My father was a very accomplished cardplayer who spent many days and nights playing cards, and sometimes he won. But on the whole, he would come home and say, "Ah, if only I had been called away from the gaming table then, I would have brought a fortune home!"

Then the various restrictions started being imposed; no school for Jewish children. I was still able to read, but after a time we had to give up the library. We continued to do our best, and I do not remember my spirits being particularly low. We were not allowed to use public transport or sit on park benches. We were not able to stroll along a street peacefully, except that when the white armband with the blue Star of David came into being, my parents and Joseph were compelled to wear it. I didn't have to because I was only nine or ten. At first people did not realize what terrible punishments they were meting out for the smallest infraction of the new laws. Being pretty and very fashion conscious, Mamma would go out without the armband, and I was terrified that someone could harm her; I was very frightened until she came back again.

We had a very large extended family, particularly on my mother's side. On my father's side I had only my grandmother, a very simple, kind, hardworking person who had very little education. She had a very hard life. She had three children and was very poor; they lived in extremely primitive accommodations in the prewar Jewish quarter, where I visited them quite regularly. To this day, when I close my eyes, I can see panoramas of my childhood in vivid colors and in enormous detail. My paternal grandfather died in 1939; he was very fortunate: he died a month after the German troops entered Kraków. He still had a normal funeral; a rabbi conducted the service, and the entire family was there at his graveside. As it turned out, he was to be the only one of all of them to have an ordinary, decent funeral. Almost every one of them would perish within the next two or three years, nineteen of them in the gas chambers.

Our extended family, with distant relations, numbered well over sixty. Only four survived. Joseph, me, a cousin on my father's side, and a boy cousin on my mother's side. The rest perished. My little brother perished with my parents.

The Kraków ghetto was set up in March 1941, and my family, my maternal grandmama, my aunts, and various relations moved into it in March 1941. But because we lived in the outer suburbs, we did not have to move at that time.[1]

We were ordered to move as late as November/December 1941, but by then I was a constant visitor and the only link with my mother's family. I visited them almost daily. We were all very fond of each other. I was the only person who was able to bring in food and small items like a table-cloth, a frock, or a pair of shoes to be sold on the outside. The money was then used to buy food to be taken back into the ghetto. The Kraków ghetto had been surrounded by a very solidly built red brick wall late in 1940. The top of it was crenellated, which as a child I thought was a decorative motif. I later discovered that those crenellations were exact replicas of Jewish tombstones.[2] That was a very clear sign, which unfortunately we did not read. Even if we had, there wasn't very much that we could have done to save ourselves.

Our family of five came to the ghetto in December 1941, by which time it was bursting at the seams, and it was very difficult to find accommodation. All we could get was a basement room, more like a cellar or a dungeon, with no sanitation, no running water. The floorboards were rotting and the walls were damp and slimy. We moved in there, to the same block of flats where my grandmama and my aunts were living on the second floor. They had a decent room with a nice large window, whereas we had only a tiny cellar window. There was a flue in a corner of that room, so we bought a little iron stove with a pipe, which we fitted into the flue. So at least we were able to do a little bit of cooking for ourselves and to heat water for washing. We had two buckets by the door, one for slops and one for clean water. I was in charge of filling and emptying the buckets. It was very hard and difficult today for most people to conceive what it is like for a woman with three children and no running water to keep them clean and fed. And what it is like to wash a pair of sheets if you have no running water and nowhere to hang them out to dry.

Mamma also continued to work for a German woman customer, who really kept us going. Mamma worked for her exclusively and she always paid in kind. So we received all kinds of goodies, which we ourselves did not eat; they were luxuries so we sold them and bought ourselves bread, vegetables, and a little bit of flour.

I was the go-between from the beginning to the end. But until my parents were deported, Mamma and I went out together. Like me, she was not at all Jewish in appearance. She had to go to do fittings, and she never went out alone. I feared for her although I never feared for myself, I was very naive. Outside the ghetto we could be stopped anywhere by a German. So Mamma hit on a method of wearing the armband and yet hiding it. She wore a very long gray shawl draped around her shoulders and arms. That way she was not breaking the law because the armband was hidden. I did not have to wear one. We visited the German woman, Frau Berger, many times at her apartment, and returning we were never stopped. When a garment had been completed, I would take it and bring back whatever she gave me.

I used the trams, although we were not allowed to, but I also walked a great deal because on the trams you had to pay a fare.

So we lived in the ghetto as a family from December 1941 until June 1942. It was normally surrounded by Polish policemen. There were four pedestrian gates and four large traffic gates. By each traffic gate there was a small pedestrian gate with a Polish policeman on duty. I knew almost every one. They were, on the whole, decent chaps. They even gave credit. One always greased their palms,[3] of course, but one didn't always have cash, so they gave credit. Except for one or two hard-liners, they were decent, and a small girl like me, so Aryan in appearance, could slip in and out. But during an *Aktion* the ghetto was surrounded by the SS and the whole ghetto was cordoned off. At the pedestrian gates the Polish policeman would still stand there, but now with two soldiers next to him. During an *Aktion*, nobody, not a pin, was able to get out. At night carts of food came into the ghetto and the Polish policemen made absolute fortunes, but they were decent and they played ball. People who had means lived very well, but for us that was different. During an *Aktion*, prices rocketed and it was very hard to buy food. The restaurants and cafés stopped functioning.

There was a registration in May 1942 for the *Aktion* to take place in June.

Every ghetto inhabitant had to appear before a registration board and present his or her identity card. If it was stamped, the person and his or her family could remain, but if not, they would be "resettled to the East." I took my maternal grandmother out of the ghetto, to the country (where Jews could still live), to a son with his wife and little girl. On my return on May 31, 1942, I caught a tram from Kraków's main station to the ghetto, where I realized that all the gates, even the pedestrian ones, were under heavy SS escort. It had never happened before, and I didn't understand what it signified, so at the first gate I stayed on the tram to the next one and the next. They were all under heavy SS guard, so I came back to the gate nearest to where we lived and I entered the ghetto. If I had not I would never have seen my family again but, on the other hand, if I had gone with my family, I would not be here today.

The only person whose identity card had not been stamped was my mother's youngest sister, Sally, so we knew she would be resettled.

My paternal grandmother went into an old people's home for the duration of the *Aktion*, and we believed that she was safe.

When it came to the registration, the head of the family would collect all the identity cards and would present them before the German arbiter. So my father took his card and my mother's. Our names as the two youngest children figured on my father's card, but Joseph, at nineteen, had his own. I was twelve and little Bartus was about eight. My father did get a stamp, so we were safe, but my aunt was taken on Monday, June 1.

The Aktion *lasted eight days, in extremely hot weather, until late afternoon on June 8. The ghetto remained under SS escort. People stayed indoors if they possibly could, but Janina saw endless queues of people being driven to cattle trucks, even children and the elderly, carrying as much as they could.*

The first resettlement took place on June 1 when my aunt Sally was taken; the second on Thursday, June 4. It was a most terrible sight. It was so hot, as if fire was pouring out of the sky. People were being driven with whips and sticks. My paternal grandmama, in her seventies, very innocent and unworldly, had been in an old people's home during the *Aktion* and now she was taken by lorry to cattle trucks at the nearest railway station. So we never saw her again.

We thought that was the end of the *Aktion* because all those who were to be resettled had gone. But the Germans, the SS, remained at their posts and didn't leave. We didn't know what was going to happen.

Tension and fear mounted; there was very little food and none coming in from outside. By Friday further posters announced yet another registration for Sunday, June 7, 1942. On that morning, Janina's father and her nineteen-year-old brother Joseph, a very fit, good-looking young man, took their identity cards to the registration center.

The cards of those who could remain in the ghetto were stamped with an SS Polizei stamp. All those to be resettled, including Janina's parents, had their identity cards confiscated on the spot.

Her father was unable to leave the registration center, but Joseph, who received the SS stamp, came to tell the family what had happened. Their mother and children under fourteen had to join their father under penalty of death by that evening.

Father was being held in an enormous walled courtyard, without a slice of bread or any water in such hot weather. It was not compulsory to take children under fourteen. As soon as Joseph came back and told us that father had been detained, Mamma started putting a few possessions together. She, my little brother, and I were going to join Father. But in the end she decided to leave me behind because I was supposed to be so very enterprising and resourceful. Joseph and I took her and little Bartus right up to the gate of the assembly point. We said goodbye to them as they joined Father there. The next day, June 8 in the early afternoon, they were led from this walled courtyard to the cattle trucks. There must have been about 3,000 of them. Joseph and I watched from the window.

When one saw these processions of people being led along the road, one had a foreboding that something terrible was taking place. I doubt if they even knew that they were going to be transported in cattle trucks. Later on they did, but this was the first *Aktion* in the Kraków ghetto.

The heat was unbearable. They had all taken layers and layers of clothes (they were allowed to take bundles of goods up to fifteen kilograms), believing that if you had no need for it yourself you could sell or barter with it, but they had no food or water, which they needed for the few days in the cattle truck. In that third procession out of the ghetto on June 8, in which Joseph and I lost our parents, younger brother, and my father's sister, they were marched in rows of five. Round about the middle of the procession came this row of five, my parents, little Bartus, Aunt Rose, and her husband.

When the *Aktion* was over, the German guards packed up and returned to their ordinary duties in the ghetto.

Suddenly there was so much space, so many empty flats, so much accommodation. But within a few days of the *Aktion* the ghetto was reduced again. Even if my parents had not been taken, we would have had to move. So Joseph and I, my aunt Regina, and my maternal grandmama moved in with our cousins—Aunt Rose's children, Sigi and Sophie—into one very large room.

Once the Aktion *was over, people believed that there would be letters from those who had been sent "to the East"; nothing was known of the Germans' intentions.*

Life returned to as near normal as possible. Janina's grandmother had now lost two daughters, Janina's mother, Eva, the eldest, and Sally, the youngest. She had come back from the country to take care of another daughter, Regina, an invalid, who had been in the hospital during the Aktion. *The family moved in with their cousins into the large, bleak room. Eventually Janina's other aunt and her husband also came to live in the ghetto. Life was precarious, with no income.*

I was the link between the outside and the inside because of my age, my appearance, and my business acumen. I was a smuggler really; I was in and out, bringing food in. People gave me commissions. Somebody would knock on our door and say, "Is Jasia[4] here? I wonder if she would take this tablecloth out to sell it for me." And, of course, I charged commission.

Thus Janina became a little entrepreneur, a considerable help to her family, and was never caught. She knew all the policemen who were mostly kind. She would slip whatever she could into their hand as she came and went.

Well, one little girl with a couple of shopping bags! I would slip him a twenty *złoty* note, which in those days amounted to a loaf of bread. If he got a hundred *złotys* during the course of the day he was not doing so badly.

So this was how we lived . . . but I think perhaps it was the courage of ignorance, really. I just drifted in and out, a formidable liar; I didn't look

Jewish and I spoke Polish beautifully—no accent, no intonation. And I could spin an absolutely watertight story on the spur of the moment. I had this ability, and I survived because of it.

We lived like that until October 27, 1942, when the ghetto was suddenly surrounded in the evening. The SS threw a cordon round it and an *Aktion* took place. Maybe there were some people who knew about it, but I was only a child of twelve and to me it came as a bolt out of the blue. In that *Aktion* I lost my maternal grandmother under very tragic circumstances. I also lost my aunt Anna whom I loved very dearly, a woman in her thirties she had been very good to me. And I lost Joseph! By the evening of October 28 I had hidden in the public baths. I was totally dispossessed; there was only Regina, my mother's sister, left, just the two of us. There were the cousins but they were only youngsters. There was very little feeling for other people's misery. It was not possible to commiserate. We were stripped of our humanity.

So by the evening of the October 28 it was over. My brother Joseph jumped from a cattle truck, badly bruising himself, scratching his face, and chipping his teeth. It was extraordinary; I cannot describe how brave he was. But he came back to the ghetto. He didn't know what had happened to me, and his first question was "Is my little sister here?"

I think after the October *Aktion*, something happened to one, that's how I see it now.

I think one became an animal, using whatever survival skills one had. It was a fight for life . . . no deed was foul enough if it helped one to survive; a terrible thing to say, but true. Joseph belonged to a labor group and had to go into hiding, but we lived, somehow. On one occasion I did not have a bed—I just slept on a headboard with a blanket and a pillow on which I just curled up. Once, when I was about twelve-and-a-half, I became unwell and was running quite a high temperature. I was feeling sorry for myself, and he gave me an apple. It was such a wonderful thing, an apple. He was good to me; he did all he could; we only had each other and we lived like that until March 1943. The Jews were being gradually moved from the ghetto in labor groups to a labor camp just outside Kraków at Płaszów. The ghetto was diminishing in size and it had been split up into two sectors, A and B. Joseph lived in A because he was working. I tagged on with him although, really, I should have lived in B because I was an orphan. Things were very, very bad by then. The ghetto was being gradually liquidated, and we knew that any day now it would be complete.

In the night of March 12 and 13, the ghetto was cordoned off, and in the morning we were in a steel trap. We knew it was the end, certainly for a child like me, small and female. Joseph stood a chance but he wouldn't let go, he wanted to save his little sister. The population of the ghetto was going insane with fear, especially people who had young children and elderly parents. People were desperate; the Germans were everywhere, shooting into the crowd. We got into Krakusa Street and, there very close to the ghetto wall, we saw a group of people crouching around something. When we got there we saw it was a manhole, and people were leaping, diving in, one after another. We took our turn and Joseph didn't hesitate. He leapt in first, held up his arms for me, caught me, and set me down. The sewer had a stream in the middle with a narrow ledge on each side and that was how we marched. I cannot tell you for how long because there was quite a long queue of maybe thirty or forty people, and there were still people leaping in behind us. We just marched along this ledge, and the further we got away from the manhole, the darker it became. We came across another manhole with steps leading to the cover, and so one of the men went up to investigate. He lifted the cover and said that we were outside the ghetto but still too close. So at the next one, we came out. Joseph and I said goodbye to each other because, as a young man of nineteen, he could never have survived on the Aryan side. He went to his camp, which was still outside. He crossed the whole of Kraków, a young Jew without an armband, wet, dirty, and covered in slime. He was terrified out of his mind, because he had to cross the whole city. I cannot describe to you how courageous he was. He got to his little labor camp on the periphery of Kraków, and I started on a two-year trek, my two-year odyssey.

Janina had no real idea how she was going to survive without money or a change of clothes. She emerged from the sewer drenched and slimy. It was March, cold, and an icy rain was falling.

She has described the first terrifying night of her "freedom" in her own book. Without preparation she embarked on a solitary struggle for survival in the countryside, trekking from village to village, knocking on doors, offering to work on farms and small holdings. Fortunately it was March, and in spring there was casual work.

I took cows out to graze and did various jobs around the farm, although I had difficulty getting placed because I was small and they wanted someone with plenty of brawn.

Potential employers were not enthusiastic but this small, frail child managed to exist, on the run, totally alone for two years, with abscesses and bleeding gums, covered in vermin and undernourished.

But she did survive, until in January 1945, when she was liberated by the Russians.

The longest period was from September 1943 until May 1944—eight months. By September they were laying off casual labor. I was very frightened because winter was coming. I was taken in by a farming family with three boys, one my age, one about eight, and a little baby. It was the harshest, most barren, most emotionally deprived time. They hardly spoke to me, and I spent most of my time in the stables looking after the cattle. Physically I was in a very bad way. By the time spring came, April, May, I knew nothing, I had never heard of Stalingrad, especially there, because the people were illiterate. I was living in total isolation.

This was Płasow, a tiny little hamlet of about twelve cottages, about two hours' walk from Kraków where the farmer took his produce to market.

Her identity was not revealed then, but there was nothing altruistic about her employers, and she was fed as meagerly as possible. Malnutrition and living conditions increased her misery.

By the spring of 1944, I hadn't washed once; there was nowhere to wash and nothing to wash with. The Polish winter is freezing. One day the sole came apart from the lace-up boots in which I had escaped from the ghetto. They bought me a pair of wooden shoes—not clogs—but shoes with a heel and a wooden sole. So I stayed on. I knew that in spring one could move around and maybe get a better "post." I did leave then, and just walked and walked. Someone did take me in, a woman who was very kind and saw the state I was in. She cut my hair and washed me in a wooden tub filled with warm water as though I were a little child, very carefully because of the sores. Her husband brought some ointment for me. They were very good to me.

Unfortunately Janina's identity was revealed by chance, and she had to leave; the penalty for sheltering a Jew was death.

She was only with them for about two or three weeks. But even in that brief time they did build her up; they fed and cleaned her, and got her "odd bits and pieces." It was almost at the end, June 1944, and she changed direction totally, with her identity revealed, to cover her tracks.

So whereas at first I was south of Kraków, I now moved north beyond Wieliczka (the salt mines). A woman helped me establish myself, my situation improved, and I came up in the world. At this point I rented a room from a very poor farmer's wife, just outside Godów. It was just a corner of a room where I had a straw mattress—a space. I ate with her because I was not doing too badly; I was able to buy myself bread and cheese, some fruit and vegetables. I paid her a very tiny rent and we got on very nicely. Then in January 1945, the Russians liberated me there, in the village.

We knew that the front was getting near, but I didn't understand any of it, except when the Russians actually started pouring into the village.

I knew then that the Germans had been chased out. I stayed for about three or four days and then I went back to Kraków to look for my family.

Only there was no family. Only Joseph came back. He had been in concentration camps in Płaszow and Mauthausen, eventually ending up in Linz. In May 1945 he was liberated by the Americans, weighing only thirty-five kilograms; soon he would have been dead. But they carried him to a field hospital and cared for him and fed him like a little baby. Gradually he started to recover and he went to a transit camp in Salzburg where he tried to get across to Palestine. In fact, the *Haganah*[5] had recruiting agents in these various transit camps, and he was negotiating with one of them.

Joseph was negotiating to enter the Haganah *in order to go to Palestine when he met a girl in the transit camp from whom he learned that Janina was alive and in Kraków.*

So the next morning he caught the train, and we met in the street! We sat for days on end and just talked and talked; we could hardly believe it.

I think target number one was education, and as soon as I returned to Kraków I became a kind of semi-domestic servant. This was with a very distantly related family, Aryans, who were kind to me. I enrolled at the local school in March 1945 until June. I worked hard and read so voraciously, I can't tell you. It was like someone who needs to quench his or her thirst. I had not seen a book for nearly six years, a long time for a child.

Eventually Janina and her brother managed to reach Italy together. With help they were able to start a new life in Britain. Janina went to a good school in Edinburgh and responded to every educational opportunity. She trained as a teacher in London, married happily, and read French as a mature student at Birkbeck College; this had been a long journey in every sense for the frightened child with two years of primary schooling. Her delight in her family and her talented grandson, Daniel, is evident. Her beloved brother, Joseph, who saved her had a difficult life in England after the war and is much affected by his experiences.

NOTES

1. As the ghetto was considered safer and more protected, families even had to apply to the Germans for entry (see illustrations of application forms).

2. See illustration of Kraków ghetto wall in *Have You Seen My Little Sister?*, Janina Fischler-Martinho's autobiography.

3. People who could be bribed were sometimes described as *Smalzownicki*; *smalz* means grease in both Yiddish and Polish, hence, "greasing the palm." Often these people were corrupt and denounced those who paid them.

4. *Jasia* is the diminutive of Janina.

5. *Haganah* was the recruiting agency for the underground military organization of the yishuv in Eretz Yisrael from 1920 to 1948. The Arab riots in 1920
and 1921 strengthened the view that it was impossible to depend on the British
authorities and that there was a need to create an independent defense force
completely free of foreign authority. In June 1920, the *Haganah* was founded.

CHAPTER 4

❧

Belgium

HENRY BIRNBAUM AND CHARLOTTE WEBER

The contrast between the accounts of Henry and Charlotte, hidden in the Belgian Ardennes with their mother, aunt, and grandparents, reflects the five year age difference between them. Charlotte's is briefer, more abstract. Henry's account is much more detailed and precise, richly filled with anecdotes, describing the fearful events engraved on his memory, events that Charlotte knows about only because she has been told, as she was too young at the time to register or to recall them. But when she describes postwar events, from adolescence, she is more precise about the illness and premature death of their mother, perhaps because as an adolescent girl she was more involved.

Their parents had been living for a while in Belgium, but their mother returned to Cologne to be with her parents for Henry's birth in 1932.

HENRY: After a while, my father, then [my mother] and I came back to Antwerp.

We spoke German and Yiddish at home, but I had to learn French, a completely new language, in order to mix with others at kindergarten. My grandparents came from Germany to live with us in 1938 and, of course, they didn't speak any Flemish, so it was all German and Yiddish. I went to a Jewish school where I also learned Hebrew, so by seven I was fluent in that language.

I remember my sister being brought home from the hospital as a new baby, and I remember her falling down when she must have been about one-and-a-half. She gashed her head against the skirting board and needed stitches; she still has the scar to this day. I remember that and other domestic events of no great consequence.

Henry and Charlotte Birnbaum as children. Courtesy of
Henry Birnbaum and Charlotte Weber.

Henry Birnbaum and Charlotte Weber at the awards ceremony
honoring M. and Mme. Morand as Righteous among the Nations.
Courtesy of John Rivkin.

It was a reasonably religious home. My father was very knowledgeable in Jewish scholarship, an intelligent man who spoke a number of languages and was reasonably well read. He was self-educated; he never went to school as far as I know. My mother also left school when she was about fourteen, but they were both intelligent people. He had his own business with a partner before the war.

The war broke out when I was seven, so I was still quite small. I can remember a great influx of refugees from Germany and, even to a child, it was obvious that some people were very poor. I remember correspondence from relatives in Poland from before the war hinting that our relatives were being killed. Although I was only seven, I can remember postcards coming that said "uncle and aunt . . . and all their family 'went to their grandpa'" who had been dead for twenty years. So we knew what that meant. This would have been after September 1939 when Poland was invaded by Germany. Belgium wasn't invaded until Friday, May 10, 1940, together with Holland and Luxembourg. I think I was aware that there was talk of war, but it didn't mean much to me, of course.

On that Friday, I was woken up by my mother very early, about five in the morning, to the sound of what I assume were bombs, although it might have been antiaircraft fire.

CHARLOTTE: I was born in Antwerp in Belgium on December 5, 1937.

War broke out and we fled to France when Belgium was invaded. France was very soon invaded too. We were with an aunt and uncle, their two daughters, and my maternal grandparents. We tried to get one of the last boats going to England from Southwest France. Somehow or other my father and my uncle got on a boat, and we were left behind. I never got this quite clear, because I never spoke to my parents about it at the time, and I only heard from other people. Anyway, France was invaded, and we didn't know what to do, so we decided to return to Antwerp. The family went back without my father and my uncle.

That I don't remember at all, I was three years old.

HENRY continues: We used to go regularly to the harbor at Royan. One night my parents were told that it was possible to get on a boat. So my mother came home to get us, and we went back to where the men were waiting, but the boat had gone with my father and my uncle. So from then on we were separated. We stayed on in Royan, but soon the Germans occupied that part of France. There were many refugees there from Antwerp, some stayed and some moved on. We went back to Antwerp.

Within weeks the Germans enacted anti-Jewish measures, things that at the beginning didn't affect me particularly. Civil servants, lawyers, and judges lost their jobs. Jewish slaughter was not allowed, so there was no kosher meat to be had. Within a year there were a lot of restrictions, in-

cluding confiscation of much property, assets, and bank accounts. A curfew was imposed, sometimes from seven at night until seven in the morning, sometimes eight until eight, with dire consequences for infringement.
You had to be in your own home at night. Being on your street wasn't
good enough; you had to be inside. In fact, our flat overlooked a tram
stop, and you could see people hopping from one leg to the other fran-
tically at 7:55 P.M., five minutes before the curfew, waiting for the tram
to get them home. So there was apprehension and a fear of discrimination. Later cinemas were forbidden for Jews, with no loitering in the
streets. You had to march everywhere purposefully, and we were not allowed to go to the park.

Many shops had notices—JEWS NOT ALLOWED or JEWS NOT
WANTED—which, at that age, made one feel discriminated against and
inferior. Then they started summoning people to go to labor camps; not
children, young men mostly. Then there was the edict of the "Yellow
Star," which had to be sewn onto the garments, not pinned or stuck on,
one on the outer garment, one on the jacket, and one on the shirt, so
that every time you changed your shirt the star had to be ripped off and
sewn onto the clean one. Soon there was a black market in stars! You had
to pay for them, and they had to be regulation stars.

Within a month or two they started picking up Jews to send them away.
Until then they threatened people with concentration camps if they did
not obey regulations. People had a terror of concentration camps. They
were supposed to be terrible, harsh places. But they started picking up
people and sending them not to concentration camps but to death camps,
which no one knew anything about. From Belgium most people were sent
to Auschwitz, where many were killed on arrival. They were extermination camps. Many people today do not know that there were two very
different types of camps, six extermination camps in Poland, and the
others were concentration camps where the life expectation wasn't very
high either. But in the death camps it was nil!

On July 22, 1942, the war had been going on for two years, and things
became steadily worse. In Antwerp there is a very popular, busy shuttle
train. One day they just stopped it and took off all the Jews; that was the
start of the mass deportations. Until then people had been called to forced
labor—like the Atlantic wall in France near Calais—but now they could
just pick up people easily because of the "star." At the beginning of the
war all Jews had to register with the authorities and had a large "J"
stamped on their identity papers. By the summer of 1942 they started
picking people up from their homes at night. They would just bang on
the doors or break them down and haul people out of bed, old people
and children, it made no difference. They would be thrown into lorries
and taken off. When the nighttime raids started we went to stay with my

aunt at night. One day, when we were going back home and were a few hundred yards from our flat, someone shouted for us not to go on because they were picking up Jews further on down the road. So we dashed into a shop owned by a friend of my mother. They took us up into their loft, and the three of us sat there while the Germans went from house to house. When they reached the shop they came into the flat, and I heard them rummaging about and talking. We had to be deathly quiet. I remember wanting to sneeze, because it was so dusty, and other silly things, such as the shafts of light with the dust particles. When it was all over and we were going back through the trapdoor, my mother put her foot through the plaster and half of the bedroom ceiling came down onto the bed.

This was one of several times when I experienced terror, particularly in the loft, hearing the Germans down below. After that we increasingly stayed away from the center of town and stayed with my aunt.

After a while we never went back to town again. When the Germans took people away from their flat, they sealed it up and no one was allowed to break the seal, because they wanted to go back in later and take things for themselves. When my mother went back and found our flat sealed, that was that.

CHARLOTTE continues: With underground and Resistance help, we went to the Ardennes and rented a flat in a small house belonging to an elderly couple. We felt that the family was too big to remain together, and it was too dangerous. Finally, a priest who lived with his niece in a nearby village said he would take two children, but only girls because boys were more dangerous. So my two cousins went to stay with him.

HENRY: We had thought of leaving Belgium and trying to get either to neutral Switzerland or Spain, or from there to South America. Switzerland was actually returning some people back across the border, back to the Germans. We thought at one time about joining some friends who had tried. We needed to find a smuggler (a *passeur*) to take us across the borders. They charged a lot of money and sometimes betrayed people, so we decided not to go. It may have been just as well because our friends were caught and did not survive. Some friends, musicians, offered to try and take my sister with them to America. I remember a lot of discussions about whether this little child (Charlotte) should go. One never knew how dangerous it was to stay.

Later on when it became obvious that things were even worse, people gave their children to strangers in the streets, begging people to take them.

My mother and the others were very resourceful, I must say. She was about thirty years old, with no great experience of life, an ordinary bourgeois housewife with two little children and elderly parents. They procured false papers (of very bad quality), and they found this person who was going to find us a hiding place. You had to become a member of the underworld, which is why I say I admire their resourcefulness, because to know how to live as an outcast and on the run is not something that comes naturally to normal, peace-loving, law-abiding citizens. That was the trouble at that time, you didn't stand a chance. The natural inclination of most people is to obey the law; but if you did that, you were dead. The only way to survive was to rebel and to refuse—to be devious.

So they got false papers but only for my aunt and for my mother. They were so amateurish that the photograph and details were just an approximate match. You paid a lot of money for these, and you took whatever you could get. My mother's was of an unmarried woman, and my aunt's, of a married woman. They just ripped off the photograph and you put in your own. The trouble was that they had a stamp on the photograph, not embossed like the passports used to be here, merely the stamp. I remember my grandfather completing the stamp circle with writing. He was very artistic but he was no forger, so it was a very amateurish excuse for an identity card. It was decided that I would be the illegitimate child of my mother, and my sister would be the legitimate child of my aunt who was married. By then they had also found a priest prepared to take two Jewish children, pretending that they were his nephews or nieces. There was a big debate going on, which I can still remember, should it be my sister and me, should it be the two girls of my aunt, or one of each? These are heartbreaking decisions . . . so I would be my mother's son and my sister would be my aunt's daughter. Anyway, they found this man who was going to find us a safe hiding place who took us to a village in the south of Belgium.

But this man was a crook; normal people don't know how to get false papers and all these things. He got a car, even though it was wartime and there was a shortage of fuel, and he took us to a city in the south, dumped us in a café, and said that he would be back in an hour, as he needed to go and finalize the arrangements. He had done nothing up until then; he only started after he dumped us. We were sitting in this café, frightened out of our wits, having ripped off our stars by then, of course, sitting with our minimal belongings around us, feeling very conspicuous in this café with German soldiers walking around outside. He came back after an hour or two, and we piled into a taxi and drove for another half hour to a village where he left us on the outskirts. Then he took us to a house in the village.

CHARLOTTE: We all remained together in this flat upstairs. My grandparents and my mother didn't go out at all. At first the couple didn't know that we were Jews, but they realized soon after and they let us stay there, and I think that actually we just paid rent, a normal rent, nothing exorbitant.

Someone must have told the Germans that we were Jews because a couple of officers came and my mother had to show our false papers. They were not very satisfied and said they would come back. In the meantime we thought we had better find somewhere else because it was getting very dangerous. Word had got around the village and no one wanted to take us in; they even told the elderly couple to get rid of us. They were wonderful people and they let us stay, we had nowhere else to go. It was winter and it was very cold. These officers did come back again but we were very lucky. They left and we never saw them.

We stayed on there until the Liberation. My grandmother died in the meantime in 1943. My brother didn't go out much, he was very frightened, and I was the one who would go out and play with the other children. We didn't go to school; I was too young but my brother didn't go to school either. I used to play with the children in the village, and I do remember being afraid of the soldiers, of the Germans, and knowing that they were dangerous. When I came to this village I actually spoke German and Yiddish, my best languages. I had not yet spoken that much French, because I was little. So I was told that I must not speak either of those languages. I am surprised that I was actually allowed out. It was very risky. This elderly couple actually looked after us. They were wonderful, but they soon realized that we were not ordinary holiday makers, we were very different because we never went out of the house. We asked them to do our shopping for us. We had no ration cards so everything had to be bought on the black market, which was illegal and expensive.

Thus the landlord soon saw that Henry's family were in hiding but nevertheless simply treated them as normal tenants, allowing them to remain in the pleasant little apartment.

Henry feels that his situation was more benign and less dramatic than that of some Hidden Children.

HENRY: I always knew who I was, unlike many people; I had to learn new names, and I had to pretend not to be Jewish, but I never went out anyway. I was with my family, my sister, my mother, aunt, and grandparents, so I did not suffer from that point of view.

Nevertheless Henry was aware of the fear and tension.

Because of all the discussions and plans of what we were going to do, I was aware people were very frightened, but because of the deception and the virtual ignorance of the fate of people who were sent away, there was less panic.

I think my mother was more preoccupied with everyday existence. She was an ordinary, kindly, gentle person so this was totally alien to her nature. She had the responsibility of the children and of her parents. It's funny . . . her parents must have been in their sixties. I am in my sixties, but I don't in any way feel incapable, yet they relied on her tremendously. My grandfather was a very intelligent person also, very knowledgeable, and yet I feel that they were much more reliant on her than I would be. My grandfather used to wear a beard, but as soon as all these troubles started in the summer of 1942, he shaved it off. I remember we all burst out laughing hysterically because he looked so weird. We were all in a very nervous state by then.

So there we all were in this village with my aunt, whose two daughters had gone to the priest. I am not sure if she knew who and where he was, so that was very stressful as well. Some people had to spend the war in lofts, in cellars, barns, or even holes in the ground, but this was a civilized little flat with a kitchen and a dining room, a sitting room and a couple of bedrooms, a toilet but no bathroom.

My sister and I, in that sense, had the easiest time possible. We were in that house for two years before the Liberation. We didn't go to school so we grew up like little savages. My mother decided she must teach us a little bit because we had no books or anything, although the landlord was a bit of an intellectual, a very nice old French man with a lovely wife. So my mother decided that she must keep my education up. I had been to school for four years by then, so I was the equivalent of the fifth form of primary school. She decided she would teach me fractions. I was making very heavy weather of it and so was she because she didn't know fractions either! So that was really quite funny. After three months, in January 1943, there was a knock on the door one day. The landlord called up to us that two German officers were there to see us.

My mother and my aunt were in the kitchen and, as it happened, both my grandparents were ill in bed. As soon as we heard Germans, my sister and I were dispatched into the other bedroom where we dived under the bed while the Germans spoke with my mother and my aunt. They said that they thought we were Jewish and they had come to take us away, but my mother showed them our so-called papers and they stayed for quite a while, twenty or thirty minutes, arguing but they were just ordinary army officers, not SS. They must have been a bit more human; they told my mother that as they couldn't be sure we were Jewish, they would go and report and then come back.

This was another episode of sheer terror. I have never experienced such terror as I did under that bed with the Germans next door.

So we felt we must get away because they would be back. It's a miracle they didn't take us with them there and then. Everybody in the village knew what had happened within five minutes, and within a radius of twenty miles everybody knew but nobody was prepared to take us in. Nobody wanted trouble. The landlord made inquiries but there was nothing doing. Everybody told him that he should get rid of us if he didn't want to be in trouble for harboring Jews, but he said, "God sent them to me, so I can't put them on the street." He wasn't religious, he was an atheist, I think, but he came out with a statement like that, which was quite amazing. He said that it was the middle of winter, "the old people are ill."

So from then on there was nowhere to go. It was January and it was snowing, there were two small children and two old people with the flu. We made a contingency plan that, if the Germans came again, the landlord would ring a small bell, and we would get out through the window. This was on the first floor so it was totally unrealistic. We set a watch on the front window to the street. I was also part of the roster of watchers. The next time the Germans came, I was on duty and I never saw them coming. Suddenly there was a knock on the door. I looked and there was this car outside; I must have been daydreaming or fallen asleep. This was less than a week after the first visit and there they were again. The landlord rang his little bell and everyone was dispatched to their hiding places or beds and the same story was repeated a second time, with exactly the same result, and then they left. I have heard it said since, much later, that the German officer when he was leaving said to my mother, "I should get better identity papers if I were you!"

CHARLOTTE: My uncle who had been with my father all those years was the first to come over as soon as the war was over. We had letters from my father, and my uncle brought us presents from him. I had always been eager to know what my father was like, so I was very anxious to meet him, and then we made the first trip to England and we finally moved here in August 1947.

My father lived in a very small flat in Stamford Hill, and my brother and I were sent to boarding school as soon as we came. My father had been doing all sorts of things during the war; he was a carpenter and an electrician, although he was actually a diamond dealer before the war like most people in Antwerp. Toward the end of the war, he started getting into business with my uncle and felt that life was more appealing in London than Antwerp. So my brother and I went to a Hassidic boarding school for two years where there were a lot of refugee children and children who were brought over from Poland without their families. Everyone was in the same situation; one didn't feel peculiar in any way. I must say I was very happy there. I adapted well and got to know my father, of course. We went home every second weekend or so. Thinking about it when I became older, I took it for granted that the flat was small and there wasn't any room for us so we had to stay in boarding school. But I suppose really my parents had to get to know each other again; they had been separated for about five years and maybe they felt they needed time to adjust on their own. One never talked about these things, one just took it as it came. At the end of 1949, my father bought a house in Hendon, and we lived together from then on. Everything was fine; I think I was perfectly happy. Perhaps later events were harder for me because my mother died when I was nearly sixteen and that was a big blow to me. I had been very close to my mother, always having been with her, without my father, in a dangerous place.

She had rheumatic fever as a little girl, and she had a mitral valve dysfunction, so she was never very strong, and I always remember having to help her along. She had a stroke at the age of forty-three. My grandfather was living with us at the time, and he had a heart attack just before that and my brother and I got chicken pox so that everyone was ill, and perhaps it just became too much for her. My father at the time was working in Belgium, in diamonds. He used to spend the week there and come home on weekends, so for about a year he was going back and forth.

Charlotte went to live with an aunt for eighteen months in New York, where she was very happy. When their father remarried, she returned to live with the family, this time in Belgium.

There she met her husband.[1] After their marriage they came to live in England, where they have lived for the last thirty-seven years.

Henry reflects on the landlord who never exploited them, never overcharged them.

HENRY: Food was short and the bread was almost inedible, I don't know what it was made of but when you put a knife in it, it came out like strands of chewing gum and it smelled foul. Coffee and beer were ersatz, but in a village you could get fruit and eggs.

The family were, of course, further restricted because Kosher food was unavailable.

We were becoming very thin and undernourished. But when we had flour, which we either managed to buy or I got when gleaning, we used to mill it and take it to the bakery to make into bread. It was lovely white bread. Even today when I eat white bread I remember what it was like then. Gleaning[2] was very tiring and backbreaking but sometimes we managed to buy wheat also. I never lost my "identity" (though he changed his name) because we kept the Jewish festivals, and my grandfather worked out when they were. He had his prayer book and other religious possessions, which for many months we buried in the garden because they were dangerous to have about. He taught me my Hebrew studies and my Bible, sometimes from a book if we had one, or by heart if the book was buried. And that's how I spent the war.

On one occasion he had to go to the dentist.

A set of teeth we cannot do without, but there was no dentist in the village. My aunt took me because she spoke French and didn't look at all Jewish, unlike my mother. We had to walk into the next village to a railway stop. There was a German guard with his rifle at the entrance to a tunnel through the mountain, talking to some other soldiers.

I remember being scared witless, the sort of terror most people never know.

CHARLOTTE: I don't think that I have been deprived. We have been very fortunate, my brother and I, being with our family right through the war. But I don't feel that I have had a terrible childhood because of this or anything else.

And you know, some people say, "How terrible!" but I don't remember that it was terrible. There was a lot of upheaval, but I think that it made me very adaptable.

Most of the people that I know who had been hidden seem to have come out of it pretty well. It is very difficult to come to terms with losing my mother, as I did when I was very young. I decided at the time that I was never going to make a very strong attachment with anyone again. It was very painful, and I thought to myself, I don't need this, it hurts too much. Then I met my husband and, well, whatever happens, happens.

Henry made vigorous efforts to obtain recognition for the village couple as Righteous Gentiles.

HENRY: I got started in 1970. It took a long time, about five years, for me to get all the documents. They had to have either the rescuers or a descendant to receive the certificate and medal. The man was dead by then. He used to write beautiful letters; my sister and he were great correspondents.

I heard nothing from Yad Vashem for months. One day when I was in Israel, I went to find out what was happening. They looked up the file and said that it was closed! I said, "You mean you have given him this medal without telling me, without letting me know? How could you do that?" They said that the file was in the archives and was no longer active. When we found it, the medal, the certificate, and all my correspondence was there with a letter from the Israeli embassy in Brussels saying that this was nothing to do with them. So they got it back and closed the file.

Henry insisted on reactivating it, and in 1990 they were able to honor the couple (see photograph of Henry and Charlotte at the ceremony).

It was a beautiful ceremony because the mayor and the whole Jewish community were there, and we had a proper "do" with speeches. I made a speech, and the Israeli Ambassador to the Common Market also spoke. Then we handed over this well-deserved medal.

Henry would have liked to become an architect, but eventually he qualified in sciences, with a BSc, a master's degree, and a Ph.D., eventually working in a publishing company scanning scientific and pharmaceutical literature, making good use of his Ph.D. and his five foreign languages. A few years ago he took early retirement.

I feel on the whole that I am reasonably well-adjusted. I go to the Holocaust Center in Hendon occasionally but not regularly. Some people go there every week because they need the companionship.

There are certain things that I am aware of. I am actually haunted by the Holocaust. I am not obsessed by it, I know the difference, but I am aware of it all the time. Not a day goes past without my thinking about it and mourning the dead . . . not a day. Not at the beginning, it came later, I don't even know when. Maybe twenty years after the war, I don't know, but for a long time now. I can hardly look at small children without thinking about how many were murdered and in what terrible circumstances.

One of the things that did mark me in the village when we were in hiding or semi-hiding was the twin aspects of boredom, just sitting in the same place with the same people for months on end, and terror. The two don't go well together somehow; they are a funny mixture and yet those are the main feelings that I recollect.

I feel very proud and privileged, I suppose, more than proud of being Jewish, which means a great deal to me. And yet I won't advertise the fact that I am Jewish, not because I feel inferior in any sense, on the contrary. For example, I would wear a skullcap on my head in the house, but I would never wear it in the street although lots of people do; I just don't, except in Israel. I have tried to rationalize this; do I not want people to know that I am Jewish? They know anyway. Why I should not want them to know when it doesn't worry me? On the contrary, I think it a great gift. I imagine that may well be a result of the war. I suppose it's inevitable that as a child being discriminated against or persecuted and told that you are rubbish must leave some effect.

So the fact that I am Jewish is the most important thing in my life, but I don't advertise it.

My children? It's funny. I have never discussed my war experiences with them to any extent. I didn't actively not talk about it. When I did my dissertation[3] in 1990, I got quite involved with the research and my children read it. Interestingly, my daughter in Israel works for Yad Vashem. When I go to Israel I stay with her. Both my daughters lived in Israel at one time, but one has now lived in South Africa for three years. They are both very Jewish.

NOTES

1. Charlotte married another Hidden Child, Janek Weber, see Chapter 3.
2. Gleaning is a backbreaking means of harvesting leftover grains by hand.
3. Henry Birnbaum, "The Nazi Persecution of the Jews of Belgium, 1940–1944: An Overview" (master's thesis, Jews College, University of London, 1991).

RUTH EISENFELD

I was born in Breslau, and I come from an average, happy, well-settled background. My maiden name was Hochhauser. I had a very happy, normal childhood in Breslau that I remember very clearly. My grandparents were nice and everybody was pleasant until the *Kristallnacht*, on November 9, 1938. We were of Polish nationality. There was a day called *Polenaktion*, when the Nazis came to collect Polish citizens. So they came for my parents but they were out. In those days they didn't take children on their own. My parents knew exactly what [the Germans] were going to do, so they left us at home with some neighbors with whom we shared an apartment. The two of us were there and I was about six, nearly seven, and my sister was two years older. Those Nazis came to collect my parents and saw us, and I thought they were nice, because I was very young and ignorant. One Nazi took me on his lap and said, "Go and find some pictures of your parents for me to look at." My sister had heard this and had locked the photograph albums in a cupboard and hidden the key. I went into the other room and said, "Where are the photographs? He wants to see some photographs, he is very nice." I remember she said, "He is not nice, they have come to take away our parents and, if they see the photographs, they will be able to recognize them in the street." She was nine years old. I remember that, it was the first shock of my life. My parents eventually came home after 12:00 P.M., because after midnight the *Aktion* against the Polish citizens was stopped. In the morning, I saw my parents as usual and lots of people in the room saying prayers because the synagogue had already been burned down. There was a man praying over my bed, and it was a surprise to see him first thing in the morning! On November 9, the synagogues and shops were burned down. I remember seeing the cupola of one of the main synagogues in Breslau burning, but I didn't understand what it was about.

You know, it was the most peculiar atmosphere in which we were living then. All the Jewish shops were destroyed one after another on that particular night. We heard all the glass flying, which is why it is called *Kristallnacht*.[1] While all this was happening, my parents started planning to hide the family or go abroad if possible. In March 1939, I was packed off to Belgium on a *Kindertransport* with my sister, Dora.

My parents stayed on a bit, trying to get out illegally, because by that time they could no longer go legally. After three months in Belgium, we were settled at Grandma's when my mother suddenly turned up, having smuggled herself through the Ardenne forest. My father arrived about three months later. He had to leave his father, an old man in his seventies, in a Jewish old people's home. He was very upset at having to leave him behind.

In Belgium everything was different. We were camping here and there.
We were no longer that lovely normal family. Family life didn't feel good.
They say that a child could pick up a language easily, so I was sent to a
French-speaking school. Antwerp is almost all Flemish but I was sent to
learn French. I was absolutely thrown into deep water, because I didn't
even know that there was such a thing as another language. I was not
prepared. Grandma had no patience, no time to explain. So I became
impossible. I forgot everything; I forgot my coat at school, and I always
left things behind. Every few minutes in the classroom, I had to go to
the lavatory because I was so nervous. The children were mocking me
and I couldn't fit in at all. My sister was in the Flemish department at
the same school, and she adapted much better. Flemish sounds a bit like
German whereas French was very different, so I couldn't pick up very
much. First of all I was dressed the German way with long, thick stock-
ings and boots. The Belgian kids were dressed totally differently with their
satchels on their sides while mine was on my back. This looked so different, so they started ganging up on me in the playground, and I couldn't

Ruth Hochhauser ("Josette Deflandre") with Monsieur and Madame
Secret and their daugher in her false identity at Tournai. Courtesy of
Ruth Eisenfeld.

"Josette" at school. Courtesy of Ruth Eisenfeld.

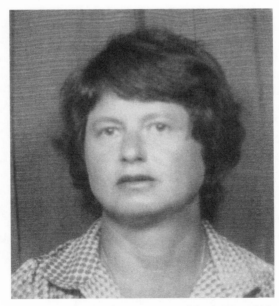

Ruth Eisenfeld today. Courtesy of Ruth Eisenfeld.

defend myself because I didn't even speak the language. I was not looked after properly and I had a big setback. Eventually, I went into a Flemish school, and I became a very average, shy, frightened, nervous little pupil. I was no longer the bright little spark I had been in Germany. I remember being terrified of the teacher, because there was no understanding in those days, no time for difficult kids.

My parents were struggling financially then. They were refugees and had hard times in the beginning and were traumatized, so they didn't have much time for us. My father had been in textiles, and his shop escaped destruction simply because it was on the first floor and not visible from the street. My father managed to sell some of his stock and come to Belgium with some money.

Ruth was desperately unhappy and unsettled.

In 1940 or 1941, we went to live in Brussels because Antwerp had such a close knit Jewish community that something horrible could happen there, but in Brussels we might be able to get lost in the general population. So we went to live there, and I was still in a Flemish school. When the Germans invaded on May 10, 1940, the German laws did not immediately concern the Jews because they were busy invading and becoming occupiers. Then gradually they started on the Jews and that meant that, after a while, we had to wear the "yellow star." We knew what we were in for by that time.

I was nine then, but by the time I was ten, life had become infernal in Brussels, because the Jews could not go out in the evening. They had to be back home by the 8 P.M. curfew. There were terrible laws preventing the use of public transport or entry to the parks. We had ration cards; in fact, I don't think they wanted us to eat. They were trying to undermine life completely and squeeze us out. As there were no more work permits, my father could not work, so it was impossible to make a living. The general population was not all that helpful either; they didn't want Jews in their houses. They were afraid of renting to foreigners, to Jews, or refugees. So we were very squeezed. My mother befriended a woman shop assistant in Brussels, because we didn't have many friends. How could we, having only just arrived, and we didn't have any non-Jewish friends. So my mother found this woman behind the counter, out of the blue, and felt that maybe, as this lady was nice, she would risk it. So she talked to her after she had bought some material. She told her that she was Jewish and had two daughters. The lady became very friendly, and my mother said it would be so nice if she could just put her daughters somewhere safe so that she and my father could just save themselves somehow.

It was necessary to split the family. Life had become so infernal, but they hoped that if we separated, maybe someone could survive. This lady said she could help because her daughter worked for the Red Cross. What absolute luck; she could have been a Nazi or an informer! This woman and my mother remained friends for a very long time. Her daughter, the young woman who was a Red Cross nurse, got us to the Château of Beloeil, near Tournai, the French-speaking part of Belgium.

We were separated from our parents but it was a safe place. Then when the Germans came for my parents and for the rest of the family too, they went into the house one way and my parents managed to flee through another, and so they escaped and managed to get to Switzerland. They fled over snowy mountains[2] and eventually joined queues of refugees trying to get into Switzerland.

They stayed there until after the war. They were very fortunate. They didn't get in immediately, because at first they were only taking people with children and, of course, my parents didn't have any with them. So they turned back, but there was a family trying to get in with about six or seven children so they "borrowed" a child and went to another border place and got in. That was another miracle! At the end of the war, they came back for us immediately. They knew where we were, and they also knew that in the meantime I had been taken away from Beloeil because I was so miserable that I wasn't thriving at all. The social worker, Yvonne Broche, later Madame Verly, and Jeanne Secret (Ruth's rescuers) had said, "Let's do something for this child."

One of the aristocratic princes of Belgium had opened part of his castle to the Red Cross to work with needy children and other organizations. They took children from very poor backgrounds, deprived and sick children, and some Jewish children as well, those not officially declared, because the Germans did not come to the office to check the list. I kept my own name there, but I don't know whether it was on the official list.

The people in Tournai (where she was eventually hidden) changed my name to Josette Deflandre. A lovely name, but I hated both of them; I didn't like my name at all, but that's what they gave me; I had no choice.

A policeman, married to the sister of the lady who took me in, had access to the Nazis, because he pretended to be one of theirs when he went to their offices, but the minute he came out he did a lot of work and later had a medal from Yad Vashem. He decided to call me Josette, which was his daughter's name. He explained, "If the Germans take you, I can go and say, 'Hey, wait a minute you have taken my daughter!'"

He could do that because I was young enough to have no papers, no identity cards,[3] so that was very quick thinking. Deflandre is a translation of a family name they have in Brussels, Van Vlaandren. So I became Josette Deflandre in Tournai. My sister stayed in Beloeil. I was extremely well looked after in Tournai but still terribly unsure of myself. I didn't like to leave my sister, and she didn't like me to leave.

It was very hard when I moved in with that family because I felt so isolated. I was taken to Tournai after three months in Beloeil.

They were a very fine family, very nice, and they had plenty of food because they were well off. They looked after me very well and sent me to very fine schools. They gave me the best possible education, as if I was their own daughter, and I soon recovered physically. But somehow I was never happy because, although I looked all right, there was always a niggle.

It's as if I had put my own children into Buckingham Palace. You know, somehow, the change for the best was hard to digest.

Through the Red Cross, we heard that my parents were in Switzerland. So I knew that they were alive and they were safe. At Christmas, and the summer holidays, my sister came to visit once or twice (although their relationship could not be recognized). It was more a psychological trauma for me because I didn't go out.

I was not deprived; in fact, I was physically spoiled rotten compared with many others.

They knew the risk but they were very generous people. The policeman who knew exactly what was going on with the Nazis warned [the family] all the time. The neighbors thought that I was a niece from Brussels, part of the Flemish side of the family, hence my rather strange accent.

A remarkable series of coincidences and conjunction of events resulted in her survival.

I was very fortunate; I would have perished if I had been left in the Beloeil children's home, because kids of ten don't lose weight and I was in the middle of growing. I was always tired. I never wanted to play or run and everybody was running. I was showing signs of deficiency. I didn't want to eat at first, because I had been brought up to eat Kosher and I started leaving things, but this was not allowed so I would hide things when nobody was looking. My sister didn't appear to have this problem in Beloeil, because she ate and she looked very well. She was a big girl. It was just me. I couldn't take it.

Also the life in the community of children was not for me. They were very rough, and if they could knock you over, they would. Nobody would be particularly friendly and would hardly talk to me. I had to go and find friends. Although I have a friendly personality I found it very hard.

The hiding family put me into convent schools. In certain places I was a day-girl and in another I was a boarder. I got on very well after a while, and I got used to the Catholic milieu. I liked it and I wanted to convert. I became very religious!

People did not talk to children then; we were just a "bunch of idiots"! We just had to follow, I was told this or that and I obeyed all the time.

I have a tendency to do that today too. My husband says that I am very obedient—compliant. But I am beginning to rebel, like today I just said, "I am going out for the day, bye-bye!"

Ruth returns to her story.

I was average but I had emotional problems, which are difficult to describe now; I had nightmares and I used to dream in German. One night I woke up screaming. We were in a sort of dormitory and there was a nun in the corner in her little *chambre*. I was in a sweat, in such a state of shock, because I was dreaming about my sister and my parents, screaming this out in German. This nun from Alsace came to my room when I was about to go to class and asked me if I was Flemish. So I said, "Oh yes, I'm Flemish." Then she said, "No, that's not true." I was in such a state because she had heard me screaming in German. She said that for having lied to her I must clean the dormitory and bring water for every girl. This woman was not very nice. She obviously detected that I was a bit different and she punished me for it. Another nun, Apollinaire, used to tell us frightening stories of devils appearing in the Middle Ages when we were having supper, as if it was still happening. The children who were not baptized would all go to hell when they die. The other children didn't care because they were all baptized. This is why I dreamed such horrible dreams, because I was frightened. I said to her one night, "Please don't tell me these stories, because they make me have bad dreams." And she said, "Ah, Josette's conscience n'est pas tranquille." Then she punished me for this as well. "There is obviously something wrong with you, my child, you had better go and see the confessor. There must be something wrong with you or you would not have these dreams." It was very, very cruel.

I wanted to be baptized but nobody wanted to do it. The curate said that because my parents were alive there would be no baptism. He and Mother Superior knew my identity. The policeman, of course, and one or two of the family were informed. But baptism was out of the question. (My sister was baptized and she felt good about it.)

I felt that baptism would lift up my sins, and I would suddenly feel different. I went to chapel and I prayed for this baptism, but then I thought, well, who's listening to me—I am not baptized! I had no entry to church. I felt such an outsider.

Ruth was also discouraged from bringing friends home in case she gave herself away.

In 1944 there was the Liberation and my parents came back—the minute they could get a train. They stood all the way, back to back. They picked up my sister immediately and went to Brussels to live at some ghastly place they found, a real slum, all they could afford. It was awful. My sister and my parents formed a new relationship. I was the outsider. I stayed another year in Tournai because, as I was fine there, there was no reason to take me away.

Madame Secret and her family pleaded for me to stay a little longer. I was quite happy and wanted to stay. I just couldn't face the poverty so suddenly. So my sister and my parents were in Brussels, and they were happy to sleep on the floor on mattresses. They only had three forks, I remember. But eventually things recovered. My parents and my sister formed a very warm relationship. For me there was a gap that has never been bridged properly. You know, I found my identity more here in England; it took a long time. I also studied the wrong profession for me, because I didn't know what I wanted to do. I really didn't know if I had any talent at all. My talents were not tapped.

Coming back from Tournai to Brussels, I was suddenly thrown into a very ordinary school with a lot of pupils in the class when I had just been in the finest convent where they sent aristocratic kids and the daughters of ministers. Suddenly I was thrown into this horrible Belgian school where the children spoke a horrible Belgian patois, and there I was, "posh." I was not popular in the class because when the teacher asked me where I came from, I said from St. André in Tournai. I was never a snob because I can't stand snobs, but they took me for one! So I could never make friends and ended up having extremely bad reports, because I couldn't concentrate on anything at all. My sister came top of the class all the time at that school, and the headmistress said, "I don't understand you two sisters; there is one at the top of the class and the other at the bottom." My sister was hungry for school; she hadn't had it for three years.

Having been an average pupil in the various convents, Ruth was suddenly an outsider and doing poorly academically. She sought out other Jewish children in the class whose aspirations were to go into couture, something for children with no academic possibilities. She thought this applied to herself.

Her self-esteem was eroded. Her career choice was a total mistake because, although she became competent at it, she found it boring, isolating, and lonely.

Through a friend who had been an au pair in London and had enjoyed herself so much, she decided to go London to live with another family from Breslau known to her parents.

The only condition was that I live with them in Camden Town at an apartment that they let out to students. I felt good here in London, because the neurosis that I had was left behind me. I felt that my identity fitted here much better. You see the name Ruth here in England is fine, but in Belgium it doesn't sound like anything! So I felt good here. In 1957, when I came over, I thought I knew quite a bit of English, but I soon picked it up and I have developed a talent for languages. Then at the wedding of another friend from Belgium, I met a doctor who eventually became a consultant gynecologist at St. George's Hospital, and we married. I felt suddenly as if my personality had blossomed. I felt that I had a good flair for languages and took lots of diplomas. But that was much, much later. By then my kids were taking O levels and A levels, and I thought I'll have a go at this, although I lacked confidence. Then I went to the Institute of Linguists, and I got three distinctions there and a pass on those exams. So I also took A-level French and got good results. I suddenly realized that I could study and that my head wasn't as bad as I had thought. I was no longer the nobody who I had thought I was.

I worked in various boutiques here in London. I hated every minute of it. You are treated as if you are dirt, a charlady, you know, people not talking to you. The girls in the shop are very nice, but the woman who did the sewing and the alterations was horrible. It was soul destroying; never again!

I married my first husband and for a time we were quite happy, I suppose, but what did I know about life? What I do know now was that it was wrong to marry to him because he didn't understand my background at all. What I told him was difficult and didn't make much sense. Anglo-Jews have not had the experience that we had (of living under Occupation). I was a completely different animal. We discovered after having three children that I was going one way and he was going another. He was advancing in his profession and at that point I felt like a skivvy at home. Somehow communication had broken down and then so did the marriage.

I had some friends and made a few more; I didn't belong to a synagogue in the beginning or anything. It didn't worry me too much, but I felt good about being here—the Jewish people here are different from the Jewish people in Belgium, that I knew.

Perhaps I didn't know what it was all about. Perhaps my whole psyche wasn't prepared for marriage.

What I thought was love, which was what I really wanted, was perhaps not what was required or what was right for him or for me. In the beginning I was deliriously happy but for a relatively short time. Then somehow when the children came along, I concentrated on them, but as they grew up and I discovered that he was having an affair, the marriage broke up. That really sealed the decision to separate. My parents were still alive and well in Brussels, and my sister as well. They were all against the divorce.

Two years later I met another man whom I married. We have far more in common because he is from Berlin. He came over in 1939 as a refugee, but he was by that time twenty-one and he was actually in the RAF [Royal Air Force] during the war. He is now seventy-nine. As I say, we had a lot in common—the whole marriage is not just sex, it is so much more. And now I realize that there is a lot more to any marriage, because you have to have a lot in common, as well as tolerance, to live with another person.

This marriage is totally different. He has brought me out; I am a completely different person. If I now speak to my first husband, he doesn't recognize me.

Fortunately, my first husband remarried someone who has three children, and these children and my children are friendly.

With my first husband I tended to acquiesce to whatever he planned, because I thought he was clever and knew better. But with my present husband, we have lots of debates, it's completely different, it's very healthy. We always forget when we have had a row because we always clear the air. My first husband was very buttoned up, so we never talked about anything difficult. We only talked about nice things, pleasant things. He knew about my background, but he wasn't all that interested somehow.

Many people hidden as children faced the comment from adult survivors, "What do you know, you were only a child."

We were always shut up as Hidden Children, because the moment we opened our mouths it might be dangerous. If anyone asked us anything, we were told to be quiet. That does a lot of harm because it nipped our personalities in the bud. We were just developing at the age of ten or eleven, when most children begin to express themselves; they just say whatever they want. And they are permitted to cry or to scream, but we were not. I didn't know who I was, what I was good for. Well, I wasn't supposed to be good at anything.

After the war the children didn't come out from under the carpet either. It was never encouraged, and so they had nothing to say until this famous reunion in America,[4] which Nicole David and others founded. The idea came mainly from her. They thought they were going to reunite a handful of Children and found that 1,500 turned up. They have it regularly now; it's very therapeutic for the likes of us because we do need to talk. We were not allowed to talk earlier on so we talk now!

Nowadays I think that I am a very young sixty-five, because I do still have a sort of childish thing. . . . I still pick up other languages when I hear them, and usually elderly people can't. I pick up from sounds just like kids do.

It's very possible that if you are not allowed to use one sense, you use another more. Like people who are blind and cannot see, perhaps they hear more. There must be something in it because it made me very aware of words and discussions, and I used to listen very much. I am a good listener. I hear and pick up.

We have had a home in Israel since 1981; we have a foot here and a foot there. I picked up Hebrew like a kid does; I sat in the class without writing down the vocabulary and just remembered it. This is what children do. It's like music, which I also remember well. All my three children are also very talented at languages. They, the ones who were available, came to Brussels for the medal ceremony[5] and they are interested in that story. But what happens with today's children? They are so busy with their own lives, and they have to make a living.

Ruth talks about her children. She likes to make a meal for them all on a Friday night. They all like to come and meet round her table but, of course, she is in the kitchen.

But I say to them when they have finished, "Don't run away, stay and chat for a while." It's very difficult, but I do actually succeed.

How has she made the transition from a Catholic upbringing to the traditional Friday night meals?

Yes, that's very hard, very difficult, because I have lost religion totally because of this mix up. I was very religious as a Catholic, then I discovered that being religious as a Jew was just the same thing really, just a different color. The whole thing I find . . . I don't know, I just stopped. I don't really care much for religion. Now, seeing what happens in Israel with all the fanatics, that puts me off religion all together. My husband also doesn't want religion, so between us we are not very religious. The children, well, my younger son tends to be a traditionalist, and he likes to go to the synagogue because he meets his friends there. It's a social thing.

They all have their father's name. My second husband didn't adopt the children. There was no need for that; their father is still alive and friendly with them, now more than when they were small. The children know about the traditions more than I do, because they went to Hebrew classes. They know their background but what they do about it . . . that's their business. They are adults now with their own young families, all very happy and settled.

Are they sensitive to the kind of deprivations that she had?

I don't like to make a point of it. It comes out sometimes in conversation and, if it fits at that particular moment, I tell them certain things. I have never refrained from telling them or hidden any of the stories, but I have also never made a special point. I think that they can piece together the whole story.

Ruth kept in touch with the Secret family who sheltered her until they died.

That is why my children's photos are in their family album. It's a very old leather album from before the war, and they put in the pictures they received from my kids.

When the family died I was given the album. The next generation was a nephew, because their only daughter died after the war. So they gave me the family album as a present and, of course, I have put in all the photographs that followed. It's a very old-fashioned one with corners. I felt very strongly about all these things.

Ruth's parents also kept in touch with the hiding family after the Liberation.

My parents even wanted to pay them (after the war). My goodness, my mother! I can still see this lady's face, she was shocked. She said, "How can you talk about money?" There were people who expected payment, but they were not that kind. No, they take a child under their roof and that's not for payment. They risked their skin, but payment doesn't come into it.

So, all in all, although there were times that were very hard when she was at school, feeling alone and isolated, there were many pieces of the jigsaw puzzle of which she had very positive memories.

The family certainly looked after me, although I felt out of place. They dressed me nicely and were good to me, and they took a pride walking with me. They liked me and, I must say, they were very good to me.

But the positive experiences came later. For example, my second marriage is a good one because I know what I want and I know what makes me tick. I never knew before what made me tick, who I am.

Ruth knows others (at the Survivor Center) who share her early experience of the Catholic religion.

The fear of hell had a tremendous impact on me, you know. I felt that if I were to be killed by a bomb, I would burn to a cinder and then burn in hell. I had worked it all out, the punishment, why we feel so guilty.

The nuns would say that Jesus doesn't listen to the prayers of an un-baptized child. You know this sort of thing goes into the mind of a child and makes you feel such an outsider. Everybody else can pray, everybody enjoys themselves in chapel, and who am I? Am I invisible?

Identity is what bothered me the most, you know, because my name changed, so it was, "Who am I? Where do I fit in?" Identity was vital to me; I really felt that I had problems with it.

I can't put a date on it, but I resolved it first of all by coming here and finding that my first name was acceptable. That was important, changing your name as a child can be a very traumatic experience, because a child has to fit into this new personality. It's like being on stage when you are an actor, you have to suddenly fit a new personality, and the name is a part of it, you see.

I have a sort of letter, which I will show you, which was given me at the Medal Giving Ceremony, and all this is written in there about my identity business and me. Because that was the extremely important feature in my life. I wanted to belong, you see, I wanted to belong somewhere and I couldn't. Who am I?

To this day, when I go back to Belgium, for example, I assume a personality that my husband doesn't recognize. He says that when I speak French, I am a completely different person, and I do seem to be.

I took Madame Verly (one of her rescuers) to the various churches in Jerusalem and felt perfectly at home in them and showed her around. Jews usually feel ill at ease because they don't want to be in a church. But I certainly felt very much at home showing her around. It always amuses my husband the way I can do this. It just comes to the fore now.

Ruth recognizes that she had to be "a bit of a chameleon" in hiding, so she can still actually play at being one. But she is conscious that she does not belong to the Catholics.

I really didn't want to shed my new Tournai identity that I had, not immediately. When I came back to Brussels, I asked the headmistress of the school to call me Josette Hochhauser, not that old name of mine. At that time I was a very bad pupil and a very miserable child, and it didn't work, so I preferred to take back my own name.

While I was living a lie during the war, I almost believed in it, you know, after I got used to this new name of mine. So I assumed a new personality of this particular child, I really did. I was successful at it, very successful. In fact, the cousins who were on that photo, the so-called cousins, didn't have a clue. They said, "We thought you came from Brussels." They told them who I was eventually, but up until then, they hadn't a clue.

A funny thing, by the way, these three people from Tournai, who are all married now with children, said to me, "But we know you. You exist in our family, you are our cousin. We never hear from you, but we know all about you." I said, "Good, so I wasn't totally forgotten then." They said, "No, certainly not, you made an impact on the family." So that is now my extended family.

NOTES

1. *Kristallnacht*, November 9 and 10, 1938, was "the night of the broken glass."

2. There were routes established through the mountains to neutral Switzerland.
3. No identity cards were required for very young children.
4. The 1991 First International Gathering of Child Survivors in New York.
5. Awards to Righteous Gentiles from Yad Vashem.

NICOLE DAVID

Nicole firmly believes that the foundation of close affection and identity she received from her parents and family in her early years helped her, after the war, to be fulfilled and lead a normal family life, to become a fully integrated member of society, despite the memories, doubts, and insecurities that remain a continuing legacy of her childhood experiences.

She was born Rosalie Nina in Belgium in September 1936 but was given the name Nicole while she was in hiding during the war. Her parents, Chawa Matzner and Munisch Schneider, had emigrated in the mid-twenties from Poland.

My father had come to Belgium to learn the diamond business, as did so many from his district around Kraków.

The community in Antwerp in the 1920s and 1930s was made up largely of Jews who had come from the ex-Austro-Hungarian Empire and later some Jews from Germany.

My very early memories, until the invasion of Belgium in May 1940, are of the protection and warmth of an extended family consisting of my parents, my father's older sister, her husband and her teenage children, other cousins, and the close friendship of two other families.

We were all like one big family, and according to the surviving daughter of one of those neighbors, now eighty-one years old, we all felt and behaved like one. Life in those prewar years was not easy. Belgian nationality was granted to refugees only after many years' residence, and work was scarce.

Every member of our extended family knew that each one of our houses was open to the others, and support was available when needed. As an only child I felt spoiled and protected. Life was stable; my parents were always there. My father was the one who spoiled me more than my mother. She was quite strict but she never hit me.

Nicole realizes that she absorbed a strong sense of her Jewish identity from her parents. They themselves came from an Orthodox religious background, though not quite as observant as their families had been in Poland. Nicole was taught to say the Sh'ma, *the Jewish prayer, every evening before going to bed, which was to be of great significance to her later.*

When the German armies invaded the country, I was three-and-a-half. We fled Belgium and joined the long line of refugees on the way to France. I remember vividly those early weeks of the war, walking with my parents on either side of me, sometimes being carried on my father's shoulders for hours. Memories of being near Dunkirk (the British retreat in 1940) are very strongly imprinted on my memory. When the Germans started bombing as we ran along, we went into a ditch. Some people were killed or wounded. My parents covered me with their bodies, and I thought "as long as they are here I will be okay." When the bombing was over we got out of the ditch and started walking again.

We arrived in a small French village, where we stayed for a few weeks. It was clear that the German armies were by now occupying France and Belgium, as well as most of the rest of Europe, and had established firm control.

As a young child, I did not quite understand what was happening, but after an unexpected meeting with some German soldiers who came to the village, I learned that, as Jews, we were in serious danger. When the German soldiers heard me speak to a small friend in German, my first language, they came over and brought some chocolate, promising to return with a doll. The next day they came back. This time my father came out and started talking to them about the progress of the war. The soldiers

Nicole aged about four with her mother. Courtesy of Nicole David.

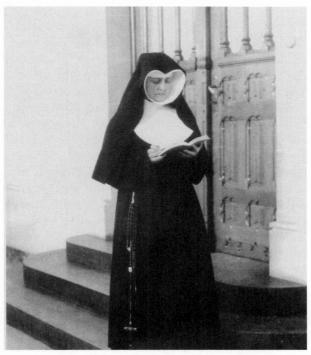

Paulette Champagne, the daughter of her hiding family, who became a nun. Courtesy of Nicole David.

Nicole with her husband, Ernest David. Courtesy of Nicole David.

were very confident, were sure the war would be over soon, as they had the strongest and also the most disciplined army. They mentioned that, if they received the order to shoot us children, they would do so. Although I do not remember the details of this conversation, I remember the soldiers and their gifts. As soon as they left, my parents explained to me that I must forget German and speak only French from now on; as Jews we were in constant danger. I grew up quickly as I had to learn to cope with it. That was the day my childhood ended. None of us, certainly not the children, knew what was happening or what the future held.

Shortly after our return to Antwerp from France, we moved to the French-speaking part of Belgium. After the economic crash in 1930, my father reverted to what he had learned from home, which was tailoring, selling fabrics, and traveling around the country. He set up a haberdashery business with a non-Jewish person. He knew the south of the country well, so when it was suggested by friends that we go to live in Profondeville, close to the Ardennes, he readily agreed. He knew that around there one could go to a farm and get food, and he also realized that it would be easier in a small place rather than a large town with a big Jewish population.

Profondeville was a pretty village, and my parents, as always, tried to protect me, despite the fact that life for Jews was being restricted almost daily. They were forbidden as Jews to have their own businesses or be treated by non-Jewish doctors and were allowed to go only to Jewish schools.

Before I was in hiding, although I remember a lot of frightening things, I also remember good things. There was a big garden behind the house where we were at first. There were three Jewish families, very close, and one family had a baby in January 1942. To me that was lovely because I had a "little doll" to play with.

During the war, Jews were not allowed to work, but my father would go every day to Antwerp to try to sell remnants of cloth, clothing coupons, whatever he could find. He would tell me that he would try and sell whatever he could. That's how he met the people who took me in. There were some non-Jewish neighbors who had heard that my father could get cloth. So they approached my mother saying that they were to have a christening in the family and the mother would like to have a dress made. My father got them some material.

When deportations started in 1942 my parents, who hid in an attic, put me in an orphanage, as I could not stay with them. But they knew that I was very unhappy. The nuns looked after us as best they could, courageously taking in about fifty Jewish children who had to share the limited space available.

Nicole had been having repeated tonsillitis and was to have her tonsils re-moved. Her mother wanted her to come home from the orphanage to have surgery. This meant coming out of hiding.

They asked these neighbors if they knew somebody who would take me in after my operation. This man said that his mother had a château and their family agreed to take me in.

Nicole never did have her tonsils removed; the Germans took her mother on the day before the operation, and Nicole had to be rushed to the hiding family, the Champagnes, at St. Servais, near Namur.

There were ten children in the family where I was hidden, of whom five were still at home. They were lovely people, members of the bourgeoisie, and strong Catholics; the parents and children addressed each other very formally as *vous*. No one was allowed upstairs in the salon unless the mother or father said so. I had never witnessed this kind of lifestyle, which was warm but formal. They saved my life and they still consider me as part of their family. I am regularly in touch with them.

When I reflect now on my experiences, my father and I narrowly es-caped deportation and death; my mother was deported while we were briefly absent from the house, and I survived the war in hiding, separated from my parents, in an orphanage run by nuns and later hidden for a time by this large Catholic family.

One of the daughters, Paulette (see illustration), who later became a nun, used to remind me to say the *Sh'ma* before going to bed.

Nicole was unable to go to school and Paulette taught her to read and write. After eighteen months, she was moved again to two different families, re-united with her father at the Liberation, and then once again separated from him and placed in a convent until the end of the war.

For many years after the war, like most of us, I did not speak about my experiences. I think the main reason was that having survived as a young child, eight-and-a-half years of age when the war finished, I was con-fronted by my father's pain as well as the knowledge that my mother and so many of our family had perished in Auschwitz.

We were told that we were the "lucky ones." We had not experienced the horrors of the camps; we were safe in convents or with families who were willing to shelter us. Because I was so young, I really did believe for many years that there was no necessity to talk about the feelings of abandonment or bewilderment at suddenly finding myself in a Christian orphanage. Perhaps we felt we had to protect our parents.

A few years ago, I returned for the first time to the café where I had stopped for a drink with my father on the day of my mother's arrest by the Germans. The owner fetched the daughter of the previous owners, now quite an elderly lady who lived next door. She told me she would never forget October 7, 1942; it was a beautiful day, and she was shopping at the greengrocer opposite our house. They heard screams and when she and the other customers came outside, they saw two women and a man being taken to the lorries in front of our house. The mother of the nine-month-old baby was begging for her child, but she was brutally thrown in one of the lorries. The witness added, "The other woman was your mother."

When we went back to Antwerp after the war, I didn't live with my father at first; I lodged with a nice Flemish family, and I had to learn Flemish. They had a daughter who was older than me. They loved music, and it was always jolly in their house. It was still a very difficult period because I felt that I had really never had a home. About a year later they moved to a larger house, taking in my father and a couple of other lodgers. This was 1945, and I was nine years old.

At school everyone had lost either one or both of their parents, so we didn't speak about it. Once again there was a very tight Jewish community. They regrouped with what they had. I think that being in Antwerp with my father, who had a very warm personality and was very loving, helped me. We had a close relationship. For a long time I felt, and I know this sounds terrible, that if one of my parents had to be deported, I was glad that it wasn't my father. Now I am wiser.

Nicole thinks that, on the whole, those who found a reconstituted Jewish community after the war were more supported than those who were "sent hither and thither."

I returned to the town where I was born. A reconstituted Jewish community surrounded me. I like the French part of Belgium, because we were a family up to 1942, but after the war we were never a family again. My father never remarried; I told him that I didn't want him to remarry. We used to go to school and find that some kids' parents had remarried so that their children were "mine, yours, and ours." I used to cringe! Of course now with divorce, it has become quite normal, but I used to come home and tell my father that I didn't want to have a stepmother and even less, half brothers and sisters.

Nicole believes that she was probably quite mature from an early age.

The first time I was told that was by a journalist of the *Daily Mirror* when she came to interview me. But you know, when I was three-and-a-half and my father told me in France to "forget that you can speak German," I began to learn how nasty the world could be. One grew up very quickly in those circumstances.

*A friend who lives in Washington told Nicole that she remembers her say-
ing, very firmly, that she would not have children.*

*By the time I made that decision I was twelve. I had actually forgotten
about that discussion. I did not want a child of mine to experience what I
had gone through, and there was the fear of losing a child in case of war.
Nicole's father suffered considerably after the war from the effects of his experiences, and she often worried about how best to help and support him.*

I married in 1958, and my father came to London in 1960. He had a
very severe breakdown after our marriage. Treatment in Holland and
Belgium didn't work. I didn't see anything else but to bring him here
with us, and we certainly didn't have enough money for my father to live
separately from us and to have help for him. Maybe later we could have
done it, but then I just couldn't see how. His first breakdown was in 1952
at the time of the Korean War. I sort of went to pieces too, because a lot
of people from Antwerp left to go either to America or to Australia. We
had papers but didn't go because the Korean War was very destabilizing.
Things quieted down. In 1956, I went for my twentieth birthday to
America to see my mother's surviving sister and brother. My father, left
alone, had a breakdown, not very severe, but after I got married I found
out that he had been ill for about a year without telling me. I was then
twenty-two, and he came to live with us. He recovered very well with
the help of a psychiatrist. It was also the time when the new drugs were
coming in and they really helped. He started work here, sorting diamonds,
and made quite a life for himself. He belonged to a Yiddish group and
organized his social life. He lived with us and got on very well with my
husband, Ernest. After a few years he went back to Belgium, but in 1970
he fell ill and came to live with us again. As before there were good and
bad periods. In his last four years his health was fragile. In the last eighteen months of his life, he finally saw a psychiatrist who had worked with
survivors; the change in my father was amazing, but by that time it was
too late. In the end my father went to Belgium to an old age home, something I never wanted. In the last few months of his life he said that if I
had allowed him to go earlier, things would have been different. Antwerp
is a very small community and he knew lots of people; he had visitors,
people in the home knew him, and he could speak Yiddish.

My father lived with us for seventeen years, and it is thanks to my
husband's love for me and for my father that the three of us got on so
well. We used to sit for hours and just chat. He was a fantastic man, and
a lot of what I am is thanks to him.

*Although Nicole sometimes worries that she might have inherited her father's
vulnerability, she generally reminds herself that she comes from a line of
strong women.*

I think I get my strength from my mother, although we were together for only the first six years of my life.

My mother was one of seven children, four sisters and three brothers. Only two survived. The sisters were all very strong women. I know that from my mother's surviving sister and also from others—cousins and people who knew them. Both my grandmothers were known to be strong women. My aunt, an extremely intelligent woman who survived and died at the age of ninety-six, was fully *compos mentis* until six to nine months before her death. When I lived in America for four years I used to go to see her regularly. We used to spend days talking but she didn't talk much about my mother.

My mother was one of the few women in her family circle who worked. She worked in a bank when she was in her twenties. She married rather late, because my grandfather did not approve of an earlier young man. My grandparents were by no means rich, but they were well established in their timber business and felt that she should marry someone of the same status or class. They approved of my father, and she was twenty-nine when they married. Looking at photographs of my parents in 1932, when they married and went to the seaside, my mother wore slacks and had her hair colored. She also used to smoke. My mother was the stronger personality of my two parents.

Nicole has a very strong Jewish identity but says frankly that she has ambivalent feelings about how this is received in Britain; she feels much more comfortable in America, where people know she is Jewish.

She used to have some difficulty introducing herself to sixth form pupils as someone who was there to speak on the Jewish perspective, though now this is changing, since the Holocaust is part of the school curriculum in Britain.

Compared with a lot of Hidden Children, I have never had a problem with my identity. Although I went to church during the war, I always remembered that I was Jewish. I feel that the fact that Paulette would say to me, "Remember your Jewish prayer" before I went to bed helped.

There are lots of people who during the war had to be "Christians." Some didn't have a strong Jewish identity before the war, and after the war they have come back confused, not knowing who they were. But there is also the perception of the outside world and being able to say you are Jewish. I had thought that the war had finally put an end to anti-Semitism and am horrified at its current resurgence fueled by the conflict in the Middle East.

Nicole believes this is due to continuing ignorance and prejudice and to the fact that 2,000 years of anti-Semitism cannot be obliterated in sixty years despite the horrors of the Holocaust.

When I go to Belgium some friends say, "She has become very English! *Très Anglaise!*" and I go mad. I suppose a lot of it is in oneself and how people are brought up and where they have lived for any length of time. I have lived in England much longer than I have lived in Belgium.

After Israel, the country I feel most at ease with is America, especially in New York, where being Jewish is fully accepted. We lived there because of Ernest's job. But having said that, there are lots of things that I love in England and that have become part of me.

Nicole feels that "rushing to counseling" can be overdone. The late Irene Bloomfield,[1] in an article on "Counselling for Holocaust Survivors," suggested much the same thing, questioning the advocacy of counseling for "one-off trauma," in the contemporary "counselling for all" culture.

It's quite true that after the war, we were told, "let's get on with our lives," and it was as difficult to ask "tell me about it" as to talk about it. As one gets older, it is natural to look back at life and realize one's vulnerability and the closeness of death.

Some Hidden Children say to me, "My children? Since I was hidden during the war, I have a difficult relationship with my son or daughter because of my war experience." Though there is no doubt in my mind that all of us who have survived the Holocaust, whether we like to admit it or not, have been traumatized by our experiences, I think it is too easy sometimes to blame every problem or misfortune on the war. This is not always a popular view!

I know that I would have turned out differently had I not been born just before the war started. But on the other hand, everybody has got something in life. What angers me most about the war is what it destroyed. How much talent, how many families it broke up, including my own.

In 1989, in New York, following a documentary film on the saving of about 3,000 children by a resistance group in Belgium, Nicole was surprised to recognize people from Antwerp with similar experiences to her own, who had never talked about them. She mobilized a small group of people to organize the First International Gathering of Children Hidden during World War II and was a moving spirit in its planning.

One thousand six hundred people from twelve different countries attended the gathering. The aim of the two-day gathering was to enable those who had survived in hiding to share memories, to remember, and to pay tribute to their rescuers. They wanted to help those who were too young to tell their story to the world at large, to tell the younger generation to be vigilant, not to let history repeat itself.

I really think organizing that conference has helped me in the same way that it helped many of the people attending who told me that by speaking about their experiences they finally came out of hiding. We understood that we were not alone and were strengthened by the support and empathy among all of us. It was a great relief to be able to talk about our history, which up until then had mostly been ignored.

Nicole feels that there is always such a lot she would like to do; she is very sociable and gregarious, and there is never enough time.

Since we first met, Nicole has again been enormously active, helping to organize and then chair another Survivor Gathering, which launched a major International Conference in London[2] in 2000. Like everything else she does, she threw herself into this task with characteristic energy but not without some cost to herself.

Children who survived the war in hiding have a foot in both camps; they are both survivors and the "Second Generation." There are thousands of individual stories of separation, terror, and physical and emotional hardship only now being heard for the first time.

But it is important to remember the good among all the evil; to remember that individuals in society can make a difference. People put their lives and those of their family at risk in order to save us, my father and me, people like Miep Gies,[3] her husband, and others who helped the family of Anne Frank in Holland, before they were betrayed.

In Belgium during the war, railway workers tried to sabotage the trains and postmen steamed open letters if they suspected denunciation and warned people of impending arrest before forwarding the letters. Social workers helped Resistance movements to save children. Many priests and convents took in Jewish children and adults. This happened not only in Belgium, but also in France, Italy, and other countries, saving many who would have been sent to certain death.

While it is important to remember the past, it is equally important to look forward to the future, celebrating the indomitable spirit of the Jewish people to survive. Most of us who have survived have endeavored to lead as full a life as possible.

For future generations it seems important to find a balance between the documentation of the horror of destruction and trauma on the one hand, and on the other, the remarkable ability of some to survive and suppress or overcome it.

In some circumstances the capacity of individuals for personal and psychological growth is remarkable, provided the trauma or "insult" does not surpass the limits of tolerance of the individual.

I think being Jewish does help. Throughout 2,000 years of history, we have been persecuted. We are bred on that, not only the Holocaust, but what happened before.

Nicole feels that what has kept her strong was a stable early life, her mother's resolve and her father's love, as well as the continued support from her husband, Ernest, who has given her the environment needed in which to re-create the continued stability that she craved.

She had a loving and secure early life, surrounded by a wide circle of supportive friends and family, was almost old enough to understand danger and, later, certainly did, but was also mature enough to think, as she now recalls, that "this is not a time for playing with dolls."

Her mother had a strong, independent, and assertive personality. Her father survived and, in the absence of her mother, gave her the love she needed, and much of her strength of purpose arose from her need and desire to care for him. The love from the two men in her life, her father and her husband, enabled her to be resolute in her approach to life.

NOTES

1. Irene Bloomfield, "Counselling Holocaust Survivors," *Counselling* 59 (Feb. 1997): 42–47.
2. The "Remembering for the Future Conference" 2000 (see Bibliography).
3. Miep Gies was the woman who helped to hide Anne Frank (see Bibliography).

SOPHIE RECHTMAN

Sophie Rechtman is a remarkably resilient, charming, and resolute Belgian who works in a voluntary capacity at a Jewish social center in Brussels. She recounts her experiences in a husky voice, chain smoking her way through her description of frightening early years, which could have destroyed the adjustment of many individuals. Although witty and assertive, her perception of the events of the Holocaust and their relevance for issues of racial prejudice and hatred today is reflectively considered. She describes how she uses these, in a gentle, creative but robust manner, when she works with school-children of different cultures. She believes that surviving positively has given her and others like her an enormous capacity to grow as an individual, and she is determined to use this as a force for good.

When you telephoned, I thought, "What am I going to be able to tell you?" Because it is all about trauma and, yet, if it hadn't been for everything that happened, I wouldn't be the person I am today. My life would have taken a totally different direction; I would not have been involved with or concerned with other people in the same way. I think I would have occupied myself exclusively with myself, then my husband, my children, my grandchildren, but not beyond them, certainly, if it hadn't been for this terrible trauma of the war.

What has come out of it has directed me toward other people. That has become my strength; in caring for others and helping them express themselves, I have become stronger. I used to crumble a bit when I was confronted with someone who was distressed. One becomes more sensitive to everything that happens, to racism, to xenophobia. Everything like that hurts us even if it's not directed against the Jews.

For myself, I just had to find some inner strength, and I've become really much tougher. Of course, you stay sensitive inside, but I think you try to be someone others can lean on, someone who supports others.

Well, first of all, my name is Sophie Rechtman; my maiden name was Granosz, and I was born here in Belgium on December 24, 1933, so in few weeks I'll be sixty-five.

I came from an extremely modest family; my father was a tailor and my mother didn't work outside the home. My parents arrived in 1928 from Poland, *Maman* was from Łodz, and Papa from a little village that no one's ever heard of about thirty kilometers from there. There's nothing there now. It's all wiped out.

When the war began, I was six years old. I should have had a little brother, but *Maman* lost the baby during the first roundups, when the Germans came knocking at the door. And then like many Hidden Children, my parents had to put me with a family, here in Brussels, with people

Sophie Rechtman with her parents. Courtesy of Sophie Rechtman.

Sophie Rechtman today. Lively educator and activist against all kinds of racial prejudice. Courtesy of Sophie Rechtman.

I didn't know. It has stayed etched on my memory. I wasn't Sophie Granosz any longer, I became Simone Legrand, and I was the "niece" of these people I'd never met two minutes before. I was no longer a child, it was all over, and the child became an adult.

I had to be careful of whatever I said. You know, at home I had been an only child, spoiled rotten, capricious, a little princess in the household one day and then suddenly, like a little mouse, hiding away the next.

First, you're not Jewish any more, you're not your mother's little girl any longer, that's all over. When you see your parents, you're not allowed to recognize them; you're not able to speak to them. Well, that really makes you realize that your survival depends on your *not* being like a child, and you can't live or play like a child any more, although I was very well treated by them, really as if I were their own daughter.

Their son had been arrested, tortured, and sent to Germany. This meant that I went into a very sad, strained atmosphere, very hard to bear.

I was completely crushed by it, I didn't dare speak. In fact, when my father eventually came back from the camps, I was no longer speaking. I would listen and I was completely obedient, always agreeing to everything, because I was so afraid, I always had to be very good; of course, they would never have put me out, but I didn't know that.

I was terrified; I would say to myself, "If ever they put me out, I don't have my parents any more, I have no one, I'm all alone, I'll be in the street, so I have to be very good." Living, thinking like that, that's no life for a child.

I was hidden there for three years, from October 1942 until the Liberation.

They tried at first to send me to a Catholic school, but obviously I had no idea of the Catholic religion. I had come from a traditional, not a religious, background. Although my grandparents had been very religious, my parents were rather traditionalist, that's to say the family just observed the High Holy Days.

For example, I remember the Festival of Pesach (Passover), huge tables with all the family—aunts, uncles, cousins—maybe thirty at the table. But my parents weren't in the least religious. I knew nothing about Catholicism, so that when I had to go to church, to confession, to communion, I was terrified.

So the Mother Superior of the school called the lady I was living with. She knew I was Jewish and she said, "Look, you'll have to get her out of this school because it's too dangerous for her and for all of us, too, because she is different from the others."

So I didn't go to school anymore, but a friend of the Grassards, my hiding family, was a teacher, and his son was a trainee teacher. He was in the Resistance, and three times a week I went to him in the evenings and had individual lessons when he had finished work, just as I would have done at school.

Monsieur Grassard, whose house I was hidden in, was very severe, but his wife was very sweet and gentle. Every day I had to do my homework, and it all had to be impeccable. If it wasn't perfectly written, Monsieur Grassard would tear out the pages and I would have to start again. Sometimes I had to do the same page four times because of one single badly written letter! Really, that was an education for life, wasn't it? That really did me a lot of good. A long time after the war, it was always "Sophie's notebooks" that were shown in school as an example of the year's work.

But I had these classes throughout the war, so afterward I immediately picked up at school, not just at the level for my age but first in the class. I knew everything that they had learned. So I was really very lucky to have had private lessons.

At first my parents were hidden in the same street as I was, so when my mother was arrested, neighbors came to tell me. They had learned that *Maman* had been recognized and arrested in the street one evening by "Gros Jacques" (a notorious Belgian who betrayed his fellow Jews to the Gestapo).

Several months later my father was denounced by neighbors in the street and arrested.

A long, long time after the war, I learned that my mother didn't even get into a camp. They put into the camps people who could work, who could still be useful to them, but there were periods later on where there were "too many workers." My mother was in a train that went straight to the gas chamber and then to the crematoria. No chance.

Much later, thinking about it, I said to myself, well, perhaps that was for the best, because I don't think my mother would have survived. She would have suffered terribly and she would have died anyway.

You try to imagine various scenarios, don't you, but I don't think that my mother could have survived in such conditions. She was a woman who loved life; she was always preoccupied with her appearance, very fastidious. She always needed to be impeccably turned out, and she was always beautifully made up. She would never have gone out without makeup, appearance was so important to her.

Then my father came back and he had been eighteen months in the camps.

Sophie's father had been in Auschwitz, had done "the rounds" of the various camps and a "death march," where he lost many of his friends. When Bergen-Belsen was liberated by the British, he caught typhus. A British officer who came to Brussels managed to pass a message for him to Monsieur and Madame Grassard saying "Sophie's Papa is still alive."

It was to be three months before he came back. He later told her that, while he was recovering, he was so hungry that he would eat lunch three times in a row at different local houses.

How he survived all that I just don't know. Three months after that he was strong enough to make the journey back. I remember the first thing that he asked us was, "Is Ela [my mother] there?" When people said to him, "No," he uttered this sentence, which cut me like a knife: "Well, she won't come back at all." For me that was the most terrible thing that he could say. He knew that if she hadn't come back by that time, it was too late. My father was one of the last to do so.

It distressed me terribly because I felt so alone and felt there was no further hope. Throughout the whole war I had been hoping, I had lived with hope, and I thought when it's all over they will come back, and we'll start again as before.

But we had to start again with totally different baggage. It was going to be a different life, for my father, for me, and for everyone, as it was for my rescuers. Their son hadn't come back (they had been officially notified by the Red Cross who told them that their son had died).

We didn't speak of it, we just carried on. She cried, he worked; you didn't speak much about these things. She always said to me, "They will come back, they'll come back," and she meant her son, my mother and father, the three people that we were waiting for. Of those three, only one came back.

I seem to remember a life lived in total silence—a huge silence. Everyone had ideas in his head and no one explained them or expressed them. She had her grief, I had mine, he had his as well, but, of course, he went out to work, and I only used to see him in the evening, whereas I was with her the whole day.

While the war lasted, Sophie was in hiding.

I went three times a week to the teacher, in the evening, and sometimes I went with her to do the shopping. There was a very big garden but I couldn't go into it. She was afraid the neighbors would see me. There was a little courtyard, and I could go out there but no farther, not on the grass, not in the garden. I could see the apple trees, I could see the pear tree, but I couldn't go out as far as that.

It was too dangerous; she wouldn't let me. Nevertheless, we did do the shopping, but not much. I was really cloistered and because of that, little by little, I really lost the ability to speak any more; I had no need to speak because I didn't have anyone to speak to.

When my father came back, we were tremendously happy, but then he had to get started again. I didn't go back to live with him immediately because he had nothing, he had to start work and set himself up again.

He had to find an apartment, and when he found that, I went back to him. First of all he moved in with his sister, who had also come back from the camps. They lived together, then she got her two children back and my father got me back.

Then Sophie's father met a cousin, a divorced woman, who had escaped deportation. They set up house together very quickly.
There began one of the most difficult periods for Sophie.

I told you that when I was very small, I had a really vile character. I really didn't accept this woman; she had effectively taken my father, and I was still waiting for my mother to come back.

When this person arrived in my father's house and I saw her in bed with him, for me that was the end of the world. At this point I had begun to have terrible nightmares; it was always the same nightmare: *Maman* rang the doorbell and no one let her in. I said to her, "It doesn't matter, *Maman*, I'll come with you." I close the door, I leave my father, and I go off with my mother and at that minute, each time, I woke up.

But I was really impossible with my stepmother. She tried everything with me, and I didn't accept anything. I would say, "You're not my mother! It's not for you to tell me that." And that continued up to my marriage, really. I was absolutely awful, awful in the house.

All I can say today is, may she rest in peace, but she was a woman without a heart. When we went to the cinema, I had to sit one row in front of them; remember I had just got my father back and, honestly, my father had been my idol. What more can I say!

So I found this period very, very difficult. On Sunday mornings I would jump into my father's bed, I was about twelve, and she treated me like a whore. She really cut me off from my father; she did everything to indicate that I was a rival. This meant that I really had a more difficult time *after* the war than during it.

It really was a dreadful period to live through, and my father was under the domination of this woman. He loved her, I'm sure, but he was torn in half by his love for his child and his love for his wife, and it was very, very hard for him too.

This situation continued right up until Sophie's own marriage. She married very young. She was only eighteen years old, but she had known her husband since she was a small child before the war. But they didn't meet again until she was seventeen or eighteen.
Earlier, Sophie had been a model pupil, but that changed when she was with her father.

That was the end of that. No more motivation. I finished my studies and went to the Athenée.[1] When I finished, my father needed to make money, so he opened a shop and decided that his daughter should become involved with it. She had been to school up to eighteen and that was more than enough!

It was a tailor's shop, clothes and suits for men. My father opened the shop for me, but it was terrible, terrible to make a girl of eighteen sell suits to men. I just wasn't made for commerce and selling men's suits. So I didn't stick it out for long.

I hadn't done any further studying or training. I remember teachers saying to my father, "Listen, Sophie should carry on studying." "No, no nothing of the sort; one has to work." This meant that I didn't do any further education, so apart from staying at school until I was eighteen, that was it, wasn't it? I got married immediately after I came out of school, when I met my husband, who is an absolutely adorable man; I've been so lucky.

I said to him, "Max, you have got to get me out of this hell. Get me out of it and we will get married." He would have perhaps preferred to wait a little, but I didn't give him a second chance, and I got married at eighteen-and-a-half. At twenty I already had my daughter.

Sophie's father was against it for practical reasons. He thought that her husband came from a family who didn't have enough money; he wasn't the husband he would have chosen for her. Sophie just wanted to get out of the house, to start a family, and to get away from her stepmother.

For me it was the two things at once. The first goal for me was to get away from the house and, in 1953, well, there was only one way of doing it and this was into marriage. It wasn't like these days. My daughter is also eighteen and she says, "OK, goodbye, I'm going to live on my own, I'll manage, I'm going to earn my living." That's what she has done; she's left the family house, with our blessing. I have set her up. I have done everything for her but, all the same, she has gone.

When I was eighteen, one wasn't able to leave the house or home unless one was going to get married. There was no question of going off to live on your own. So for me it was the only way. Of course, once I was married and had my own little territory, I decided I would like to have a child, and I would give my child everything that I haven't had myself.

At that age you are very idealistic, you want to do something wonderful, and you hope that everything will go as well as possible, and yet sometimes you idealize everything; you are not living in the real world. Like everybody else I made lots of mistakes when I was a young mother, but I think that I would do exactly the same if I had to do it again.

Sophie had no mother to help or support her.

I didn't want anybody because I already had my husband's mother and my stepmother, but I didn't want either of these two when my daughter was born. The only person I wanted was Madame Grassard, who had hidden me. She was like a mother for me; she really became my mother.

Sophie speaks affectionately of Madame Grassard, with whom she was in contact until the end of her life.

My daughter had her own two grandmothers, my mother-in-law and my stepmother. For her it was normal. But my "aunt," as I call her (Madame Grassard), was more like a mother.

And yet my stepmother was really an extraordinary grandmother to my daughter. How things can change! She wasn't a rival any more, she wasn't in her way. She adored my daughter and it was mutual. My daughter actually took it very badly that I never liked her; it was so difficult for her to understand. She became a wonderful grandmother.

I even blame myself, saying to myself that, after all, it wasn't her who was bad, it was me. I know I was really awful, but things were as they were, so I don't reproach myself too much; that's how it was.

We reflect that there was much less understanding then of the emotional needs of children who had had such experiences.

I want to tell you something. The big problem with Hidden Children and people who have been deported, I am not the only one, is that people had just one word for us all, you were "*lucky*."

The deported had been lucky because they had come back and yet people blamed them. People said to themselves, "Well, if he's come back, God knows what he has done, what he had to do to survive." How often did we hear that!

So the majority of deportees stopped speaking because nobody wanted to hear them. It was too horrible, people didn't really want to listen. The Hidden Children were completely ignored.

For our part, we didn't dare speak because we had learned what the deportees had suffered. We said to ourselves, "Well, compared with that, what we've gone through is nothing." So when people then said to us, "You were lucky," we knew this was true; if at eight years of age I had been sent to the camps, I would have been killed. It's true; I was lucky, I survived.

But no one asked, "How did you live?" "What was it like?" "What were you doing all day?"

So we kept it all inside ourselves; we could never discuss or express it. So I dealt with it myself; I say I "cured" myself, because in my estimation, I recovered from a serious illness and I got better all by myself.

When Papa died and I was all alone, I cried, but otherwise I never cried in front of anyone. I don't know how to cry. I kept it all inside. Now it is all finished for me—I don't cry anymore. So I hardened myself, I became very strong, and decided to do something with my life.

That's why I say I am different now from how I would have been, because at a certain point I said to myself, "Why did *I* survive? There must be a reason for it." If my mother didn't survive, my grandparents, aunts, no one came back, how did I survive? And I felt for those who had been deported, and I said to myself, "I have to do something for them. They suffered so much."

Maurice (who came into the room briefly) is a former deportee. So I said, "Maurice, I want to do something for you. I want to do volunteer work for the deportees." So until recently, when I created the Association of Hidden Children, I worked for the Union of Deportees. I did their administration. That's how I came into the Jewish community, little by little, saying to myself, "If there's a message to pass on, if there is something to do, you have to help people who have suffered more than you have, not thinking of yourself but rather, 'I have to help others.'"

But it wasn't until 1991, when there was the first meeting of Hidden Children in New York, that I fully realized that we too were victims!

People said to us, "You too have suffered." And that for me was something very important, to have our suffering recognized. Finally somebody had listened to us; people were asking us questions in the general discussion, and it went on from there and was tremendously important.

For Sophie and others, it was a kind of validation to be recognized as survivors and victims of the Nazi terror. They have had to fight for legal recognition at the governmental level in Belgium.

She hoped that soon they would have the official status of "victim." It would not mean anything financially, they only want to be legally recognized as casualties of war.

I think that that has allowed many people to say, "Well, at last I exist, in the sense that my suffering has been recognized," which is very important for them.

Sophie agrees that victims of a car accident or a train accident may say, "I am a victim for life; I am suffering."

But she feels strongly that the opportunity to talk about their experiences now has allowed them to become stronger, more self-confident.

Being recognized as a victim of war allows you to move forward. The man who was sitting here when you came in, well, he was like Mr. Anybody, just like all of us, but he has become our archivist. Every day he is at the ministry doing wonderful research for everybody, for people who want to look up their rescuers. He wouldn't have said that ten years ago, that wasn't his job—he was a furrier. It's absolutely extraordinary what this man has become. It's really good.

Everyone has truly grown through this experience, creating this association (of Hidden Children).

Sophie talks animatedly of the wonderful creative work the association has unlocked in those who lived in silence for fifty years.

Huge silence, yet everyone just managed and got by. It just shows what people can do. The result is extraordinary.

Obviously, everyone in the world has problems; there are people whose children blame us for having talked too much, and there are people who blame us for not having talked *enough*. There are children who blame their parents for having left, blame Judaism, have terrible identity crises; all of that's true, but overall the result is positive. We were there, we have experienced it. Of course, there are problems—the problems of identity, problems of divorce, which people have always had anyway. You can't blame everything on the war either. There are people in real difficulty, it is true, but over all I certainly feel there are positive things.

Sophie describes the creative and imaginative ways in which their experiences are used to educate schoolchildren, with a mobile exhibition that travels the country.

We tell them when we meet these children that we were all witnesses. We tell them what a Hidden Child is and what the rescuers did for these children, the positive aspects. We don't linger on the sad history of Hidden Children. We look at what these people did during the war and why.

I tell them how people opened their doors and their hearts to these unknown children. They hid us at the risk of their lives.

They adapt their talks to the developmental age of the children, explaining, no matter how young, how they can take some kind of responsible action to counter prejudice and racism.

Sophie feels that in Belgium there is still much anti-Semitism, racism, and an extreme right-wing, racist party; the situation is complex because of divided loyalties of political parties, as well as the language divisions between French and Flemish speakers.

Racist tracts, like those the Nazis sent out, are distributed; no one does anything. In fact, there is a law against racism, but it is insufficiently precise. Before this law was passed, the extremist parties made a terrible leap forward. So I say that we have always got a role to play, to alert our youth and say to them, "Look, this is what a racist party is, this is what extremism is, this is where that led us before; we are going to explain to you how it could affect you too."

To get there you have to review the past through our experience. It was necessary for "healing," recognition. It was necessary to be recognized in order to move forward; it was necessary for me to work for the deportees, for the Jewish community. I've never really earned very much. My husband has always managed well. I used to go to the office every day, and I earned peanuts but I wouldn't have done anything else for anything in the world.

And her daughter?

Ah, my daughter, my daughter, she thinks I talk too much about all of that, that I have spent all my life in the Jewish community, and she says she's had it up to here, "*Maman*, keep quiet, that's enough." But we've had so many injustices, it is important not to accept them.

Sophie speaks with enormous satisfaction of the way in which she works with schoolchildren of different cultures, such as Muslims from North Africa, for example, to dispel misunderstandings and myths.

One day I began, "Hello, I'm Sophie and I am Jewish." This little girl, maybe fourteen or fifteen years old, put up her hand immediately, and I said, "Have you got a question already?" She said, "Are you certain that you are Jewish?" I said, "Absolutely, there is no doubt that I'm Jewish." And I continued to talk. Then she again put up her hand, and she said, "You're really called Sophie?" and I said, "Yes, I'm Sophie. Wow, we'll have to stop here; there's a problem! We can't carry on like this because you're not going to follow anything I'm saying, so let's find out what the problem is. Tell me what's bothering you and why you don't understand." From her I learned that she understood that Jewish women have names like Rebecca, Esther, Sara, so she did not believe that Sophie was a Jewish name. Secondly, she understood that all Jewish women wore wigs "like you see on the television reports." You know, like very religious Jews. For her, Jewish women didn't look like me. So I explained, "Look, there are Jews who are religious, there are those who are not religious at all, and there are those who are a little bit less," and so we could carry on.

Once I was at the Deportation Memorial, where the names of all the deportees are inscribed. I was there with Maurice Pirol, president of the deportees. We met a group of young Muslims and told them, "These are the names of all the people who were deported." He showed the names of his parents, and I showed the names of my parents and my family. When we finished, a young girl stood with her head against the wall. I asked one of her classmates, "Is she unwell—has she got a problem?" And they said, "No, Madame, she's saying a prayer for the people in your family who died."

And I said, "Maurice, we've won. Today we've won. There is an understanding. They will go home saying they have spoken to Jews, and at last there will be a dialogue!"

Sometimes I say to these children, "Fifty years ago, the Germans wanted to eliminate everyone except those who were blond and had blue eyes. Which of you here would have survived?" Perhaps there would be two or three children with blond hair and blue eyes and I would say, "Right, you could live, and all the others would be condemned to death." That made them think. Even the little ones look at each other and think "Mmm" and I say, "Yes, that's what Nazism was; it was intolerance, it was racism."

We have had an extraordinary opportunity to have this association and to be able say to young people, "Careful, pay attention. We have lived through something absolutely terrible but, nowadays, it's about *you*, we've just been talking about *you*."

There's a time for everything; the time for going over the awful experiences was quite necessary in my opinion. I think it was necessary in order that the entire world could learn about it, to obtain this recognition. I think that that was the case, certainly for me. When I said to you I never cried, that's not true. At New York (the First International Survivors' Gathering in 1991) I cried for the very first time. I even cried so much, in the Belgian group, twelve of us, that I didn't even dare to look at the others. That's when Elie Wiesel (the distinguished Jewish author and survivor) asked for forgiveness from the Hidden Children. He said, "Forgive me for never having asked any of you what you suffered." Because in fifty years no one had asked us anything.

Nevertheless, I look at the whole picture and I feel that overall it is positive.

Sophie talks of meeting other Hidden Children for the first time after seeing them in a film in which they had all, separately, taken part.

When I saw this interview I was very moved, and when Janek (see Chapter 3) came to Brussels, we fell into each other's arms. We hadn't known each other before, but we just fell into each other's arms as if we were members of the same family. It was completely extraordinary.

NOTE

1. Athenée is the Academic secondary school in Brussels.

CHAPTER 5

~❧~

Holland

BERT WOUDSTRA

Bert, a robust and cheerful man in his sixties, still lives as he did during the war, in the north of the Netherlands near the German border. After the deportation of his father to eventual murder, he was hidden in a variety of ways, sometimes with his mother, but mostly alone. His experiences were often terrifying and isolating, and occasionally involved dramatic clandestine rescue by members of the Dutch Resistance. Later on he regularly had to leave his temporary hiding family at night to sleep on an empty boat, alone except for his little dog, when German roundups threatened.

He shares with most of the Hidden Children I have interviewed a positive view of life, high intelligence, and sense of humor. None of this prevents him from expressing feelings of anguish at the fate of his father nor how this and the dangers he experienced during hiding have affected him.

His school progress was profoundly affected by the war, but he has nevertheless been successful in his career and has founded a large and loving family.

Like many survivors, he regards it as a duty and a privilege to take part in educating his community, especially children, about the facts of the war and the Holocaust in particular. He also actively devotes himself to repairing relations between the German and Dutch nations and engages in other forms of volunteer, benevolent international work.

I was born in 1932 in Enschede, a town on the German border with Holland, the second son of Jewish parents. My brother is nine years older. My grandfather came from Friesland, and my father was the youngest of twelve children. Our name, Woudstra, is Friesian. I don't know when it became Jewish, but the name goes back three generations.

Bert Woudstra aged 12, a rare photograph taken in hiding. Courtesy of Bert Woudstra.

Bert Woudstra, successful business man, campaigner to improve Dutch-German understanding, and charity worker. Courtesy of Bert Woudstra.

My grandparents moved to Hoogeveen in Drenthe because there was no work in Noordwolde, their province of Friesland, and then to Emmen, where my father was born.

I had a German/Jewish mother who was born in Westphalia in 1895 in a very small village called Meudt. As a young girl, she trained in a textile shop in Mengede, owned by my father's eldest brother. Through him my parents met in Germany, and they came to live at Enschede. My father was the founder of a ladies outerwear business, and he worked with my mother to build up this firm in the early twenties.

My father was very liberal for the time, but my mother came from a very strict Jewish family. Before the war, we had a very good life. I didn't have much of a relationship at this time with my elder brother. I was the youngest, and I was more into sports and active things.

Bert's brother was very artistic, and this led to clashes with their father, so the elder brother left home at this point, and Bert found it very difficult.

We were all on holiday in France in 1939 when the mobilization started. At age seven we saw the war memorials from World War I in Belgium, which I remember impressed me very much. Then in France we could see all the soldiers coming; it was an anxious time. My mother said, "Is it good to go back to Holland? Is it not better to go to England?" So we drove to Calais. It was very difficult to get permission to drive that long way because fuel was restricted. So finally my parents said that we would live in Holland because the war would not come there. My brother went to Rotterdam, and we went to Enschede. I attended a very famous private primary school. My father hired a teacher to give English lessons to both of us. I see the book still in front of me, *The Berlitz Book of English*, with nice pictures and text. But I didn't know why I had to learn English so suddenly. All my father said was, "You never know."

It was nice to learn some English words each week. Then suddenly in May 1940 the war started! We were living in a house above our shop, a type of Harrods, not a department store but very high class, specializing in ladies wear. My father was always dreaming of having an old house, away from the business, and we moved just after the war started.

On May 10, it was a typical night, I remember hearing on the radio that the Germans were coming.

My grandmother in Germany was still alive and came to live with us. She was eighty-five, which was very old in those days. I learned that my mother's brother, Jakob, was captured and was in Dachau, a concentration camp. After he came out of the camp we went to see him, and he had bandages around his head and so on, very terrible. He got special permission from the Nazis to attend his mother's funeral in Holland. After the funeral he didn't go back to Germany but flew to Brussels. In November

1939 he committed suicide. His wife, Paula, and his son, Siegbert, were also in a concentration camp at Theresienstadt, and they did not survive. His daughter, Beate, flew to England and is now living in the United States. More refugees came to us from Germany. My father helped them socially and financially too, to buy a house and so on. My uncle Emil and aunt Jenny from Mainz came to live with us. Their son, my cousin Werner, had already lived with us for two years and was very nice, like a second brother. So with the start of the war it was very strange to discover that people, friends, whom we had visited three times a year, had started a war against us! How is it possible that part of my family living in Germany came to earth to overwhelm us? It is crazy! Anyhow it happened. We moved in May or June 1940, I think, to a new house.

Bert learned at this time that his father had sent some capital to London and had thought of going to England but changed his mind; he realized why he had had English lessons.

So we go back to the new home, and it all looks fine to me. We got our first electric Frigidaire instead of an old one that we put ice blocks in. We had a garage, and I had my own room with a very nice bed that you could shut into the wall. It was all fantastic. But, of course, it was not so fantastic because the circumstances were bad. I didn't get it at all. Then it came very slowly to us. We have to wear a star and I have to leave my school. We had to give our radio and bicycles to the Germans. We needed permission to go on the streets after eight o'clock. So bit by bit, I realized that something terrible was going on. Then in September 1941, there was the first *razia* (roundup) in Amsterdam, and 120 Jewish people were arrested, including my father. They were put in a school building not so far from us, and the next day they were brought to a train and taken directly to Mauthausen. After two weeks we got a message from the Germans that my father had died from a heart attack. It was typical, 120 men had died of heart attacks! Either the Germans had made a joke, to disturb our minds and he was still alive, or it was a reality. We were very sad, and my mother had a total collapse. I still hoped, one or two years after the war, that perhaps my father was coming home. Many of my uncles and cousins were arrested the same night, so a whole group went away. Then it became more serious. There was a committee of Jewish people in our town who were the contact between the Germans and the Jewish population, and they advised us to go away. The Germans said that we had to report the next day and take everything we needed because we were to go to a camp. And we said, "Oh, no!"

A friend's parents hid us for the first few weeks. A Protestant priest, a fantastic man who helped more than a thousand Jewish people during the war, hid my mother and brother.

I was with a family out of town who were very rich people, textile factory owners. I was there for some weeks.

Bert was placed with the gardener who lived in his own house nearby. He had no contact with his mother at this time.

He pauses for a long time.

I think I was worried about what was happening to my mother and to my brother and my cousin.

The first family I stayed with was the Jannick-Benedict family; the mother was of Hungarian origin, a very nice woman who died two years ago. I loved her, she loved me, and I loved my friend. The father was also a very friendly man, and people were very nice and helpful to me. The saddest thing for me was to be hidden in the gardener's house—it was a very bad period. The boss of this couple, Mr. and Mrs. Hilbrink, was a Mrs. Van Heek—a very well-known name in the local textile world. Her husband had died four years earlier, so she was a widow, a fantastic woman who did very much work for the underground organization. She was very much against the Germans and Nazis.

The gardener and his wife who had to hide me had no choice and were not happy with that. They were not really unfriendly to me, but I was very lonely there, and it was a very sad time. I felt that they were afraid. One day I heard from Mrs. Van Heek that there was a young man living in one of her townhouses with his family, also hidden. His father was an orthopedic surgeon who lived in my neighborhood, so Hans Neeter came to me and we played indoors because we couldn't play outside. It was very nice, so I felt better.

There was no school, though. I was really hidden; I only got out to the open air at night.

I only had my Berlitz book—no other books or toys. I played with things in the farmhouse, I made my fantasies, I hid in the attic. I learned how to go in and pull the door closed, and I could be hidden there. One day Mrs. Hilbrink said to go up quick, and I went and closed the door. There was just space for a chair and a little battery light under the roof. Then I heard the doorbell ringing; the door was opened and a very loud voice says, *"Is hier Bertje Woudstra?"* (Can I see Bertje Woudstra?) And I thought, oh God, this is a terrible signal! And I felt dead, but then I thought, I have a false name and even these people did not know my name, "Bert Sonneveld." Then the man came in. It was silent and I heard talking, talking, talking, but I couldn't hear what was going on. After half an hour Mrs. Hilbrink came up and asked me if I knew a dentist, Dr. André Noordenbos. She said that he was downstairs and that I should come down. So I went down. Dr. Noordenbos said, "There is a fatal situation; the Gestapo is making a *razia* around here in two or three hours.

I had a patient from the Gestapo, and he said he was in a hurry because he had to do a *razia* in Boekelo, and I knew that you were there." And I was thinking, "Pow! let's go!" He had a red sign (stolen by the Resistance) on his car that showed he was a medical doctor.[1] He had put this on his car and had gone to try and find me in Boekelo but already the road was closed. He was stopped by Germans who said that he couldn't enter the area because they were working there, and he must wait for some hours. But he said that he couldn't wait because he had to go to a child who was very, very ill and would they please inspect his car and let him go on. Perhaps when he returned, he might have the child with him, so they should let him through very fast to the hospital or it could die. He was fantastic, a bit of a gangster. He put bandages around my head and said that I must behave as a very seriously ill child and lie down in the car. I must take everything that I have with me, and he would try to get me out. But he could promise me nothing. And it worked; when we drove away the soldiers were saluting as we went through. But the same day my friend Hans was arrested with his whole family. After the war I heard that they had all died in a concentration camp.

We went to the house of the dentist who was living near a big military airport, and he had to go in through a gate with a special permit until he was within the perimeter of the airport. So as I was just a child, I was very safe in that area living with his family. They had four children around my age and older. It was a fantastic house in nice surroundings. I could play outdoors in the fields, but I couldn't go to town.

That was the start of the hidden period with the family of Noordenbos. He was like a movie star who had many loving affairs (laughter).

His wife, Geertrui, was unforgettable, a real mother to me. The children were fantastic, and I am still in contact with them. He was a kind of actor—larger than life. At that time, there was a character called Jack Boss, a detective in dozens of little World War I books for kids of my age that cost a quarter of a guilder. When you looked at that man (Jack Boss), it was Noordenbos! He was a lady-killer. His wife was exquisite, and when he came home it was normal and cozy, and he looked as if he was never with other ladies. It was very difficult, but it was a very warm situation.

My mother was then hidden with a family in town, and she asked the priest Overduin, who had a contact with my foster family, to bring me for one or two nights to be with her. Noordenbos arranged it. So after about five months I went to my mother. She was living in a room in a small house, and it was a very emotional reunion. I was there for one day, and I should have been there for two or three but my mother got a message, a letter. She opened it and I saw she was getting pale.

Bert and his mother were being blackmailed for 25,000 guilders; they should pay immediately or the writer would denounce them to the Gestapo. They contacted the priest who believed that the owner of the house had written the letter. He called Dr. Noordenbos, and within a half-hour they put their luggage in the car and rushed them away. It was feared that Bert and his mother could be traced to the Noordenbos household.

This was a terrifying period; so although we went to the house of Noordenbos, every night we took the car, a German DKW, and drove it into the woods, camouflaged it, and my mother and I slept in it.

Nothing happened. But we had slept in the car for, I think, fourteen days, which I found depressing and horrible. Every night we were waiting in terror. Are there lights of cars coming? We had to make new plans, so my mother got a new address. I stayed with Noordenbos for some weeks, and then we were together again. We went to the north of our province, and my mother stayed in the house of a Mr. and Mrs. Holstein. But it was a little bit difficult having my mother there for a long time because of other things they had to do, such as helping English pilots to survive. The Noordenbos family felt that it was no longer safe for me to stay there. They had a sailing boat in the north, by some lakes, and they asked a farmer if we could go there. We had to pay, and I never knew where the money came from. They were simple agricultural laborers, a Protestant family, very nice people. We got a room with cupboards in the wall containing two double beds, and we had one each. I could play outdoors, I didn't go to school, but I could go on the farmland. My mother couldn't go out at all. Then a second problem came.

The priest brought Bert's German Uncle Emil and Aunt Jenny to the same address.

His uncle was difficult, dictatorial to his nephew, pro-German, and complained bitterly about sharing food, to Bert's embarrassment.

We had a piece of meat that was cut into seven parts, and we all got a little bit, but my uncle complained because he was paying. I didn't like that at all.

In September 1942, Bert's brother, Egon, and his cousin joined them. They had come to ask advice about the chance of going with a passeur [2] *who could take people to France and onward through the Pyrenees to Spain.*

Of course, you had to pay for that. The next day the guide came to us, a Dutch man, to tell us what we had to do. It was arranged that one day they would send a card to a friend of ours in Switzerland who would return a coded card. After two months, we got a message: they were free. So my brother and my cousin went to Spain and then to Canada, in the Dutch army. My brother joined the Royal Air Force.

Then the priest said, "It's a good way, they have succeeded, so it is not unthinkable to go the same way." My mother agreed, and the man returned and told us to meet him at Amsterdam Central Station in two days. "You have to pay several thousand guilders to me, I will give you tickets and false passports, and you will go to my contact in Paris. He will take you to the South of France." So in two days we traveled by train to Amsterdam. It was very dangerous. We were in the central hall of the big station; Germans were walking in and out. Our big friend came with a smile and everything was OK and asked for the money. My uncle asked how we could be sure that he would come back with the cards and pass-ports. The man said, "I did it for your son, you can trust me."

Bert's uncle was suspicious, so the passeur left his watch as a guarantee.

   He never returned. They went back to the farmer but it was no longer safe.

My mother and I went to an old fisherman, Berend Miggels, who lived in a huge house at the end of Lake Beulakker in Jonen. His wife had died some years ago, so he was alone except for a lady who helped him in the house. My mother didn't like the situation there because things were a little bit primitive. One day he gave me a little boat and he said, "That's your boat, you must take care of it." He was perhaps sixty or sixty-five, but to me this seemed very old; all his children were grown and gone away so he was happy to have a little boy around. The lady who looked after the house was a little bit angry at having hidden people in the home. It was very isolated; you couldn't get there by car, only by bicycle, boat, or on foot, but I had a fantastic period there.

By this time Bert was about ten; he made a sail for the boat and went sailing and fishing, going with Berend Miggels in the mornings at 3:30 A.M. to empty the nets before going back to bed. In the evenings they repeated the process.

Sometimes Dr. André Noordenbos would come along in his sailboat and say hello. But after six months the housekeeper, who was not happy with us there, said to Berend that if the Germans came along and found us he would end up in a concentration camp or be shot. So it became very dif-ficult; it was dangerous to hide Jewish people; they risked their lives. Berend was a very strict Protestant who went in his boat to church in Blokzijl every Sunday; we had to pray at every meal and read the Bible three times a day. My mother didn't really accept this, but I was reading the Bible and I was praying. I understood that people were trying to help us, my mother did too, of course, but she was more distant. So she was not so upset when one day Berend said that we should look for another address. Noordenbos objected, but Berend said that his housekeeper would go away, which he didn't want, or she would make trouble for us.

Noordenbos arranged through the chain of underground workers for Bert to come to his family again and his mother to Twello, near the very old

"Hanse Town" of Deventer with a Mrs. Nel Huber, a friend of his mother-in-law.

When it became too dangerous to live so close to the airport, the Noordenbos family decided to go to Twello. The mother-in-law, Mrs. Ten Cate Hoeddemaker-Blijdenstein, was a very nice old woman, the widow of a gynecologist who lived in a big villa. So we went to that house with all our belongings. I met my mother again, and I could often cross the street and go and see the mother of your (author's) friend Jonne,[3] and Edo, his younger brother. My mother didn't come out. There were more people hidden there.

I don't know for sure how many people were hidden by Mrs. Huber, six or seven maybe at different times. My mother was very happy there. She was a very good cook, and Mrs. Huber was not, so, *"Voilà!* You take over the kitchen, you are my cook, *Tante* Florry." So it worked well; she was baking cakes, whenever there were ingredients available, and was called "the best cook in the world." This was a very special household: free, respectable, welcoming, artistic, interested in history and music, cultured. So I was also very happy there. My mother had a fantastic time there. With all the ups and downs, there were many problems to tell about. Mrs. Huber also went to prison. It was unbelievable the atmosphere and the way they acted. Jonne was studying (medicine) so I met him only three or four times with Olga, who later became his wife. There was also another sister, Petty, who worked in the Resistance, and Edo. He went to school. I didn't, but he lent me books. We stayed there from, I think, 1943 to 1944, and it then became too dangerous. There was heavy bombing of trains, and there was a train crossing near the house. We survived many attacks by British fighters. It was a sad time because I was thinking of my father, my uncles, and cousins and brother, but at least I didn't have to worry about my mother. That was one side; the other was that I was having a fantastic time, a good life!

There was just one postcard from Switzerland to say that Bert's brother was alive. Then the mother-in-law of Mrs. Geertrui Noordenbos warned against the whole family staying there, it was overcrowded and the bombing was severe; so the Noordenbos' decided to go to the waterside, to the north. Dr. Noordenbos had bought a houseboat. And the whole family went to it on the Beulakker Wiede, a pleasant lake.

In 1944 we went to a small village school in St. Jansklooster where I had been before. The headmaster, Mr. Schreur, was a fantastic man who knew about my situation.

Life was becoming even harder in Holland, but Bert and his friends were encouraged to be very independent.

We had enough food; we could buy milk, butter, eggs, cheese, and so on. The Noordenbos family had flour, and the baker would bake bread for us so there was no shortage. Many refugees from Amsterdam came on old bicycles, sometimes without tires, to look for food. Mother Geertrui said we can invite everyone to eat, but we can't give them things to take away. So every day we had five, six, seven people around our table. It was a very interesting time, quite amazing. At that time I was twelve and had to go to the farmers with money to buy milk. We were trained to negotiate the price by ourselves, and we were trained to be self-confident, to look after ourselves. We planted trees beside the road, because such trees in winter are needed to warm us—right? So we were cutting and sowing for ourselves, and we got punished by the officials but we still did it.

At the end of the war, the hard winter of 1944, when we were skating to school, the atmosphere was getting more and more serious. In wintertime our houseboat was lying in a canal near the bridge in Ronduite, a very, very small village. The Germans had put dynamite under the bridge, ready to blow it up, with soldiers waiting in a car to watch only 100 meters from our houseboat. So it was dangerous, but we had a sailing boat, a yacht with an engine, that was also hidden. We were friends with a yacht builder, Huisman, whose son, Wolter, was in our class, and so we were sailing and working on the wharf. We took the engine out of the boat, in case the Germans took it, and hid the boat in the reeds. Then Mrs. Noordenbos's aunt Geertrui said that it was too dangerous for me with the Germans nearby. So I went every night, alone over the ice, to sleep on the hidden yacht. It was dark and a little damp. I was strong and self-supporting, but sometimes a RAF bomber or fighter came shooting ships and cars on the road, and I didn't like it. I did it because I knew that I had to do it for the family, because if I was arrested then they were responsible. I did this for about three months, throughout the winter. I had the company of a little dog.

Afterward we said it was not so good to take a dog with me, because when people came the dog was barking. Then in April 1945 the war ended, and the Canadians came to liberate us. After some days the Canadians came and we drove with them to Vollenhove, a little liberated village. There were no Germans there, and it was very nice that the war was over! But at that moment I had bad feelings; I was worried about what was coming. Was my father alive, was my mother still alive?

Bert's mother was still safe with the Hubers, but he was worried about who would still be alive.

No travel was possible at the moment, so we had to stay in the little village of Ronduite. After two weeks Noordenbos came. He was still living in Enschede alone, well, alone with one of the girlfriends!

About three weeks after the war ended, we heard that my brother was alive in England and my cousin was in Belgium. He came one day in his jeep, and my brother flew one day in his airplane to Enschede Airport, so we were all together. My brother and my cousin were both officers so, of course, as young people we adored them. He took us in his car, and we went home to Enschede.

I think coming back was more difficult sometimes than being hidden. Nobody wanted to contact you or ask questions; you were like a sick person. I came back to my school, but now I was a little behind and had to go into a lower level. This was all right, but even the kids in the class, including Jewish kids, never asked me where had I been. We didn't talk about it.

One of the teachers was very nice to me. He knew I was thinking about my father. The headmaster gave me some tasks in the school as he thought that I was more mature because of my life experiences. We had school camps near the lakes where I was during the war, and nobody else had my experience, so I was a big shot! I had to go and give instructions about sailing, rowing, and so on. So I had a special place, and I think the headmaster gave me the task to give me some self-esteem.

There was a bad period when he was struggling to attend a school where he knew that his father had been briefly detained before deportation.

The school was the one where my father was brought after the *razia*, and I used to take him bread every day for three days before his transportation to Germany. I would go up the stairs and every day I would "see" my father there; it was terrible for me, I didn't imagine it.

Bert's wartime experiences affected his education, and he eventually lost heart in pursuing further studies. He went into the textile business, initially with his brother.

I was married and we had children; I have a fantastic wife, and I adore her. She was the first who listened to my life story and shared my sadness and so on, and I think that without her I would not be who I am now.

I learned that you need a long time to survive your thoughts and your experiences.

So from about 1960, I was active a little in politics, in committees, trying to build a bridge between German and Dutch people. Some people said I was crazy, that you shouldn't talk to Germans as long as you live. But the initiative in attempts to build bridges after the war came from Germans. Yes, there are good Germans.

After the war I tried to be a Dutch citizen, not a Jewish man.

I don't forget that I am from a Jewish family, but I don't believe. I think God is dead. When such things happened, there couldn't be a God who is seeing this. So for me it is over. I am an atheist in a certain way. I am fighting against being labeled and discriminated against. My religion is my choice and your choice, but my land of nationality is a given fact. And that is very difficult sometimes to explain. Every time I heard, "Oh, you are Jewish," or people saying bad things about Jewish people when I was younger, I didn't react, but now I react.

I wouldn't call it directly anti-Semitic but the labeling is still there. I find it during my work and I find it in society.

At the start of the war we had to leave our schools and were put in a "Jewish School," which I found so discriminating. And one of my big problems still is that I react in that way because I wanted to be a Dutchman. I think through history people have thought that they cannot trust Jewish people. In some circles you still see it. I am a member of an international service club, and I have learned that sometimes when you meet people you become aware that they are anti-Semitic. Not so often, but I have experienced it. I am a Dutchman and I am still upset about the conduct of people in general; we are still fighting and making wars and no one learns. It's terrible.

The traumas disturb the lives of countless children and adults for years and years. When will the momentum come in this well-developed world with all its scientific knowledge so that we don't start wars any longer and give every human being a chance?

The inhabitants of the region in a fifty to sixty kilometer circle around Enschede, called the Euregio, meet each other sometimes in the Netherlands, sometimes in Germany. We have a sister organization in Germany, and we have two presidents, one Dutch and one German. The organization is called *Nooit Meer, Nie Wieder* ("Never Again"). We do a lot of work in schools and high schools in Holland and Germany. I have brought one of my speeches for you. We talk with young people and older people, also with people who were in the Wehrmacht. Sometimes you meet people who learned nothing and sometimes it is very difficult.

My niece is married to a German boy, a fantastic man, and she is also fantastic. He works in Holland and she is an English teacher, and they are very special people. His father is a very important man in Basle near Arnheim in Germany, very rich with a big business. He was in the war, in the Netherlands, and when I met him recently he spoke for the first time about his experiences, but he doesn't feel that he did anything wrong. He says he was very good; he was an officer and did nothing against the Dutch inhabitants. So I said, "But your system was sick."

When will we solve conflicts or differences by talking or by the intervention of an International Court, and not by weapons?

NOTES

1. Doctors and dentists in European countries carry the emblem of the caduceus on their cars, red for doctors and green for dentists.

2. A person who could secretly enable escape to a neutral country for money. Not all were honest.

3. The distinguished Dutch pediatric pathologist, Dr. Jonne Huber, whose mother, Mrs. Nel Huber, sheltered many Jews in hiding, originally introduced Bert Woudstra to me.

MILLY HOROWITZ

Milly was a baby in Holland when she was concealed by a Catholic family and has had to piece together much of her early history with the help of other people. She was clearly lovingly cared for, and some of her worst deprivations were most apparent immediately after the war when she was returned to her traumatized parents. She has found it difficult to discover that on her false papers she was designated as puella esposita, *a foundling, to conceal her Jewish identity, but she was amused to learn that her fictitious date of birth was given as that of the Queen of Holland. After the war, when she had to apply for a passport, she was designated as stateless.*

I was born Amalia Steinberg on January 1, 1942, in The Hague, Holland. Although we went back to The Hague after the war, mother soon remarried, and then we moved to a very small town called Roermond in the southern part of Holland. It is, in fact, nearer to Germany and Belgium than it is to many towns that people associate with the Netherlands. That is where I grew up until I was sixteen, and then I was sent to Amsterdam to school. There I stayed for two years and, when I was eighteen, I was sent to London. I have been here ever since.

I had a rather mixed education, that is to say, I went to a Protestant primary school, then I went to a convent school for one year, which I absolutely loathed, and then I went to a nondenominational school. To finish it all off, I went to a Jewish school for two years.

I think my parents were afraid because there weren't any Jews where we lived and, although I had some Jewish education at home because my parents were quite religious, it is a very difficult thing to understand for Jewish people who were born and grew up in London. I don't think my children can imagine what it was like living after the war in a small town where the Jewish population had been virtually wiped out. I think that, apart from us, there was one complete family where everyone returned safely, but I think that was only because the husband was the head of the *Judenrat*;[1] people did not take kindly to him for that reason, but he and his whole family survived. Other than that, there were bits of families, half-families, and quarter-families, and I think altogether about fifteen Jewish souls of various ages. I was the only Jewish girl of my age.

Roermond at that time had a general population of about 25,000 and 99 percent were Roman Catholic, with a very small Protestant minority.

The result of all this peculiar schooling meant that I never finished anything in particular and never stayed anywhere long enough. The positive side of it is that I am very tolerant of all religions and whatever people want to believe, as long as they don't force their beliefs on other people, which I don't like at all. The other negative side is that I am isolated and

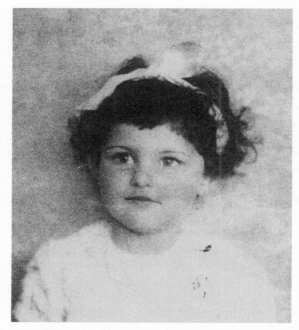

Milly during her hiding years. Courtesy of Milly
Horowitz.

Milly after the war. Courtesy of Milly Horowitz.

The painting Milly received from her foster parents as a wedding present in 1961. "In happy memory of the terrifying years that you spent with us." Courtesy of Milly Horowitz.

that I never learned to belong to any of them because I certainly wasn't Roman Catholic or Protestant, and every time I went to a new school my stepfather would say, "She is not allowed to take part in any religious instruction whatsoever; she has got to leave the class unless you are reading the Old Testament—otherwise forget it."

Milly today. Courtesy of Milly Horowitz.

Milly finds it strange that she did not find this embarrassing at the time.

I accepted everything. I must have been the most accepting child of that generation. I think everything they did with me and to me I just accepted for some reason. The only incident I can remember that I did not accept was when I was twelve and at a convent school where all the teachers were nuns, some of whom were quite nice, some of them weren't. The only male teacher we had was a singing teacher, and all we sang were German songs. I got really fed up with that after a little while, and I stopped singing until they noticed. I said, "I don't like all these German songs. Why can't we have something else for a change? You know, let's have a song in English or French."

We did learn all these languages at the time, so why always pick German? I think they must have realized there was this Jewish girl who had survived and had some feelings about this matter. It was never mentioned again, and we did get more of a mixture after that. That does stand out in my mind very strongly.

We were also near Belgium, which was probably very nice but, on the other hand, because I was stateless I couldn't go anywhere. Even if our school went on a day trip, I had to have a visa for the day, which was a nuisance, so mostly I didn't go. You know, I was actually born with Czech nationality, which I have lost.

I have no memory of my infancy or even of later years; it is as if I have pushed it all away. It wasn't a particularly happy time for me; I was a very lonely child, although I did have this one brother, but he never lived at home, I never really knew him. Unfortunately, my mother put him into an orphanage after the war, because she just couldn't cope with both of us, and she was getting married again. I didn't know this strange woman, and so she had a very hard time with me. My stepfather didn't want my brother; he just wanted this one child, me. I didn't know this at the time, obviously, but I discovered it later. So I grew up as an only child, basically. I wouldn't say it was a hostile environment, but I think perhaps if my mother and stepfather had not been religious, if I had just been like the other few Jews in town who were not religious and were allowed to mix normally, I would probably have had a much more normal life. Because we stood out, you see. We were this one teeny-weeny little island in a totally different environment, and I was also brought up to believe "Gentiles are no good." Now I don't believe that myself, but this is how I was brought up.

Yes, I remember my stepfather saying that at regular intervals, yet he was a very respected man in the little town where he had lived before the war. He was hidden all through the war in a village nearby, but his only son perished, and he came back. His first wife had actually died of cancer just before the war, and there was nothing left, nobody. They had to start from scratch.

He originally came from Warsaw and left Poland, I think, when he was eighteen or nineteen. He should have been drafted into the army, but he was not going to fight for either side if he could help it, and he simply walked away to Germany. He lived there, quite happily, until 1933. He went to live in Holland, which wasn't quite far enough, but it had been neutral in the First World War so . . . you know . . . it was quite logical. He knew that area because he had done business with that part of Europe.

We had textile shops but he never talked about his work before the war. I think he had a very interesting past; when she was doing her journalistic training, my daughter tried to record it on tape but there was such a language barrier, it was very difficult. So I don't know how far she got, I should ask her.

Milly's parents lived in Holland before the war, in The Hague. They were both immigrants.

My father was from a place in Czechoslovakia, which is now in Ukraine. My mother came from a village in Galicia in Poland. They met in Holland and married and then had my brother before the war.

I was born the first day of 1942, and my father just about saw me and then my mother thought that it would be a very good idea if we all went into hiding. Then I became ill with dysentery or diphtheria. The Germans were very scared of contagious diseases so they kept away. I went into hospital and I got better, but while I was in hospital, I had a swollen eye from a mosquito bite. The doctor was very nice and suggested that I stay there. "She is safe here. You might as well keep her here a few more days." So my mother asked him whether he could find a hiding place for me. I think I probably went from the hospital to various places (one never went straight to anywhere), and one party didn't know about the other, because it was better if they didn't. A few years ago I went back to my hiding place to find out what had actually happened, because my mother never told me. She left me there to go into hiding with my brother somewhere else, and eventually they were caught, so the people who had been hiding them were killed.

This was in 1942 or 1943, I don't really know. My mother and brother were taken to Westerbork, the Dutch transit camp, and from there to Ravensbruck where they spent quite a long time. From there they went to Bergen-Belsen from where they were liberated in about May 1945. They were both extremely ill, far too ill to travel, so I don't think they came back to Holland immediately, not until the British doctors nursed them back to some signs of good health. When they returned to Holland, they couldn't find me because we had moved four times during the war.

The family who sheltered Milly were afraid of the numerous collaborators in Holland, although, as an ideal "blond baby" and a little girl, she was less conspicuous.

The family was childless and had always said they wouldn't give her up unless her parents came back for her.

I was found eventually through the Red Cross and then went back to The Hague and joined my mother's only surviving sister, who had come to Holland with her before leaving Poland and all their other eight brothers and sisters behind.

I must have been somewhere between three-and-a-half and four.

She had no early recollection of her mother.

In 1947, when I was five, my mother remarried, so I don't remember The Hague. I wasn't allowed to attend the actual wedding, but I do remember arriving at a station, and I must have been very small as I remember there was a huge distance between the bottom of the train stairs and the actual platform. I remember being very scared. It was a steam train, I do remember that.

Milly feels that she had had "a very good time" in hiding.

My mother always said they took great care of me, but after the war she severed all contact with them. I never saw them again. My "hiding grandparents" came to my wedding, though.

I only discovered two years ago, when I actually went back to Dordrecht, that my foster mother had run off with a priest. Now I don't know whether that was during the war or after, and it may well have influenced my mother's decision not to have anything to do with them, because we don't mix with people like that (laughter)! I found my "uncle," the twin brother of my foster father, was still alive, but not my foster parents, obviously, nor were my "grandparents." I must have had other "cousins" and "uncles."

They were at my wedding. I don't remember, but I did have photographs of them there.

They sent me a very nice present when I got married, and it hangs on my wall. It was especially made for me, a hand-drawn picture that depicts the quote from Exodus, you know, when Moses was found in the bulrushes. There is a little basket with Moses on one side and a basket of leaves on the other. The text says "In happy memory of the frightening years you spent with us," 1942, and the date of my actual wedding. Yes, that is very special; it hangs opposite my bed.

Milly did not consciously look for information until two years ago, and then only on the insistence of her boyfriend. Her ex-husband was never interested in her background or her past. She believes he was ashamed of it.

She also discovered, when her mother "blurted it out," that she had been baptized during her hiding period. She had not known about this before.

If I had, I wasn't conscious of it. It never occurred to me. And I thought, "oh, how funny."

Milly told her husband.

"Oh, guess what, you know, I was baptized a Roman Catholic," I said. "What does that make me, a Roman Catholic Jew or a Jewish Roman Catholic?"

Apparently he had known about it for years.

For Milly this was the last straw and crystallized the feelings she had held about her marriage for some time. She decided to leave after twenty-six years of marriage, nearly nine years ago.

I think my family were ashamed of the baptism, although my mother had said, "Oh well, you know, it was only a bit of water, it has long since dried!" But she still felt bad about it. They tried really hard to exorcise this "Roman Catholic streak" in me. And I must admit, for a little while when I first arrived in Roermond when I was six, seven, or eight, perhaps, I used to go into church and sit there. I didn't actually say any prayers, but I felt sort of happy there for some reason. It was the Roman Catholic cathedral; Roermond was actually a cathedral city. It was the local bishop's seat, and they had had several very nice cathedrals. They are all closed now but then the door was always open. Eventually I grew out of it, and it had no meaning for me. On the other hand, I didn't like going to synagogue, I still don't. I mean I had a lot of it because my husband was very religious, and I was forced by my stepfather and my husband, you know. I didn't actually rebel, but I didn't like it at all and, since I've left, I don't ever go the synagogue. Now I have a Roman Catholic boyfriend, Jacques, who comes from that part of the world and who is much more understanding and tolerant. He said it would be a very good idea if we went to Dordrecht and looked, and we found everything. We found my registration of birth, a false one, and my baptismal certificate, written in a big book, a register of 1943.

The lady who helped us find it took out a white card and said, "Oh, I'll write you a registration card." I said, "I don't want one of those, I'm Jewish!"

Jacques looked at me, and he was really hurt. I said, "I am Jewish, I'm not Roman Catholic, you know I'm not" (chuckles), and I think it wouldn't have been valid anyway because I was not baptized in my proper name, I was a fictitious child! They had to do it in order for me to be more realistic.

Milly sees this as a token of her survival.

I've got the photocopy of the actual registration; I've got photocopies of everything. Ah, it was very traumatic because the first thing we found in Dordrecht was a little war museum. It was about Occupied Holland under the Nazis, generally, with a little Jewish section of the exhibition, which I liked very much. And I explained who I was and why I had come. Incidentally, I discovered Dordrecht was a beautiful city. It's very pretty, very old, and lovely. It's well worth a visit.

So they said, "Well, do you know your name, what you were called?" and I said, "Hofstee," so they went through the telephone book and found four different Hofstees. He rang them all, and we found my foster father's twin brother. He was married and lived in a sheltered old age home just outside the city; we went there and they were very, very nice. He remembered me, and he recalled Marie, his sister-in-law, changing my nappy on the table. I said, "Tell me something, my mother always said that both my foster parents were nurses." And he said, "Not at all." He said his brother was an ambulance driver or an orderly. I'm not sure what my foster mother was, but my foster grandparents had a chip shop or something.

It appears that I spent more time with them than with my foster mother. I asked him if he knew that I was baptized. He said, "Oh, yes, I was very against it, and I told them so, but they insisted." "You shouldn't do it without her mother's consent." But they did it anyway.

Her foster uncle was able to tell her in which church she had been baptized. But with the bombing and destruction, the records had been moved from place to place. Eventually she traced them. She was also able to trace a house she had lived in.

I said to Jacques, "I can remember the house that we lived in, and when you opened the front door there was a staircase going straight up. I don't know whether I dreamt it or whether that's true." And, of course, I didn't knock on the door of the actual number where we'd lived, but we passed some other houses where the door was open, and when I looked inside there was a staircase going straight up. There were lots of churches nearby, I remember that.

What I didn't remember was the enormous amount of water in Dordrecht. It had formed where the two big rivers of Holland come together. It's huge; there is so much water and lots of canals and old, old houses, a really pretty little place, quite near Rotterdam.

So there I was, and I asked my foster uncle, "Where do I find my birth registration?" He said, "Oh, you had false papers. You were brought to us via a Protestant clergyman by the Head of the Police, that's how you came to us."

I went to where he'd sent me to find my registration of birth and asked the girl, explaining who I was, and she asked me if I had some sort of identification. I gave her my passport. Of course, in British passports you only have your married name, not your maiden name like on the Continent, you keep both. I said, "Well, that's really me." After some searching the clerk returned looking upset. I found that I had been registered as a foundling and that really upset me very, very much, because I had never known this, you know. Then Jacques looked at it and said, "Look at the date of birth, look at your birthplace. They make you slightly younger." Apparently they had given me the Queen's birthday, April 13. And so that is my second, my official birthday (laughs)! But they obviously did it on purpose.

I've still got that; the Dutch were very thorough, very bureaucratic. After the war they actually wrote a little note saying that this was a false registration and that this person was actually born on January 1, 1942, in The Hague, under the name of Amalia Steinberg. But I managed to get my birth certificate from The Hague, which I had never had before. It gives my mother's name, the time I was born, quarter past two in the morning, and the name of the member of the hospital staff who registered me.

These revelations and proofs of her past are of enormous significance to Milly.

Apparently, I was given the names Maria Josepha from Mary and Joseph. I saw that in my baptismal registration I was baptized Maria Josepha. That's all I know. I've never been called my real name, Amalia, I've always been called Milly.

Milly very much wanted to know "Why, what possessed them to hide me and take me into hiding? Because that was a great thing to do."

Her foster uncle said, "We couldn't let them kill innocent babies and children, we couldn't do that!"

Years and years later, when I was married and living in London, my neighbor told me that while I was on holiday some people came from Holland who desperately wanted to see me.

They didn't leave a name; do you know what they left? They left a little lock of hair, a little blond curl in a little box, and some photographs. They must have been my foster parents.

After the war Milly, her mother, and stepfather tried to rebuild their lives in Roermund. There was a synagogue, rebuilt on the site of the old one, a very small Jewish population, and several fragmented families.

So there we were living in Roermond. It was not a happy time. My mother was exceedingly nasty and was always shouting at me. My stepfather, I think, meant well but was a distant, very dictatorial, and very, very strict man, very controlling. He put me in the coal shed whenever I was naughty. I don't know now why that was, because I can't even remember being naughty, and I'm always told now that I'm actually a very sweet person, which I don't accept. I can't be, you know, because my mother always told me I was horrible and my stepfather used to put me in the coal shed.

I was a very difficult eater. I always had tummy aches, and when I was eleven I had my appendix removed in desperation, because they couldn't find anything wrong with me. Food played a very important role because there had been such a shortage before. I know that my mother was always very loath to waste anything. I had to eat everything that was on the table whether I liked it or not. My papa would say, "Well, if you don't eat it today, you'll get it tomorrow, and if you don't eat it tomorrow . . ." and that's how it was. And so I have been more lenient I think with my children.

But there were things, foods, that would not come into our house. One of them was turnip, because that's what she [her mother] had in the camp, turnip soup. I don't even know what it looks like because that never made an appearance (chuckles)! Papa always said that he survived the war by eating dry bread and onions. When he came out, he had nothing, no clothes, nothing. He found a suit that had belonged to his son on his Bar Mitzvah, which fitted him perfectly.

They have very peculiar laws in Holland. In Holland you are given your father's nationality, which was Czech in my case. After the war my mother married Papa. He wanted to adopt me, and I was told that he couldn't because he was too old, unless I stayed in Holland until I was twenty-one, but I left when I was eighteen. I got married when I was nineteen, and I became British.

Had Milly ever made any connection between her mother's harsh treatment of her and of her time in the camp?

Well, I did. Years later I once asked my aunt, who was actually very sweet-natured, the total opposite of my mother, and I said to her, "Tell me something, was Mama always like this or is it just because of the war?" because she really reduced me to tears. My aunt said, "Oh, no, she's always been like that. She's always been selfish." Now, it's very easy to say that, but when I look back at her life, I only know that she came from a family of ten. She was the eldest and, at the age of thirteen, her mother died in childbirth; there she was with all these nine children to bring up and with an elderly grandmother who moved in with them. When she was nineteen, she said, "Right, that's it, I've had enough, I'm going," and she went to an aunt and uncle living in The Hague (who perished in the war, so I never knew them). I think they treated her like a skivvy. She never said much about them; they were very wealthy and she lived with them. She took this one sister with her who begged her to take her to Holland. I only know that she had one brother called Benjamin who died when he was very young. And I suppose my mother had terrible guilt feelings about leaving them all behind and surviving when so many other relatives didn't. We have no photographs, I have no names. There was one other sister, but there were only three girls and seven boys. When my daughter was born, my mother wanted me to name her after her one other sister and her grandmother.

Milly's earliest memory was being called "dirty Jew" in the street in Roermond where she lived as a very little girl. She thinks she probably always had very pretty clothes and things, which the others didn't.

We lived in a very horrible neighborhood for some reason, which I also could never understand. Papa was a very proud man, very educated and cultured, and yet we lived in this horrendous slum. Many years later I asked his business associate, who was my so-called aunt with whom I was very close, "Why did we live there, it was so horrible really?" and she said, "Well, because there were no houses." After the war there wasn't anything, and so you took what you could get; then afterward she said, "It was very convenient for the shops." We could always go home at lunchtime, and as we got older it was very convenient for Papa, so we stayed there. At the back of his mind he always thought, "Well, when I retire I'm going to live in Amsterdam, so why bother, we might as well stay here." But they never retired to Amsterdam, they retired to Israel. But by that time, in 1965, I was already married and living in London and was expecting my second child.

I read a lot, I was always reading; I think that was my retreat from the world. I was always found with a book in my hand. My mother used to hide my books on top of the wardrobe, because I wouldn't do my homework.

I got here when I was eighteen. I met my husband-to-be almost immediately. He was quite friendly with me. Then my uncle from London asked, "Well, why don't you send her here?" I was sent to London because I had some surviving brothers of my real father and uncles and their families there; they'd already come here before the war.

I just finished school, came here, and went to Pitmans, I think basically because they didn't know what to do with me. I didn't want to study, which I think caused disappointment. That was in 1960, long before the European Union. I was stateless, and I still had this little paper saying "nationality unknown or uncertain" (laughs). I do remember coming here with my mother who had Dutch nationality. I didn't, so they searched me from top to bottom, everything. My mother was so angry and, of course, they didn't search her because she had a Dutch passport.

They had all been naturalized. My stepfather, my mother, and eventually my brother. I was stateless; I've never had Dutch nationality.

I didn't quite finish Pitmans. I think getting married seemed the solution to all my problems. Probably, even then, at the back of my mind I felt that nobody really wanted me. You know, here were my parents, literally shoving me off to my aunt and uncle in Stamford Hill, and my very sweet-natured uncle with the long beard, who would say, "If you're not home by eleven I'm going to lock the door." I would then have to go to another uncle who was a bit more liberal minded.

But Milly was unhappy, married to a much older man.

I told my parents that I was getting divorced, and my father said, "I'm not a bit surprised, I've seen this coming for years." My mother said, "I don't know what you're on about, he's a good bloke. He doesn't run around with other women. He doesn't beat you up. What more do you want?" She never understood, I don't think, but my stepfather did.

After her first child was born, Milly was unwell.

I think I was very depressed; I was in hospital for three weeks because my stitches went septic. I knew absolutely nothing about babies. I had never encountered or held a baby before. Nobody I knew had babies, not in my circle, because you know, I only knew old people, and there I was with a baby. I think I just coped somehow.

I think all my life, looking back, I have coped very well, thank you very much, but on a sort of mechanical level anyway; I don't know about emotional level. But she was a very sweet little girl, a very good baby, and my mother-in-law said, "God is very wise to send you such a good baby because, if she wasn't, you would have thrown her out of the window by now." She was a good child and very easy and very independent from a very early age and knew exactly what she wanted, where she was going, did what she did, and just got on with her life. And Stephen, the next one, took a lot of my time.

I had very easy pregnancies, good healthy ones, no problems, easy births.

I was brought up very proper and clean, and everything had to be just so. I got quite friendly with my neighbor who was very nice, but it was all so alien for me. We lived in a suburb, which was so English; it was wealthy, and we were relatively poor really. And I had to make do.

It sounds as though her infancy with her foster parents was very nurturing because she was strong enough to cope with the later difficulties. One of the reasons she made contact was that she considered herself somebody functioning reasonably well.

I think I just functioned on a very superficial level. I went through all the motions, you know. I got married, I had children, and I brought them up, and everybody tells me that I have done a wonderful job. But we all do our own thing. Sometimes Jaques says, "You have not had much fun in your life." It is true; fun is not a word that occurred in my life at any time; I didn't ever have fun. I didn't have fun as a child because I wasn't allowed to, and I certainly didn't have fun at home with my parents.

But in the past few years, Milly has settled into an understanding and acceptance of her difficult childhood experiences. She has grown into new phase of confidence.

Unlike some Hidden Children who were old enough to mourn the separation and loss of their families, she shares with other very young children a sense of security of early years with a loving "hiding family," all the concrete proofs of which she has established in the past few years with the encouragement of her supportive partner Jacques. That early foundation clearly buffered her uncomplaining and compliant personality to enable her to withstand the difficult postwar years and an unsatisfying marriage.

NOTE

1. *Judenrat*, Jewish administration under Nazi occupation.

ANITA WAISVISZ

Anita now lives in Israel, where she was taken soon after the war with a group of orphaned Dutch Jewish children. She and her elder sister survived when she was hidden by a family in the countryside. Despite a simple, rather rudimentary life, she retains affectionate memories of her "hiding mother."

Contemplating a photograph of herself in early childhood, she feels sad for the little child that she was then, who was soon to undergo so much separation, upheaval, and unhappiness. She was cruelly treated by a postwar family and has experienced multiple difficulties in her life since arriving in Israel, including the death of her only daughter in childbirth. Despite this and serious illnesses of her own, she has retained her confidence and self-esteem. She now works as a receptionist for her niece's private surgical practice in Tel Aviv.

We sit in Anita's cool sitting room in a Tel Aviv suburb, shaded from the fierce sun outside. Like Anita herself, everything is bright, immaculate, and hospitable. She describes a life full of tragic events, even after she came to Israel. Despite severe chest problems, she remains lively, stoical, and strong.

My name is Anita Waisvisz. I was born in Amsterdam on December 25, 1933.

My mother was born in Kraków in 1895 and grew up there. When she was sixteen she came to Holland with her parents, where she met my father, born in 1894. They got engaged in 1918 and married in 1920. My father's family was originally from Galicia, but for many generations they were in Holland, in The Hague. I don't know if my father's family was religious or not, but my mother and grandmother were, my father less so. But I remember the plates and the cutlery on Pesach, such a big annual occasion. We were just a nice religious family.

I think we moved to Antwerp, Belgium, when I was about six months old in June 1934. My sister was much older, so I grew up by myself with a few friends. My father was working in Holland at Phillips[1] so he came home only at weekends. I adored him; I was very, very close to him. We lived very quietly until the war and, when it began on May 10, my maternal grandmother was living with us and my father was in Holland and couldn't get home until a month later. We had very good friends, a writer and his wife, who was Jewish, leaving for England. I remember they said to my mother, "Please come with us to England; a man by himself will manage." But my mother didn't want to leave without my father. Even on the last morning their son came in and said to my mother, "Auntie Hella, please, please come with us." Our life would have been very different if she had.

When the war broke out they came and took my grandmother away to a home for the elderly. She was deported and so were my other grand-

Anita Waisvisz at school. Courtesy of Anita Waisvisz.

Anita (*2nd right*) with her hiding family. Courtesy of Anita Waisvisz.

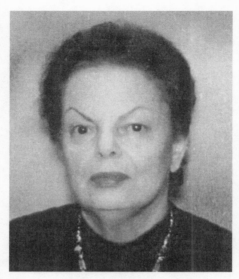

Anita today. Courtesy of Anita Waisvisz.

mother, an aunt, and my parents. My father had a very large family with lots of nephews and nieces, but only one or two survived. When he came home he thought that it was best for us to return to Holland to be with the rest of his family.

The family was smuggled out of Belgium to Holland in a large lorry transporting cheese. They remained together until 1942 despite the restrictions imposed by the Germans. They were forbidden to go to the park or to use public transport.

We couldn't visit non-Jewish friends, and I had to go to a Jewish school. They put the younger children in one room and the older children in another and that way we could study a bit. I have a picture that was taken very shortly before I left home.

Anita stops to show me a photograph.

It's funny, I look at her and I don't see myself. I look at that child and I really pity her because she was so trustful. Look at the eyes, so open and so full of trust.

At the beginning of 1942 everybody was told to report to the place where the Germans were collecting all the Jews; people had to bring all their luggage with them, and they were deported from there. So in July 1942, according to my sister, my father said, "One of these days we will be sent for, but we won't go."

Anita's sister made contact with a woman who worked for the Underground in Holland. First her sister left home, with the woman's help, then a place was found for Anita.

I was eight-and-a-half years old. The night before I left, I came in to say goodnight to my parents and there was a young woman sitting there with them. They just told me to say hello to the lady and go to bed. I had this feeling that something was going to happen, I couldn't sleep. I just knew.

In December 1941 I had had a doll's house, not new, but lovely, and every evening before I went to sleep I put everything in order. I had to leave it behind; it was only a toy, but I remember how sad I was.

Next morning when I went in to my mother's room she said, "You are going on a holiday; its best that we all leave home for some time. So you are going on a holiday with very nice people."

She packed my suitcase with all my clothes and then we sat down and she said to me, "We have to change your name; instead of Waisvisz, it will be *Wisser,* and we must change your place of birth." I had to say that we had lived in Curaçao because I looked very dark, with curly hair. We (supposedly) came to Holland in the beginning of the 1940s for a holiday, then my parents went back, and we stayed a little bit more with the family and when war broke out I never saw them again. That was the cover story! They told me I must never tell anyone about it, it was a secret, but after the war they would come and bring me home, and *then* I could tell people about it. But, you know, I never told anyone, ever.

My mother told me never to cry during the day because that bothers the people you are staying with, and they can't help you. "When you are upset, you must cry at night." I have never cried in the daytime, never in my life! I went through so many sad experiences and never cried. You know people say something and you stick to it. Now that I am quite old I can imagine what it must have been like for my parents.

An old lady came to the house, she was probably in her fifties, but to me that seemed old. She told me to say goodbye to my parents and I went with her. If I met anyone who recognized me while I was with her I should ignore them. That seemed silly because I met my neighbor, who spoke to me and asked where I was going, and I just carried on, which he couldn't understand.

The elderly lady lived in a very big house. The Germans had interned her husband who had been in the Second Chamber of the Dutch Parliament. So he wasn't at home, but I think there was still a son living there. I was lost in this very big house. I was given a little room under the eaves of the house, and I was suddenly alone. Her son told me not to walk around in the house because if anyone saw me, it would be very dangerous for them. There was a very nice housekeeper who brought me a meal, and there were lots of books I could read.

When I look back, I never complained because I understood the situation. You couldn't change it; it has to be that way, but for a child only eight-and-a-half years old it was difficult. I just said "bye-bye" to my parents and here I am, sitting alone in a room under the roof! Very early in the morning, at about six or half past, I was allowed to go out. The housekeeper would come, and I would get a bit of air and then go back to my room.

Anita, a very obedient child, stayed with them for two months. She feels that she remained very compliant, even as an adult.

Returning to her early life, after two months, she was taken to the village where she was to stay for five more years, two of them postwar.

I came there in September 1942 and I remember my "aunt." I called her Aunt and then later Mother. She opened the door and she was a big Dutch lady and, when I saw her, I felt that here I would be secure. Even though it was small village and they never kissed you or hugged you, there was something about her. You felt that nothing could hurt you—very strange. She was very religious, a Protestant, and when they asked her if she would be prepared to take a Jewish child she said, "OK, but I won't hide her; she has to go to school the next morning because that's the best way. If they see her after a few months it will be strange." So I started going to Christian school; I went to church and everything. I really believed, you know. I came from a religious home so in the evenings I would say first a Jewish prayer and then a Christian one, but after a couple of weeks the Jewish prayer got shorter. I really, really believed. I went to church, I learned the Bible, and felt really at home there. I spoke their dialect. After the war when my sister came to visit, she couldn't understand me. It's quite different from standard Dutch, not as different as in Friesland, but it was difficult to understand.

I was very lonely for my parents, although they wrote to me undercover until they were picked up when somebody denounced them in 1943. We learned from the Red Cross after the war that they had been in Westerbork in Holland and then they were gassed in Sobibor on May 12, 1943. So it was very short.

Anita learned after the war that, when the Germans took her mother to the railway station to put her on transport, she refused, saying she was not used to traveling without her husband.

And you know, they let her wait for my father! She was very strong; I think that I am very like her.

We were bombed very often because the very nice village where I was hidden, Aalten, was close to the German border. I went to school and made friends. The lady, who was a widow, had three children, and we also had to give a room to Germans. There were also collaborators, a couple who used to see me come out of school and they would say, "We know you are a Jewish child, and we will send a car tonight!" I was lying in bed and I heard a car, and I was so afraid thinking they were coming to pick me up. But, thank God, it always went away. They were all caught in the end. There were also lots of young Dutch men who refused to go to work in Germany, so they were hidden with the farmers there. It was a very big center of the Resistance.

In January 1944, Anita was terrified when there was a roundup in the church. But a very dark-haired farmer's wife passed her off as her own child and spirited her out of the church.

There were always times when you were afraid, but you didn't complain. Even when I was very sad thinking about my sister and my parents, it seems unbelievable that we never made a scene and we never cried. Today I just can't understand it! Every situation that happened later on in my life, I always accepted it and that's not good. But that is because of all the things you went through during the war. You had to accept everything; you couldn't say no, and you had to do what you were told.

After the war finished my parents were not there anymore, so I stayed another two years with the family. They told me a very funny thing. One time we had a German officer billeted there. We were not allowed to use electricity, but when he came home he could put it on. There were no sweets anymore, but he brought home chocolate or sweets from the German PX, and sometimes there would be some chocolate beside the plate at breakfast. I would ask, "Is that from Günter?" Auntie would say, "Yes, why do you ask?" and I would say, "I am not taking anything from Germans."

After the war I refused to go to Germany or Austria. I know they are not all guilty, but I always say that you need a sieve with big holes to keep the good ones in and let the bad ones fall out.

Anita stops to ply me with some coffee and ginger cake she has just brought back from Holland.

When my sister came for the first time after three years, she told me that [our parents] were not coming back. I never believed that my father had died in a concentration camp; I always said that he was in Russia and that some day he would come back. Even when I was nearly nine months pregnant, when it got dark, I had to close the curtains because I had the feeling he was walking around the house. Can you imagine? I thought he was afraid to come in. After I gave birth it passed. After the war I remember going to school one day, and I saw a man walking a few meters ahead of me and I decided, that's my father. All the way to school I ran around him because I thought that after three years he won't remember me. So I ran in front of him and by his side, and I was so disappointed it was not him. All kinds of very strange things happened like that, because I wanted him so much to come back. When we were young and were preparing to come to Israel, hardly anyone had parents. Out of twenty-three, perhaps two or three had parents, another three or four had either a father or mother, but most were without. In the beginning I didn't miss him that much because nobody else had parents, so you were used to it. But after I gave birth to my daughter I felt it terribly because there were no grandparents. I must say I miss them much more today. It's funny, as I am now sixty-five. When I look at the television and see a man who is in a home for elderly people, whose son or daughter comes to see them, I start crying. I never had the opportunity to take care of my parents; I don't even know what their personalities were like or how they thought about certain things. I think that is one of the things that bother me most. You know, if I had no pictures I wouldn't remember how they looked, nothing at all.

I went to a concert at the Philharmonic and I sat and thought how I had never had the opportunity to go to a concert with my mother or father, and the tears rolled down my face. Now that I am older I think I miss them more, not that they would have been alive today, I think they would be 102 years old! But it is funny how I react now; I am really surprised about it. For years you put it away and don't want to think about it.

But now, Anita explains, when she starts thinking about something she is able to "switch it off" if necessary.

Anita and her sister are quite unlike each other. They are not usually taken for sisters.

I didn't grow up with family like she did; she went and stayed with different relatives, but I didn't. I remember my grandmother in Holland and my grandmother in Antwerp, but I never visited them; my sister was eighteen-and-a-half when she left home. She also went to visit friends of my parents after the war; she was very close to them, but I didn't feel comfortable with them. It's odd.

I wanted to be Christian and join the Church, so I went to see the reverend when I was thirteen and told him. He was a lovely man and said, "You come back when you are eighteen and we will talk again." But I stupidly told my sister who thought that she was going to lose a Jewish sister. So she went to a friend in an organization working with children who had lost their parents. This organization—I hated it!

Anita's sister made arrangements for her to go to visit a Jewish family in Rotterdam at Christmas 1946. Initially they were kind, but soon the mother behaved very unkindly to her.

I continued my studies and in April 1947, at the Passover holiday, I took my little suitcase and I went to them (at that time food was still rationed) for a week. After that I packed my suitcase and said that I was going back to Aalten.

The Zionist woman refused to let Anita return to her rescuers. Essentially she was engaged in a power struggle for Anita's Jewish identity.

I had stayed with my "aunt" in Aalten for five years, and she put her life in danger, not only her life but also the whole family. They didn't tell her that I was leaving, and they didn't tell me! She was an awful woman, the one in Rotterdam. I always say that from April 1947 until September 1948, until I went to prepare for Israel, that was *my* concentration camp! She made my life hell. She took me for money and she treated me like dirt. She isn't alive now, thank God.

The woman even intercepted Anita's correspondence, and the husband had to give it to her surreptitiously.

I told my sister how awful she was, but she wouldn't believe me, because when she came she was so sweet! All the time I was there, every night when I went to bed, I cried. I was so unhappy and I thought of eloping but I had no money.

Anita was not allowed to contact her hiding mother, who eventually came to Rotterdam in search of her.

I was so happy to see her because I thought that she had come to take me home. The "fish wife" (I always called her that) started screaming, "Where are the rations for Anita? You didn't send them." *Tante*[2] said, "Well, I didn't know she wasn't coming back." Imagine, I had stayed with her for five years and that was the first time that she heard that I wasn't coming back. She had on a black coat and I put my arms around her, inside the coat, because I didn't want her to leave. I said, "Take me home! I don't want to stay here; I want to come home with you." She didn't know how to leave, because I didn't want her to go. She went home and after two or three weeks she had a nervous breakdown from the whole thing; it was terrible! That was such a trauma. I felt very unhappy there. Nobody believed me, but I had to get out. They were preparing to go to Israel, they were very Zionist, and they wanted me to go to a very religious Jewish family. You know, like a football, like a parcel. I didn't want to go.

As Anita was in Habonim, a Zionist Youth Movement, she went to the head of the Pioneer group asking to go to Israel. Being under fifteen she was accepted only after she described her wartime life in the village, helping with the washing, working on the land. Given a chance to prove her abilities she convinced them. She left the abusive woman in September 1948, after eighteen unhappy months. The woman's cruelty was compounded by Anita's sister's refusal to believe in her ill-treatment. She also later discovered that some relatives of the woman knew what she was like and would have helped her, had they known.

I think she was indoors for three years, hidden, but it was not that, it was her nature. She was so awful. I said later that I would have loved to poison her. She just made my life hell! I think that if I had been with a different family and had love, things would have been otherwise. I am sure of that. But you can't change anything.

I got married very, very young, and I wanted a family, lots and lots of children. I have a very good friend who was in Auschwitz-Birkenau during the war who always says to me, "You know, none of the people who came back after the war, *nobody* was in a normal state." I heard from friends of mine who stayed with uncles and aunts, it was awful. Everybody tells the same story.

The same friend told Anita "it was much more difficult for you, because you were alone; you had no one to tell how you felt. You were in a much worse situation than we were, because we were all close together, and we had each other."

I was lucky that I came to that village and to such a lovely family; the two daughters are like sisters to me, and I was always very close to my "aunt." I always trusted her, you know. Even if I was out of order and she took my arm or my ear, she did that with all the kids. I adored her.

Here in Israel we remember all the Jews on Yom Hashoah.[3] My grandchild is seven years old, and his class had to prepare the whole program for the day. He asked me, "Grandma, could you write something that you did during the war?"

Anita was invited to talk about her experiences. Her grandson was amazed to discover that she had been a church-going Christian believer and wondered why she could not just "play it, just act as a Christian?" A teacher was also incredulous that an eight-and-a-half year old had never revealed her true identity.

After the war when my sister wrote a postcard, the first one that was not written undercover with my name on it, Anita Waisvisz, my "aunt" said,

"Ah, that's your real name." I said, "No, it's a mistake, she doesn't know my name!" because I had been told I couldn't tell anyone until my parents came. But she said, "Here your sister has written your name." I said, "No, no, she has forgotten it; she hasn't seen me for three years" and so on. Unbelievable.

Nobody could change my ideas or my way of thinking. If I decide to do something, I do it. I mean in personal things, not in studying or something like that, but because I was always very sorry that I didn't go in for nursing as I had hoped.

Afterward Anita became ill with sarcoidosis at the age of twenty-seven and was in hospital for six months. Today she has much reduced lung function; she finds the hot, humid weather and pollution in the Israeli summer very trying. She talked of her relationship with the other children in her hiding family.

It's funny, they never thought about it a lot, they just accepted me. The youngest one with whom I am very close said, "I just never thought about you being Jewish, never." I always had very good contacts with them, but not so well with the son. But I think he had his problems because he grew up without a father. I always felt that he was jealous of the closeness I had with his mother. Even when I came for a holiday his behavior was very strange.

The two girls were older than me, the youngest, with whom I shared a bed for five years, was three years older. We are still very close. At least, instead of my own family, there is something left.

In August 1950 we left Holland and had a few lovely days in Paris on the way to Israel. My sister came the year after me. We went to the kibbutz in Galatea and lived in tents, even in the middle of winter with rain and lots of wind. We were all so happy to be here that it didn't bother us, and we were young. It was there I met my first husband, and we got married when I was seventeen years old. Through the whole situation I had only one wish, to have another family, to set up another family. I was fixed on it; I was much too young to marry, but I got pregnant and I was eighteen when my daughter was born.

Having survived so many hazards, Anita's subsequent life has not been easy, either. Her only daughter, Tamar,[4] died after giving birth of a very rare complication.

After Tamar's death I had to function because when Ehud, the baby, came to us, he was six months old, and he stayed until he was three. That's the thing that saved me, because you know you are living in a balloon where nothing touches you, it's a very strange thing.

But it is very hard, you know, you have to be very, very strong to get up in the morning and face life like a normal person. People don't like it if you are bothered or you are acting differently, so I put on my mask every day and I go on. That's the very hard part because, even after thirteen years I miss her very much. They always say that "with time . . ." but it's not true.

We were very much alike in character, so that now it's not just her I miss but the fights we had! She was full of life, so when she came into the house it was just filled up with her, she was very spontaneous. But you do get on because life is much stronger and you have to. I thank God that we have our two grandchildren because, otherwise, I don't think I would have any reason to get up in the morning!

Anita pauses again to show some photographs of her grandchildren.

My husband was also Dutch and that was a big mistake because of my temperament. I am half-Polish and, from my father's side, I had a grandmother from Portugal, so I have some Spanish blood. During the war my husband was in Bergen-Belsen. I don't think he went to high school and the difference in education . . . well, when you are seventeen, you can do anything! He never read a book or anything and, you know, I couldn't live with it. He was a very good person, he loved our daughter and he loved me, but I couldn't take it, and we divorced when she was two years old. His brother came and talked me into letting him take care of my daughter because he had already suffered so much in a concentration camp. I was all alone, and when you were divorced in those days, in 1954, it was the biggest scandal possible! Even my sister was also very ashamed and, all of a sudden, you have no friends, you are all by yourself. So when we divorced I signed her away, and I didn't see her for five years, he didn't let me.

Anita has been with her present partner for forty years.

He was born in the old city of Jerusalem and is a lovely person. He gave me the will to live again!

Anita believes that her own character was quite like her mother's. So she was like her mother and her daughter was like Anita, perhaps also like her father, also a very strong character.

You know we sat *Shiva* (mourning), for seven days—and people came, it was such a tragedy for the whole village here because, for ten years, she tried to have children and then she had two boys and wasn't there any more. Everybody who came in was crying, but I didn't shed a tear. I said, "Me, take something? Don't worry, I won't cry."

At night? Oh yes, at night I banged my fist on the wall because I was very angry also! Terrible anger because although life goes on, it's not the way it was. It takes the shine off everything; there is no more shine. You have to be strong. When I see on the television families who have lost one, two, or more sons, I think, who am I that I should complain. But still your own suffering, your own sorrow, is your own, and you have to deal with it. The strangest thing is that nobody speaks about her anymore. It's like . . . I mean I love to talk about her, but when I mention her, people don't like it. They are uncomfortable; they don't know how to take it, what to say. For me that's very strange; she lived, why shouldn't I talk about her? Of course, you are never the same again, but after a very short period I said to my husband, "I won't let myself go down because then to get back in the saddle, to step back in to normal life, is much harder." You can't let yourself go. Sometimes it's very hard, but I think I am very strong, and I think one of the reasons is everything I went through. That makes you very strong.

If you go under it's very hard to come back. That's what I think, because it's much easier to let yourself go. I remember saying that I just wanted to sleep for a year, not to think or feel anything, but that's impossible. Only the bears sleep for a whole winter; they are very lucky!

Anita had been doing volunteer work, but after Tamar's death, her niece, Anat, an ear, nose, and throat surgeon, asked her to work as a receptionist in her new clinic. That was ten years ago.

I do secretarial work, reception work, and make appointments. I keep an eye on things that they are running smoothly, twice a week, in the afternoon; eight hours a week is enough. I also did it for my grandchildren, because I think it is good if they see that their grandmother is still working. I like the contact with the people and the patients very much. Instead of a nursing career, it's some compensation.

Anita managed to have her hiding mother declared Righteous Among the Nations at Yad Vashem.

She got it in Amsterdam in 1982, with fifty other people. It was very emotional, really something. All her children were there and, the year after, her youngest daughter and husband came for a visit and we planted a tree at Yad Vashem. That tree today is now very big, very nice. I felt very good when she received it because she was such a . . . it's very hard to describe her. During the war she was never afraid. I think she got a lot of strength from her religion. The only thing she was afraid of was thunder, she would make us hide under the table.

But she was never afraid of the Germans or the bombardment. She always stood outside the cellar with the men during the bombardment, with her daughter screaming at her to come inside. But she paid no attention and stayed outside with the men. I always called her *Tante* but, after she went into the home for the elderly, I started calling her Mother.

What has kept Anita strong?

I think first of all my husband gave me a lot of strength. During all the years, I must say everything, even the war. You had to be strong, and I think it kind of adopted you and went along with you. Also, of course, character. It's not easy always, but you try to keep it up.

I also think that it is being Dutch. There is something in us that just doesn't let go very easily. You have to be strong.

NOTES

1. Phillips, now Royal Philips Electronics, a large electrical company based in Holland.
2. Anita's "hiding mother," her rescuer.
3. Yom Hashoah, Holocaust Day of Remembrance.
4. The name in Hebrew means "date," the fruit.

BASIA BONNEWIT

One of the difficulties Basia had to endure, not altogether uncommon for Hidden Children, was the conflict of "loyalty" between the hiding mother and her own mother who survived to claim her after the war. To some extent they have never been able to resolve this.

Her mother, who also endured separation and hiding during the war, was intensely jealous. Her personality has probably always been rather difficult. Basia is now settled in Israel with her family, including her mother, and she tries to maintain a balance between expressions of affection to her own ageing mother and her large hiding family still in Holland. She exemplifies those Hidden Children who experienced this difficulty on the return of a parent or other surviving relative.

She married Benno, another Hidden Child from Holland.

Basia, an only child, was born in Holland in November 1939. Her parents were of Polish and Russian origin and had emigrated to Holland. Her father was working in a factory in Amsterdam, which was suddenly taken over by the Germans, and all the Jewish workers were taken away.

Basia's mother took her initially into hiding and then, to avoid detection, had to send her to an orphanage where she remained for about six months. She has a vague recollection of it as being "terrible." About six months later someone told the director of the orphanage that the Germans knew that he was hiding children. Children with blond hair went to the north of Holland, and the dark haired children, including Basia, were sent to the south.

My mother had been married for only four years. She married in January 1939, and they took my father away in 1942.

They took me to the south of Holland where there was a group from the underground. One of them is still alive today, and we keep in contact with him. My foster parents wanted a child from Rotterdam because it had been badly bombed. So my hiding mother went to the underground to choose from a whole row of children, and she chose me. I don't remember anything until the time she chose me, but after that I remember everything. One of the problems was my own mother, she was very jealous.

I was with the family for three years; I only realized that a few years ago. I was like their own child.

The couple were childless following a mining accident, which disabled Basia's foster father. His wife was a nurse, and they had married against her family's wishes.

He told me later that many people injured in mining accidents just lay in bed and did nothing. But he wasn't like that; he wanted to learn so he

Basia as a child. Courtesy of Basia Bonnewit.

Truus and Hermann. Courtesy of Basia Bonnewit.

Basia with her "hiding mother" Truus van Oosten. Courtesy of
Basia Bonnewit.

carried on reading and writing. They were fantastic people and were
married for forty-four years until he died thirteen years ago. I was with
them for three years and, for me, they were my father and mother. It was
a big family because she had ten brothers and sisters, and he had eight,
but the family accepted me as "Truus and Hermann's child." I called them

Basia today. Courtesy of Basia Bonnewit.

aunt and uncle at first but, one day when I fell and hurt myself, I screamed out for Mama and Papa, so from that time that was the way it was.

I remember that the bed my "father" was in was very high and by a window that looked out over an open field. The Germans came and they were shooting so we lay under the bed. That happened a few times, so we would go to one of my hiding mother's sisters. I can't remember that I was scared. My "aunt" told me that once the Germans came in when I was asleep, looking for Jewish children. I was dark and they were blond, but she told the Germans that her part of the family was dark and that she was the only one who was blond. That saved me!

My mother found out where I was and managed to make contact. Then the problems started. Truus and Hermann started to tell me that I had a mother and, of course, to me it was crazy, because *they* were my mother and father. She traveled from Amsterdam to the other side of Holland, and it took her three days! One day I was standing by my "father" while he was peeling potatoes, and I saw this woman standing outside and asked him who it was. She came in, and it was very difficult because, of course, I didn't accept her.

After about two weeks she took me back to Amsterdam. There were ten people because, after the war, my grandmother was there and a friend, Nathan Durst, with his sister and my uncle. My mother's sister came back from Bergen-Belsen, I opened the door and there she was and she was completely bald! There were another two cousins, ten people all together, and I was the only child.

Basia's mother, grandmother, and uncle had been hidden in Haarlem together.

I can't say she caused problems then. After the war I went to a non-Jewish school where they started calling me "dirty Jew" and things like that, but I had no idea, I was only seven years old. They threw me in some water, and then my mother sent me to a Jewish school.

At this school Basia and a little boy recognized each other. They had played together when they were both in hiding; neither knew the other was Jewish. He, too, now lives in Jerusalem.

Then I had problems with sleeping because I was scared that my mother would go away again. I used to keep going out of the room to see if she was still there, then I started vomiting and all kinds of things. So she took me to a psychiatrist, my mother was very modern; she is still alive at eighty-six. I went maybe three or four times. He would just talk to me and that was it. But every year, nearly every year, I went back to the south of Holland.

I remember after the first holiday I spent with my foster family, I re-member sitting in the kitchen crying and screaming that I didn't want to go back to my mother. During the years it got better, but I always have a very strong contact and attachment to them.

Basia was so close to her foster family that her reaction to her foster father's death thirteen years earlier was profound. He had suffered kidney problems following his long years of immobility.

My mother started with her problems about ten years ago. Sometimes, out of the blue she says, "Your bond with Truus is much stronger than with me." So I tried to explain that it is completely different, it is from three to six that you get all the love, and that is very important.

It is sometimes quite difficult, unless you know the context, to know when Basia is referring to her own birth mother, and when to her hiding foster mother. Sometimes she uses the word "mother" interchangeably.

My mother's sister is still in Holland, and she was sick so we decided to go to the south of Holland for a few days for her birthday. From my mother's family of ten children, seven of them are still alive, aged from seventy-eight to ninety-five, a lovely family. I called and said that we were coming, and she was very happy because two of her other sisters were staying with her. They are all widows so they stay together for birthdays and holidays and their families cope.

The first time that I talked to my "aunts" I asked them what they thought about the war. Their reaction to me was very positive; I was completely surprised by it. We talked quite a lot. She also has a brother of ninety who came on her birthday, a tremendous guy. His name is Jack, a real gentleman. When he left he said to me, "You still belong to us," and so did her sisters.

My husband to whom I have been married for nearly thirty-six years always said that I should still be living in Holland; he says that the minute I get to Limberg I relax. The last time we were in Holland I didn't tell my birth mother about it, and she didn't even ask. I didn't tell her about the aunts or talking about the war, nothing. Suddenly my mother said to me, "When you were three years old, you left me." I left *her*!

A friend, also hidden, told Basia that it was normal; they always say "you left."

That gets worse and worse, although my husband helps me a lot to get over it. Funny!

I don't know if I have much more to tell you. I went from the elemen-tary school to Jewish high school. I knew my husband already from fourth grade; we were in the same class, the same synagogue and the same organizations.

What had happened to him during the war?

He was also hidden, a little further north in Brabant. He was together with his parents; he lived in one house, and they lived next door but his parents saw him every day. He finds it difficult to remember some things, but now he is talking about it, although my in-laws, who died a few years ago, never did. My husband always says, "It was 1939 to 1945, then five minutes later it was the start of 1946." My sister-in-law was born in 1946 and doesn't know anything and, as my mother-in-law died nine years ago, there is nobody we can ask. There are only cousins alive but not the old ones, and they never talked about it. They talked once to my son, Danny, when he was sixteen. Now slowly other things are coming back to my husband, but he can't ask anybody because they never talked.

One of the problems for my husband is that he believes that, as far as my in-laws were concerned, he didn't exist because his sister was born after the war—a beginning—but he was born before! So it was quite difficult, and we suffered from that until we understood. We only started talking about it when my mother-in-law was already dying. Then it was too late; we couldn't ask anybody.

My mother talked a lot about it, about the past, and my aunt also talked a lot about Bergen-Belsen. We talked about the kids, but in our high school class there were only two, my husband and Jack who I knew in elementary school, who had parents. When I make a list, some are OK, but most of them have been in therapy. It sounds funny to say that it is good if you are taken away from your parents.

Basia's daughter feels that perhaps she transfers her worries on to her children.

She talks a lot with my mother who said, out of the blue, "Your bond is much closer with her [my daughter]." So my daughter gets mad, very upset, and starts talking to my mother, calms her down because she can handle her, say whatever she wants. Then my mother calms down.

I never wondered why she gave me to that orphanage. It was something that had to be done, and I was quite easy-going or so my mother told me. After the war when I came back with her to Amsterdam, I was used to praying before eating and before I went to bed, and my mother was very good, she let me.

What was that transition period like, from a Protestant home back to a Jewish one?

I was very easy, that was my luck. I remember when I was still in hiding when I went to church, I watched everybody to see what I should do.

Then when I got back to Amsterdam, I sat and waited for the prayer before a meal, and my mother said, "We are not used to praying." I don't remember that she said that we are Jewish, so I stopped, but for a long time I prayed before I went to bed, and she let me. Then probably I stopped.

Basia's parents each came from a Hassidic family, but when her mother was eighteen she broke away and became assimilated.

My grandmother was very religious, but after the war my mother didn't keep a Kosher home. I started going with my grandmother to synagogue until she died, when I told my mother that I wanted her to be Kosher because, otherwise, I can never invite friends. So my mother changed the whole thing. She didn't do it for her mother but she did for me, that's what she told me.

Then when we were married, my husband also got a religious education. I didn't drive on Saturday because I hadn't for years and years. We actually started driving on Saturdays when we came here, to Israel. Now we are not religious, we are traditional because we are Kosher at home; my kids have it at home. I never told them to do it, but they do it. I don't eat meat outside the home because it's not Kosher. For instance, on Friday evenings, we do the whole thing with candles and so on. My husband goes to *schul* nearly every Saturday, and on the holidays the kids go too.

My mother remarried in 1972. She always said she would but only when she wanted to, not because she needed a roof over her head. She wasn't lonely because there were two sisters and their children who always spent the holidays together and everything. Our family is very close, sometimes a little too much, because everybody knows everything about everybody!

Basia's mother and stepfather later moved permanently to live in Israel.

My stepfather was like a father to me; he loved my kids and died five or six years ago when he was eighty, ten years older than my mother. He was religious, and it suited my mother because everything she knew came back. Now she is in an elderly home about a half-hour away.

Basia's mother had learned to speak Hebrew quite well, but the whole family speak Dutch together.

When we came here, to Israel, and the children were small, my husband said that we would speak only Dutch at home. It would be a help when we travel, because we go to Holland a lot.

Dutch survivors have their own association, Elah.

I am a member, I don't need them, thank God, but once a year they have a whole day like a reunion or study day. You can choose to do whatever you want; some paint or make a drama, but I always go to the group who are talking. You can talk about what is inside because you know a lot of the people. This was the first time that I started talking openly about the jealousy between my mother and my aunt. Someone started talking about jealousy, and I realized for the first time what this was, I had never realized it.

I think I am more scared than people who had a normal background. Not long ago we talked about it with people at home.

Basia expressed amazement that, despite the war, she was comparatively unscathed, although she did transiently have some problems when she was little because she was frightened that her (birth) mother would leave her again.

I couldn't get pregnant probably because of the lack of vitamins during the war, so we adopted our children. It was not just me but lots of women didn't get pregnant. Anyhow, when we got here we adopted the children. We got Danny when he was ten months, because they try to give you a baby that is a little like you. That was then, now it is a lot more difficult. Danny is now twenty-eight, and we had Karen when she was three months old.

Basia was very stressed for a time with one baby of ten months and one of three months.

My wise neighbor said, "What you did is much more difficult than being pregnant, because you have nine months to get used to having a baby, but you get a phone call to say 'come and look at this baby and see if you want it.'"

Basia's mother and stepfather were very supportive at this time.

She helped me a lot. Danny was ten months and Karen was three months and was in a terrible state. She had been in an incubator at birth because she weighed only one-and-a-half kilograms. When we got her she was only four kilograms, and we didn't sleep at night so my mother came during the day. She said to my husband, "During the night you sleep on the couch, and Basia and Karen will stay in the bedroom because you have to go to work and you need to sleep." So she came during the day to help me.

Even when I had to go away for the weekend, they would stay here or the kids would go to them.

But as Basia's mother aged it became more difficult. She was very active until the age of eighty-two and theoretically could do whatever she wanted. But with increasing age she became more critical and angry with Basia.

As an only child I get all the anger and everything. She talks quite a lot about the war, that I went away, and she says that she didn't see me from three to six; I get that quite a lot. But I am now at that stage where I don't care!

After high school Basia worked in a hospital laboratory, but the war had affected her concentration, and she did not quite finish her qualifications.

She worked very happily in two Amsterdam hospitals for some time before emigrating to Israel.

My mother always wanted me to be a nurse, but I said, "No, that's not for me." I wanted to carry on with the same work here, but they would not accept me without my doing the training and exams from the beginning. So I said no.

On the suggestion of a friend, Basia trained to be a beautician, despite her initially limited Hebrew.

I worked at home for about twenty years. It was very easy because I didn't have to leave the house. The kids were small so when they were sick, I didn't have to ask somebody to take care of them or send them to school. They remember that I was always home and say that this was fantastic! I worked for twenty years or more, then one day I said, "That's it, enough." Then I started doing volunteer work visiting people, and I have been doing this for many years now. I work with social workers who tell me who needs a visit.

She and her husband and daughter have been much involved with committee work concerned with cystic fibrosis.

He has never been so busy! He is studying psychology at the university because, when he was younger, his mother always told him that he couldn't do it and wouldn't let him. So now he is doing it for fun! He is going on a course to make his memory stronger and sits on several committees. I help him and also we do separate things.

Basia reflected on the discussions taking place between former Dutch hidden children at the annual meetings of Elah (their association).

They say that so many had the same problem, and it gets worse. I have a cousin on my father's side who was hidden in Friesland in the north of Holland. She loved it there. Her mother found out where she was and took her away to foster parents in Den Haag (The Hague). She had a breakdown. I talked to her quite a lot and she said, "I don't know what would happen if I had stayed in Friesland."

Basia's aunt told her about a man who came to the south of Holland as a baby and stayed on there after the war.

He didn't know, he was a baby. When he was about six or seven he came home and said to his parents, "They say that I am Jewish." So his father said to him, "Later I will explain it to you." But they never explained anything. He got married there and had children and the parents died. Then when he was clearing out his parents' things, he found boxes with letters from his parents and a letter from his real parents to his foster parents. Then he found out that he was Jewish. He later went to Auschwitz and found out about eighty of his family. He discovered that he had a sister in Amsterdam, and now he has a lot of problems!

My aunt told me that he was Jewish, that he feels Jewish. He may have known for years. He is my age or maybe a little younger, but he is still looking. My mother told me everything, which was very important, she talked a lot.

I know from somebody about two sisters who stayed with an aunt and uncle, they were the best friends of my parents and they didn't come back. The girls never talked about it with the aunt and uncle. The younger sister who was my age died when she was thirty.

My mother many times wanted to talk to her about her parents but she didn't want to know. So she went into hospital and was lucky to have a doctor who knew she was Jewish and asked her if she had survived the Holocaust. Then the whole thing came out, because she had two boys who didn't even know that their grandparents were really an aunt and uncle. Because of not talking she got sick, but from that time she agreed to go into therapy and is now a completely different person.

I can't explain my feelings about my aunt (Basia's hiding mother, Truus van Oosten). I feel very comfortable over there. First of all she is a very special woman. I always talked to my birth mother about everything but I can't anymore. I can talk a lot to my aunt, much more than I did years ago.

Basia and her family applied to Yad Vashem for the Righteous Gentile recognition for her hiding parents, Truus and Hermann van Oosten.

We did it in about 1976 or 1978. He was paralyzed but we had all kinds of plans to get him here, to Israel, with chairs and everything. Then he got sick with his kidneys, and I went to Holland. She came here for the first time, but for him it was too difficult to come and so one of his brothers stayed with him. She came and I called Yad Vashem and said that we wanted to have the ceremony here, also with the tree.[1] So we did the whole thing, about twenty years ago.

You know, last year we were in Washington and went to the Holocaust Museum with my brother-in-law and sister-in-law. There is a big wall with all the names from Holland, and we found her name, Truus van Oosten. I took a picture and sent it to her.

When we were there it gave me the feeling that we still belonged.

Basia has had other difficulties recognizing special events in her foster mother's life, which have caused her upset and embarrassment.

We said that we were going to Holland for their fortieth wedding anniversary, and my mother said that she would come too. I didn't know what to do; I looked at my husband, and he didn't say a word. I felt that this was something special for me, not for her. I knew that if she came, she would be talking and my husband and I would not be able to talk. A mutual friend intervened and, to this day, I do not know what was said, but my mother is still mad and talks about it whenever it comes up.

We went to Holland for their fortieth anniversary, and it was unbelievable. First of all, the brothers and sisters from both sides were all alive. So we had lunch just with them and then there was a party with all the brothers and sisters and all the children, altogether 200 people. The people I had grown up with. It was very emotional, I loved it, and it was fantastic. I felt terrible that I had not wanted my mother with me.

Later they asked me about my (birth) mother, and when I told them that I hadn't wanted her to come, they understood. I loved it, but for a long time my mother was very upset and very sad. When my husband said that he wouldn't go if my mother went, I knew that I wouldn't be able to go without him.

Had Basia's mother been jealous and manipulative earlier in life? Was it a part of her personality?

I never felt it; maybe it's just as she is getting older. Earlier she had been very active and busy. I just don't know. My husband has asked me the same thing. The feeling that I just wanted to go with my family, by myself, felt terrible, but I still can't explain it. I just didn't want my mother to be there! Can you understand?

If we are with people she still talks but she never asks anything about it apart from asking after my aunt, who suffers from rheumatism like my mother. But she asks nothing else, and I don't tell her. I always used to tell my mother everything but I stopped. Her jealousy is quite strong, and it gets worse. Yet after the war my mother used to push me to write to the family and see how they were. "You must write to them," she would say, and she sent me back to see them; she built the whole relationship.

Yet Basia can easily identify and empathize with her mother's emotions at leaving in the hope of saving her.

It's very complicated, but one day I said to Benno, "Suppose they take away the kids?" When Karen was about three or four I said, "Suppose it came to war and they take away the kids!"

If we are in a shopping center and a child is crying because it cannot see his mother, I feel terrible! I have been like that for the last few years, and I think, "my God, they took me away when I was eight." This kid is crying for his mother, and I never did that. This has only been for the last three or four years, and I don't know why.

NOTE

1. An avenue of carob trees at Yad Vashem, planted by survivors or their relatives, honors "The Righteous (Gentiles) among the Nations."

CHAPTER 6

❧

France

BETTINE LE BEAU (MICHAELS)

Bettine's happier experiences began when she finally arrived in a rural French village on her own, after a series of frightening escapes and journeys throughout France with her mother and brother, which culminated in incarceration in the holding camp of Gurs, in Southwest France.

She seems to have been a resourceful and cheerful child who has always had an innately positive outlook, although she was, like many similar children, unhappy when her brother turned up and removed her from the hiding family in which she had become established. She became a comedy actress in England, specializing in character parts such as chirpy French maids. She now teaches classes in Positive Living and runs a Yiddish language group to survivors at the London Survivor Centre. She is a lively, vivacious extrovert who looks and sounds half her age.

My name at birth was Bettine Fallek. My Yiddish name was Brandl, and now my married name is Michaels and my professional name is Bettine Le Beau. I was born on March 23, 1932, in Antwerp, Belgium, and I am now sixty-three years of age.

Before the war my father was a furrier and, at that particular time, we lived in Brussels. As war broke out in 1940, my father used to come to London to buy furs from the Hudson Bay Company. He heard what was happening and phoned my mom to say he was coming home, and she told him to stay in London, and she would take the children and try to get to Paris. From there she would join him in London. "It's silly for you to come back here where there is war; what are you thinking of?"

Bettine with her brother at the Camp de Gurs.
Courtesy of Bettine Le Beau (Michaels).

The farm at the village of Souspierre where Bettine was hidden, 1944. Courtesy of Bettine Le Beau (Michaels).

Bettine at the farm a few days after it was hit by a German bomb, August 30, 1944. Courtesy of Bettine Le Beau (Michaels).

Bettine, lively entertainer, with her sculpture of Prime Minister Ben Gurion. Courtesy of Bettine Le Beau (Michaels).

My mother was a very confident lady, so she changed her money into gold pieces for easy currency. The trains were all full, so she decided to take a taxi all the way from Brussels! We went to the Consul in Paris, but they told us to come back; this went on for days and weeks. In the end France declared war and we were stuck.

I have a big brother, Harry, four years older than I am.

Then afterward we adopted my little cousin, who was always considered my little brother.

So we were stuck in Paris and, because there were so many people, we were sent to a village near Bordeaux. Every week you had to report to say you were there. Then they came with big lorries, and they took all the Jewish ones and their families and sent us to an internment castle.

I had grandparents living in Antwerp, but my mother's relations were all in Poland. Both my parents were born in Poland, my mother in Łodz and my daddy in Kraków. We were very Jewish but not religious. I know everything about it, but I don't think we practiced it. We were traditional but not religious, like I am now.

I went to school in Brussels. It was a nice school, and I enjoyed it. It was a Jewish school but not a very religious one. Harry, of course, had to do his Bar Mitzvah.

I suppose in hindsight I remember my mother crying when she got letters from Poland, and things like that, but I didn't realize what it was. I knew that something was wrong, but I thought that maybe somebody was ill or something. I remember there were parcels and a lot of crying whenever something from Poland arrived. But as a child, you know, you are just full of yourself. I wanted to learn and I wanted to do things; I was a great show off.

Probably you sense the tension in all this. When we had to go on the train, my brother would go first and save places and not let anyone sit down. He would push and get things for us, because he was now the man of the family and the situation brought it out more.

The castle, Masgelier, that we were taken to was very nice when I think about it. I went to visit afterward and it was nothing, but at the time, when we were young, everything seemed so big and wonderful. It was a real castle with gold and paintings and big fireplaces and everything. But all the families had to sleep in a dormitory together, men, women, and children. Everybody talked, and it was difficult to sleep. I remember Mr. Ehrenreich who wanted to talk and tell stories, and other people wanted to sleep so there were arguments. Some people were affected mentally. I remember there was a nice gentleman who my mother said had diarrhea.

Well, some of us were smuggled out although there were dogs. I remember my brother going to bring back loaves of bread and beans. He had plus-fours, and he put them in the plus-fours and left the beans. So when he came there were no beans, but there were quite a lot who did go out undercover and bring food. So it wasn't bad; it wasn't wonderful, but it wasn't bad.

We were there for I don't know how long, perhaps a couple of months. Then big lorries came again, and they took us to a concentration camp called Gurs, near Pau. There it was very bad.

What was the transport like on the way there? Did you have any idea of where you were going?

No, you are just put there, but I wasn't frightened, you know. I'm an optimist, and I always think it's going to be all right. They separated the children from the parents, and we were put in a children's barrack that was like a hut made out of cardboard with tar on it—right? We had to cut out windows, and we slept on straw mattresses. It was filthy, there were rats and mice, and we didn't have much food, but I suffered more from cold than from lack of food. I have low blood pressure, and I was crying because I was so cold. I couldn't feel my feet or fingers, but the food, I will explain about the food.

It was very democratic. They brought black bread to the children every day and that was cut into hundred gram slices, very little. We were thirty in the barrack so it was cut into thirty pieces and was then put on the floor. Then each of the children could choose, a different child chose first each day and we took it in turns. I had my brother with me and when it came to choosing the bread it was a big performance. I was going to take this one, but he would say, "No don't take that, take this one, it is bigger." And you know to take a piece that is bigger, it's a big thing. The corner piece looked bigger so there were always fights about it. The one who was last to choose got the crumbs, and we used to lick our fingers and pick up the crumbs—a crumb was so wonderful.

Then they used to give awful soup made out of pumpkins. Then a kid found out that there were pips of the pumpkin somewhere, so everybody went to find these pips, and we used to put them on the floor and wait for the sun to dry them, and then we would open them up and eat them because we were so hungry. The food wasn't given on plates, you know, it was given in tins, like sardine tins, and these tins would get rusty, so all day long we would take earth and rub the tin so it wouldn't get rusty. So this was our pastime. I do remember the Red Cross sometimes gave the kids a spoonful of jam, and one of the kids found out that if you beat that jam it became twice as much. So as soon as we got the jam, we started beating it because the food, you know, was very restricted.

Each day it was bread and soup and that was that. I mean we were starving! And I was cold, I was so cold. We could see our mother now and again, but she wasn't in our barrack block. She was in aisle L I think; I remember aisle L but I don't know why.

Then this is what I heard afterward: Somebody approached my mom and said that they could smuggle out ten children. Was she willing for her two children to be smuggled out? My mom said yes, although a lot of mothers said, "No, where are my children going?" So I remember I was smuggled out, and we stopped one night in Limoges with a family. I found out when I went to the reunion in Paris two years ago that it was the OSE (*Oeuvre de Sécours aux Enfants*) with the Jewish underground who were the instigators.

I was taken to this foster place, in Limoges, just for one night, I remember. It was the first time I was given a bed with sheets, white sheets. Even now when I change my sheets it's a pleasure. And what did I do? I wet the bed! I felt terrible!

Anyhow, the next day, we were taken to the children's home in Corrèze. There were lots and lots of children there, and I said to myself why do they all have German names? There was Trudi and Brigitta and Helga and Margot, and we were in France. But now I realize these were children that had been sent to France like a *Kindertransport* for safe haven. But they weren't in a safe place. When I arrived there it was the worst time of my life, because I was separated from my mom, really separated, and they just took everything I had. I had a dress that I never wore, which I kept for best, and that was taken from me, but they said that everything was communal and that when I had my shower I could choose whatever I wanted to wear. It was first come, first served! But I didn't want to part with this dress; I just didn't want to part with it. Then I had lots of lice, so nobody wanted to stand next to me. They put some powder on me and a scarf—they didn't want to die, those lice—and everyone moved away from me, right? I was the only one with the lice! Anyway, I had this powder and lice and I wet my bed and nobody liked me.

At lunchtime we all sat at a long table, and they would pass around a plate with big pieces of bread with butter, and when it came in front of me I started looking for the biggest. Everybody said it was terrible, and they called over the *monitrice* who said, "You don't do that here, you take the piece nearest to you." But she didn't say it in a nice way, she really told me off. So I thought nobody loves me, and I was under the impression that all grownups should love me, and she didn't love me either, and I have these lice and I wet my bed, I'm not with my mom, and they took away my things.

How old were you then?

Eight, just eight-and-a-half.

They asked me what schooling I had done and, as I am always a show off, I said that I could do more than I can. So they put me in a higher class and the teacher is speaking, but I am not listening to him, and he has the book in his hand and he said, "Repeat what I said," and I couldn't. So he takes the book and hits me on the head and all the lice powder went on him, and he got annoyed and kicked me out. So I felt this teacher doesn't like me, the girls, the kids don't like me and, worst of all, these lice don't want to die. So they decided to cut my hair. They sent me to the doctor because he was also the barber, and he cut it.

My brother tried to escape but they caught him in the next village. He went with another boy called Jacques and, when they were caught, the monitor or the headmaster said that they were to be put in quarantine and no one was to talk to them, even me. He said that they think they are *two heroes* but they are just *two zeros,* and nobody must talk to them. So I couldn't even talk to my brother, anyhow. So there I was, unhappy and miserable but, being kids, you soon make friends, and when I made friends everything was OK.

Then there was an announcement: Any kid that has a relation in America is being sent to Marseilles and from there by boat to America. I said, "Me, me, me; I have a rich uncle in America."

So my brother and I, with some other kids, we go to Marseilles. We arrive at Marseilles and America declares war! So we go back to the children's home. Then they said that they were going to take some of the children to Haute Savoie and smuggle them over to Switzerland. My brother and I and some of the other kids were taken to chalets there, I think it was near Aix-les-Bains, to wait our turn. Every week there was a group of kids smuggled over to Switzerland, and I am waiting for a long time. I'm wondering why I am always the last, and I realized at a reunion why. They sent the children with an accent, the German kids, first. I could pass for a French kid and my accent was OK. I was supposed to go with my brother the next week, but they caught the kids who went the week before and that stopped me going. You see it's all fate! So back I go again to the children's home.

So we stayed there a little bit longer, and then it was really bad. The home had to close down because the Germans would have taken it, and now they took the kids and changed their names and put them in families. I couldn't be with my brother because he was four years older, and so he couldn't be put into a home, he had to work. He worked as a shepherd, and he had a horrible time with a woman farmer who was always drunk and used to beat him. He used to be two months with the cattle and not see a soul on the mountains, because that is what a shepherd does.

They changed my name from Fallek to Frettière, and they told me to say that my father was a prisoner of war and my mother was dead. They said how much people will love you and be nice to you, but don't say you are Jewish. Even today I say to my friends, "Don't tell me any secrets." I don't want to know because I hate keeping something to myself. My husband says, but you know I have to talk to you! But I say, "No, only tell me nice things."

So they sent me to a farm in Souspierre, near Montélimar. So we were at this farm with another little girl, whose name was Henni Benanfeld. They changed her name to Henriette, and she also had a story, you know. We knew we were Jewish, but we both knew we mustn't say. The people there were the lady farmer that we called *Tante* (auntie) Marthe, and her husband was *Tonton* (uncle) Abel; they were in their forties, and they were wonderful.

They were really lovely people. I went to the school in the small village where there were seventeen kids of all ages. I made friends with another little girl. The lady who looked after us was very, very considerate; as soon as someone came to visit her she would send us out. She knew that we couldn't speak up, and it's a terrible thing if somebody loves you and you just can't be open with them. So this was the relationship; they were very affectionate, and they took us to town in Montélimar. She had a brother and a sister-in-law who used to come at Christmas and Easter, and it was like a real family. Now, unfortunately, they have both died, but I still correspond with the brother who lives in Nice, and I went to see them last year with my husband. She sends me nougat, and I send her English chocolates at Christmas. As for Madame Marthe, the one who saved me, she is one of the "Righteous Gentiles." I made sure when I went to Israel that she was there, and I was so happy I have done that.

I went to school, and while I was there, there were a lot of the French Resistance hiding in the woods not far from us. We were in a valley, the woods were on the right and the road was on the left, so when there was shooting the lady used to take *casseroles*, you know pots and pans, and put them on our heads. There was still danger and often someone who was in the Resistance used to come with a gun, and the farmer would give him food to take back with him. So he was a very good person, not just to the Jews. He was a Protestant, not a Catholic, and apparently when there is a minority in a country they are more helpful—right? So I think it was a pastor who approached him about my little friend and me. We even went to their (Protestant) temple (church), but I always felt I'm Jewish. You know Jewish people say, "We are the chosen people, we are the cleverest, we know this and we know that." Which is very good, as any psychologist will tell you, for self-esteem, and if you want to think positive, think big.

After I had been there quite a long time, my brother arrived and now he had lost his charm; he was very brusque. Instead of saying thank you very much for looking after her he says, "I have come to collect my sis-

ter; what food have you got that I can take back?" Because he was ready
to survive, he had to buy food from villages and sell it in the towns, and
that's how he made his money. The people were taken aback and so was
I, but it was wonderful the way he actually came and collected me, but I
didn't know about this until later.

How did you feel about going?

I had no say. If they said come, I went; I was a very good girl. I had to
accept it; I just had to accept it. But I must say, I have always been an
optimist, and when I was in the concentration camp, all the kids were
crying and saying, "I will never see my daddy again" and things like that.
I always said that everything will be OK. When I was on the farm, I also
said that everything was going to be OK. I have this attitude, which I
am blessed with, in which I always say it's going to be all right.

In Canada last year at another reunion, I met this little girl that I had
been with, and I said to her that my brother wasn't very nice because he
just "*schlepped*" me away without giving me the chance to say goodbye
to her. She said that was her worst time because, when I left, nobody came
to collect her for six months, and she thought that everybody had forgotten her. We all have little vignettes we remember, and I remember that
when I was on the farm, the farmer had a special breed of chicken, very
small, miniature chickens. He gave me one of these chickens and one to
Henriette, the other little girl and, whenever my chicken laid an egg, it
was for me, a very small egg. When my brother came for me he said, "I
believe she's got a chicken; I want it!" So we put this chicken in a box
and we went on the train with it and we arrived at my mom's with this
chicken at a little village called Beaulieu. When my brother came and
collected me, half of France was already liberated by the Allies. I asked
him how he found me. He didn't know, but he does remember how he
found my mom. There was, in Lille, I think, a Jewish organization and
it was there that they contacted my mother, and she said, "Oh, I want
my little Betty." He said, "Leave it to me." And so off he went. My side
of France wasn't liberated, so I don't know how he managed. But in
French we say he is *débrouillard,* which means he takes an initiative. When
I ask him now how he found me, he says he doesn't know. He can't remember; he's blocked out quite a lot, compared to some. I don't remember much, but compared to him I remember a lot.

Anyhow, he brought me back to my mom and, to survive, he used to
go to the villages, get meat, and sell it in the big town because there was
a form of Black Market. Then one day I remember I was with my mom
in the forest, with some other people collecting blackberries, and the bells
were ringing. My mother said that somebody must be getting married,
but it wasn't; it was the end of the war!

So then my mother said, "Right, we are going to Paris to the consul."
And we all went to Paris.

Where had her mother been all this time?

After Camp de Gurs my mother was sent to Rivesaltes and from there
they sent her to another concentration camp. She said what had saved
her life was two gold pieces that she had sewn into her bra, so instead of
being sent to be killed she was put to work—right? But she again doesn't
talk much about it. She never wanted to talk about it.

When I went to the reunion in Canada we had workshops and there
was a therapist who was asking how it had affected relationships between
the new generation and the Holocaust survivors. It's amazing how we
are all different; some of the children said that their parents never talked
about it. Another group of children said, "All we hear is how they didn't
have food and how much they suffered and I am fed up to here with all
this 'suffering.'" So you have differences. My mother never talked about
it nor did my brother. I do because I like talking, but when I first started,
when I first came to this country, people weren't interested. They didn't
want to hear, until after *Schindler's List* and then, all of a sudden, people
wanted to know about it. Now I go to schools and tell them about it.
Even among Jewish people now they want to know, and the English
people who weren't in the Holocaust are interested now, where they were
not before. I never gave the whole story to my children. I told them little
things about the bread and such, but I never told them the whole story.
But now they know; I don't think it affected them.

My son loves it when I speak Yiddish. He says, "Say that again, say it
again." He is very Jewish, and he has become very religious, not pious
but Kosher. When I give him a biscuit, he has to look on the packet to
see if it's OK. I say, "Eat them, I'll take the sin. If you don't know, it's
not a sin." But he says, "No, that's not the point."

So Bettine was reunited with her mother.

Now my dad, who was here during the war, he was like "Dads' Army."
He helped in the air raids or something. Before we went to Paris, my
father arrived in the village, I don't know how he got to know about it,
but he arrived in the village and I remember it was wonderful, he was
wonderful. He was walking in the fields, and it was great for him because
he had been in the town, and he said, "This is wonderful to be with my
family in the countryside." Then he said that he would make everything
possible for my mom and us children to go to Paris and then to England.
So my father went back to London and we went to Paris. England didn't
let anybody come in then.

I gave a talk the other day to Holocaust survivors in Redbridge. Actually, I take Yiddish groups every Wednesday for Holocaust survivors in Hendon, but this was Redbridge. I asked them, in Yiddish, to introduce themselves and say where they were during and after the war. They said that after the war they were in camps, and they said that they couldn't come here. They had to stay in camps because no one would take them; it was very difficult.

So even though he was established here, my father could only bring in the children, not his wife, my mother. So we came, and then there was a very nice rabbi here who helped a lot by giving my father a false marriage certificate, which said that they married in London, which they did not. Because of this he could bring my mother over a few months after we had been here. Then I was sent to school, but the relationship between my mother and my father wasn't the same, and that was very painful.

My mother had some friends who were also furriers and, when we stayed in Paris, we stayed with them. They had two sons who had been killed, but they had somehow managed to survive because they went to Nice. Nice was not occupied by the Germans but by the French *Milice*. Anyhow, they had survived and my mother found out that they had gone back to their apartment, so we stayed with them. They are dead now, but they were very nice. We were just there for a few weeks although, of course, my mother was there longer. I didn't go to school until I came to England.

And that is my story! I was twelve when I arrived in England. I would like to say something about my little brother, OK? My mother had an older sister who was killed, who lived in Poland, and she had a younger sister, Sonia, who lived in Belgium with her little boy, Solly. Now after the war everybody tried to find out who was alive, and my father asked about them. He was told that Solly Silverberg was alive. How did he survive the war? Well, apparently his mother, Sonia, was put in a cattle wagon, and she had Solly in her arms. He had his name and everything on him, and there was a good German soldier on the platform, and he made a sign to my aunt to drop the baby and she did. A lot of mothers wouldn't, you see. So she dropped the kid, and the German soldier took him to a priest, and he put him in a home and, thank God, he had all his identification on him.

My father brought him over to London for a holiday with the intention to go on to America. My auntie said she was too old to look after a child but, because of his personality, he was so loving, we thought, we are not sending him, we are keeping him. We had a dog and instead of saying, "Is this your dog?" he said, "Is this *our* dog?" and instead of calling my parents auntie and uncle, he called them Ma and Pa, the same as us. So that's how I came to have two brothers.

Bettine had many separations from her mother.

As I say, if it happened now I think I would grasp the situation more and would be more frightened, but then I have this nature. I mean many things have happened to me, and I say, well, I'm growing. Each time I have a problem, I am growing, but God somehow doesn't give you one problem; they come in clusters. I don't mind growing, but not so quickly, not all at once. I don't think it affected me; I am not bitter. My Holocaust groups say that every day is a given day, and they have been chosen to be alive for a reason, and they enjoy life. They are much happier, my group, than people who have not suffered in the war, because I have friends who have daughters and sons who go to psychoanalysis and they take Prozac. Nobody in my group takes Prozac; they enjoy themselves especially now that we have the Holocaust Centre in Hendon, where they play bridge, they write, and have entertainers and people like me tell them jokes. It's wonderful; they don't have chips on their shoulders. Of course they cry sometimes.

MARCEL LADENHEIM

Marcel's father had already been in one of the early rafles *(roundups) of Jews from Paris and had been deported, via one of the French assembly camps, Beaune-la-Rolande, to his death in Auschwitz. His mother was struggling to survive with two small boys when she became mentally ill. Her children would certainly soon have been found and deported had not Marcel, then about age four, taken himself and his younger brother to a neighbor's house and simply asked for shelter.*

His hiding family were two Italian sisters, one of them a dancer at the Folies Bergères, who had "no love for Jews" but nevertheless took care of the little boys throughout the war. Marcel is certain that neighbors were perfectly aware of their Jewish identity, but they were never betrayed. He and his brother are examples of children who were hidden visibly, that is to say, they were able to go out, and even to school, but with a false identity.

Although the personalities of the sisters seem to him now to have been eccentric, it was a warm and affectionate household. From time to time a wan figure would come to the house from the hospital, never daring to come in. After the war, the brothers were taken to relatives, Orthodox Jews, in the north of England.

This was the hardest time of loss, dislocation, and deprivation. Cosseted and loved by their hiding mothers in Paris, they had no say in their transportation to England, to a household that was cold and affectionless. They had no religious upbringing, were extremely unhappy, and missed the warmth, language, and culture of their French foster family.

Marcel clearly felt isolated during this time. Eventually he qualified as a dentist. He is a thoughtful and reflective man, looking forward to his retirement, sometimes a little anxious and perfectionist about his work but never incapacitated by these traits. He is stronger and more resolute than he sometimes believes he is.

I was born in Paris in 1939, and I lived with my father and my mother for a few years at a place called Passage Bradis, in the tenth *arrondissement.*

My parents had emigrated from Austria. My father was a furrier, and my mother was a model of some sort. My father was taken away in 1941 to a camp in Beaune-la-Rolande, in the center of France for a year, then transported to Drancy and then to Auschwitz. Meanwhile my mother and I lived with non-Jewish people. I remember going to theaters and pictures, often, to escape from reality.

Subsequently I heard that my mother was taken away to a mental home. It seems that she broke down when we were living with those

Marcel Ladenheim as a baby, with his parents. Courtesy of Marcel Ladenheim.

people, and she tried to attack a man with a knife. I stayed with these people who were friends to some non-Jewish Italian ladies, Olga and Esther, farther down the road. Apparently, when I was about four, I knocked on their door and said I wanted to live with them and they took me in.

A lively little boy when "hiding" with Olga and Esther, the two Italian sisters. Courtesy of Marcel Ladenheim.

Ma petite Olga et Ester,
cheri
J'ai recu tes journaux je
te remerci beaucoup il m'ont
fait bien plaisir ça m'interasse
beaucoup Maintenant - j'ai
beaucoup de timbres Je crois
que j'en ai 1.000 ou un peu
moins et l'ecole moi et Père
font un rôle juif parce que
je ne suis pas juif et il n'y a
pas Noël Je t'embrasse bien
fort en esperant de
recevoir une lettre de toi
1948

A poignant letter to his two rescuers sent about
four months after leaving France, 1948, explaining how confused he feels by his new identity
(*'un rôle juif'*). Courtesy of Marcel Ladenheim.

Marcel Ladenheim today. Courtesy of Marcel
Ladenheim.

Olga and Esther and their friends were kind and friendly, and the re-action was "Fine, if you want to have him, have him, we don't particu-larly want him anyway." Obviously having a Jewish boy in Paris with the Germans around was a little bit dangerous—particularly a boy—a girl is safer.

I lived with Olga and Esther from about age four to six, until 1945. After the war my mother came to take us back to Passage Bradis, but from what I can gather she really was in no position to have us. She was ill, badly traumatized, and apparently the neighbors complained that we were really not being looked after.

My brother, Henri, was born in 1941 when my father had been taken away to the concentration camp.

As I get older it doesn't get any easier to tell because I think, typically, you don't talk about it, most people haven't talked about it, and it's only recently that they tried to come to terms with their suffering.

After the war, when I must have been seven, I stayed with my mother for a very short period of time. I did go to school throughout, I think. I wasn't really hidden,[1] I was just protected.

After the war I went back to my mother who really wasn't fit to look after us. I can still remember her going out and looking for work unsuc-cessfully. Even at that early stage, at six or seven, you understand the sig-nificance of unemployment; it's a very traumatic experience. I stayed with my mother for about six months; then I can still remember the police coming to take her back to a mental home outside Paris, and I went back to Olga and Esther. My brother went to Olga's boyfriend. She must have been in about her mid-thirties at the time and was a dancer at the Folies Bergères.

It must have been very difficult. Olga would tell me that my mother came and refused to come in. She was obviously very, very traumatized. This wasn't that particularly unusual when people came out of concen-tration camps but, in this case, this was a woman with a child and a baby, and it was really avoiding the Germans. She remained in a mental home for about ten years after that, and I didn't see her again until I was about eighteen. It was a bit of a stigma, you know, having a mother who is mentally ill.

So I stayed with Olga and Esther until I was nine in 1948. They didn't have children; I was their child and they were kind. I went to school and apparently did very well. But Olga says that she was asked to go to the school and the teacher said, "He is very disruptive." I must have been very wild, which amazes me now. "He is very wild; it has got to be curbed somehow. He fights all the time." She said, "Oh dear. How is he in school?" so they said, *"Ah, il est le premier"*—"he is first."

These were the happiest days of my life really.

Then my aunt and uncle came from Manchester to get me. They managed to get me an Austrian passport, and I stayed in Manchester with them until I was about eighteen. But quite frankly, as far as I am concerned, that was the most traumatic phase of my life, because Olga and Esther, even though they were Gentiles, were very, very kind to me.

Were they your paternal or your maternal relatives?

My aunt was my mother's sister. They didn't have any children, they were obsessed with religion, and they were very, very cold. They were very bad years and it was tough. I wasn't religiously minded.

No, you hadn't been brought up like that. Had Olga and Esther tried to raise you as a Catholic?

No. I think my brother was probably baptized. I don't think I was. I did go to church occasionally but there wasn't any big push. You can well imagine with Olga's lifestyle that she was hardly going to be too Catholic . . . but her sister was, interestingly enough, and she was quite devout.

The major trauma as far as I'm concerned was the fact that these people weren't very nice; they were very cold. And when I say "not very nice," they left to go to Israel when I was eighteen and went to University, and I literally didn't hear from them again. I had to look after myself.

Olga and Esther had probably taken terrible risks although they weren't aware of them.

What did you find out about your father's fate after Drancy and Auschwitz?

Nothing really, but we went to France about four or five years ago, and on the way back I noticed Beaune-la-Rolande. Suddenly I thought, that's the place. So we stayed, and I did a bit of sleuthing.

I discovered that there was an annual meeting in the "*Place*" and I realized, only recently, that there was a whole network of child survivors. I got in touch with an organization in France called *Fils et Filles des Déportés Juifs*[2] for children whose parents were deported. This opened a completely new chapter for me, which has been very useful.

Marcel's aunt and uncle did not speak French.

They were from Austria and spoke German, so I picked some up. But they were miserable years. I was thinking about my meeting with you and, as I went through my life, I thought the whole thing sounds a bit miserable, although I am not a particularly miserable person,

I don't feel unhappy.

My brother took to religion very well; in fact, he is very religious now, which is ironic because he was baptized. He now lives in Israel and has a very large, very Orthodox family and I keep in touch with him reasonably

well. I remember my mother saying, "look after your brother," and I've
always done so, which has become a little bit strained lately. I'm about
to retire and he writes, "My kids want to be educated" and I'm thinking, "I've got enough commitments, don't thrust anything more on me
now." A few months ago I also got a letter from him saying, "By the way,
your uncle and aunt are about to retire. We want to put them in a home,
and you're going to have to provide to a certain extent." These are moral
dilemmas that I'm about to face, but it doesn't worry me that much.

My brother is an engineer who went to the University of Manchester
to study mechanical engineering, and I did dentistry. My aunt left when
I was nineteen and in my first year, and I almost never heard from her
again. Now I realize the significance of this. I didn't even get a birthday
card. It sounds awful but it is only now that I think, "oh, that wasn't very
nice, really."

Basically my maternal relations who live in Israel haven't been particularly good to me. Only now am I looking at it from a different perspective. You know, I think to myself, "my children come to me, they got
married, want money, need clothes, and things, they've got a certain
amount of security," and I must say that at the time I really didn't. Fortunately, while I was a student, I lived with a very nice ultra-Orthodox
family. My aunt and uncle had made sure that I was going to stay in an
Orthodox home. It was more or less very *frum*.[3] I stayed there for about
four or five years, and they were very restrictive. There were a lot of things
I couldn't do, but there was warmth in the house and that made a big
difference.

I was always going to do medicine, and I was accepted at Manchester,
Sheffield, and Leeds, but my uncle in Israel said, "You know, Marcel, if
you wanted to come to Israel you'd be far better off with dentistry."

I came back to Manchester and I said I wanted to go to dental school,
and they accepted me.

It was attractive in the same way that now, instead of medicine, people
go into computers because that's where the future really lies. Dentistry
did hold a very good financial future.

So I chose dentistry and, this is the misery of it, I'm so sorry I did
dentistry; I am totally unsuited, basically, because I'm not really manu-
ally very dexterous. With dental school, you don't realize until about the
third year that this isn't for you.

I've met a lot of people who regret doing dentistry and people of my
age, who will say, incidentally, "I had a heart attack a few years ago."

I did have a heart attack a few years ago, and I could have retired. My
colleagues all said to me that it was a golden opportunity to get out of
it, but I haven't got that many other interests, so I am trying to see it
through for another year or so.

It is very lonely. One of my problems is that I'm not very steady with my hands anymore; I've got a tremor, but I take beta-blockers for my heart and that's steadied it.

I qualified in 1963 and met my wife in Israel. She is American and, after returning to America, she came to England where we got married and started a family in 1965. We had our first child in 1966.

I do get very sad, and I don't think that I've really come to terms with the death of my father in particular, it still upsets me. My one big problem is, with people, I still feel uncomfortable. Number one is always a fear of rejection; although on a day-to-day basis it's not very important. When I was younger, if I were to go to a dance, I wouldn't really go up to the girl because I would fear rejection.

Marcel's problems in adolescence were for him worse than in his formative years with Olga and Esther, which were actually very warm, loving, and caring years.

Those two or three early years did set me up okay. It was a very important time, and Olga will say to me sometimes, "You know, *tu es comme moi*, you are just like me." I do think I am very much like her. She's really like my mother. She's still alive and I phone her twice a week.[4]

Coming back to Olga and Esther, you kept the relationship with your hiding mothers?

No, it broke down when I was with my aunt and uncle. They weren't going to let me go back to France because Olga and Esther were "non-kosher" in many ways. When I look back on it now, there were five breaks from people I had become attached to. Very big separations, you know, from parents twice and from Olga who was like a second mother as well, so, it must have been terrible.

I lived in Manchester with a man and wife who had both been in Auschwitz. I lived with them for five years. I knew that the wife had suffered from a little bit of depression, but then she had actually been in Auschwitz. She only once said how bad it was. But when the Russians came to liberate Auschwitz it was even worse. And that was it, end of story. She never said anything else.

You were never encouraged to talk about it; I think that they felt a little bit embarrassed, a bit awkward. You know, you don't ask how was it in the concentration camp.

Marcel said that he gets very anxious sometimes. About big things or little things?

Ah, both. I would worry about a patient coming in on Monday with a difficult extraction; you know, that would prey on my mind, or I would worry about my children marrying somebody not quite, not very suitable or being unwell. Yesterday I was worrying about a practice problem, and I didn't know how I was going to cope with it.

I like to be liked. I suppose that I really desperately try to please, and that's basically one of my faults. Perhaps because I didn't want to be rejected, I always wanted to be nice. Certainly, seeing my maternal relations, none of them is like that; they are all fairly aggressive, domineering. One or two of them are a little unpleasant; none of them is, you know, condescending.

Marcel was hidden by Olga and Esther and there were probably restrictions that he was not aware of at the time. In adolescence he was treated by his aunt and uncle as though he had no right to be there. It is paradoxical that, when he was not safe, during the war, he was treated very warmly and, from what he said, it sounds as though he felt quite secure.

If somebody said to me the real trauma occurred after, it wouldn't surprise me. For me, there was a tremendous amount of domination. Religion just didn't mean anything to me at all. I wanted to watch football and have girlfriends, but I didn't have these things, and I can still remember my aunt chasing me with a knife around the table because we were forever at loggerheads.

The bad part of my upbringing was really from ten onward when it was, to me, really bad.

I really didn't get in touch with Olga and Esther until they went to Israel. Olga and Esther were very nice people. "If you want to come back, that's fine, that's great," Olga said and was always there to give me five pounds if I needed it. Even now, when I go back, it's "I'm going home." But there was a break for about ten years where I really did miss out on a lot. Yes, no question about it. I wouldn't have been Jewish now.

I can remember getting the coach from Manchester to London and then to Paris. In those days it was a bit of a journey. So it was like going home, but those two or three years were definitely the best. We both still like to talk about it.

She does do some racist talk: "*Les Noirs,*" "*les Arabes,*" which is how people talk in France. You just need to have been attacked or something you don't want and you become racist. She would even say to me, "I've got to say you are a little bit Jewish yourself," and I'm thinking "that wasn't a compliment."

I think what happened in France is that, although a lot of the French were anti-Semitic, there was a very strong liberal trend among them. She almost certainly didn't like Jews, but she saw a little boy and she took him in. This was a liberal thing. She had to do it as she would if she saw a man beating a dog. She would go over and say "stop beating that dog." A humanitarian streak does exist in France.

Of course, as far as my children are concerned, I was a disciplinarian when it came to education. I wanted them to be able to earn their own living, but as far as religion is concerned, I was very lax. I couldn't say, "You are coming with me to the synagogue."

My wife and I don't think the same way about our daughter's non-Jewish friends. [My wife] is much more accepting. Her sister and her uncle married a non-Jewish person, and so being American, this isn't of such importance. To me it was important because I've been indoctrinated in that sort of way. Furthermore, I knew that this would cut me off from all my relations.

I would say that having a family was very important to me. I've nobody else, let's face it, on my father's side, and I'm not particularly keen on my relations on my mother's side.

I do know that I have got an aunt and uncle in South America, but I've never made contact. I would love to meet them. I've got a cousin in Argentina, and we've written twice but then it petered out.

I wouldn't go to Germany or Austria on principle, I'm afraid. I may not be racist, but I am anti-German, because they did such terrible things.

My children don't understand it, but then it's in my lifetime, you know. They [the Germans] took my father's life.

I think the second generation phenomenon is a very, very interesting one. Because I hear of too many examples where children have behaved rather strangely, and I think a lot of the survivors assume that it was something to do with their surviving.

His children are identified?

On the contrary, *au contraire*, they're distancing from it. It's almost as if they know something has happened. It's almost as if they don't want anything to do with that story. They want to get away from it. That, I think, is very strong.

We lived in Kingston, which is a non-Jewish area, and they always had non-Jewish friends. None has had a Jewish friend. They don't want to know. I can think of a few [instances] where the kids have either gone off to Australia or one has become very, very religious, and one has become the other way. You can't believe it. Only last week a man died, he was seventy and a member of the Holocaust Group, and one of the boys didn't even turn up for the funeral, and the other one wouldn't say the prayer (*Kaddish*—prayer for the dead). Obviously, there had been a rift between the two generations where the boys have disappeared.

What about truth telling. Was that an issue?

I don't think it was that relevant. Personally, I find I can tell a little lie, "I'm sorry, we can't come on Thursday because I've got a headache," with ease. But a big lie, well, I couldn't do it to save my soul. If I had misbehaved, that sort of thing, I can say, "Well, I went to see Dr. Bluglass" (Marcel laughs) as a red herring, you know. But ah, I don't like to do it.

That is not because of what happened in wartime, that you had to invent a history at school?

No, I don't think so. Personally, I find telling lies difficult. There are people who are pathological liars; you probably meet them in your profession. I would say I am exactly the opposite.

It may also have to do with the "liking to be liked."

Could be, yes. Yes, it could be.

How else does he feel it has affected him?

I feel, particularly after my heart attack, as if I can cope with just about anything, even dentistry. I do feel that if you put your mind to it, you can do anything, except learn how to play the piano and play for Manchester United.

I think you can do anything. When it was suggested that I should do dentistry I thought, "Well, I can't. I'm not very good with my hands," but I thought to myself, "but if I push myself I know I can do it," and I did do it.

That seems to come from a very optimistic center.

Well, it's a bit like me; it's difficult to pigeon hole. When it comes to big things, I've survived them, but I'm unlucky, you know, in the small things. I'm optimistic in that respect. But I am pessimistic about difficult tasks.

I think, "Oh my God, what if she developed septicemia?" or I would grab hold of the tooth and think, "this is going to break." In a small way, there's this pessimistic streak.

My one negative thing, apart from wanting to be liked, is that I never feel comfortable with people. I've only one or two friends, and I will see somebody and think, "Oh, I would like to meet that person," but after ten minutes I think, "I'm boring him, I want to get away now."

We speculate that some of that has do to with the age at which he came from one country to another. It cannot have been very easy coming from an upbringing in France to cold Manchester and cold people. When Olga and Esther were rearing him at a formative time, what were they, optimistic or pessimistic?

I think I would have said both. Esther was like "the woman," and Olga, the one who is still alive, is the one that went out to work. She was the attractive looking one with a whole lot of boyfriends and, yet in many ways, she assumed a male role.

Olga was more of an optimist really. She was basically optimistic.

Perhaps that's where it comes from.

Could be. But if I said to my wife, "I'm optimistic," she would laugh.

I really think I enjoy life. Here again, particularly since my heart attack, every day something good happens, you know, like today I came here and there was nothing to pay on the train! And I think "that's nice" (Marcel laughs). I do appreciate life, although my wife doesn't quite perceive me like this.

We talked earlier about denial. Where does Marcel think he sees himself?
There is a difference, isn't there, between really enjoying life and putting on a bright face while feeling pretty miserable underneath?

My philosophy basically is that, if you can have a few hours of pleasure a week, you're doing very nicely.

How does Olga remember Marcel as a young child?

She talks about it all the time. I was like a king, a beautiful, beautiful boy with curly red hair, and I think to myself, "you should see me now!" the best in the class, so good, in fact, that I was sent to the President of France because one boy went and I was really quite good at school. I wasn't that good in England mind you.

But I never seemed to catch up. You know, I was all B's at A Level rather than all A's.

It was difficult because, not only did I have to learn English, I had to learn Hebrew as well, and I hated every minute. Really, it was misery. I've got to say this.

I've got a few photographs, although she's kept the majority. She has a beautiful flat, and she has acquired Louis XIV replica furniture. When you go into that flat you think she's got style and taste.

She's got the letters that I sent her when I came to England all wrapped and laid in a box, and she won't let me have them. She says they're hers. And it's very, very moving, the letters of a nine-year-old, in French of course.

She'll read them and then forget it! They are her prized possessions. She's quite happy about me reading them, and I think that they would make a very interesting little book. It's all *"Ma Chère Petite Olga"* "My dear little Olga"; there is obviously a little bit of optimism, but there is obviously misery underneath (see illustration of Marcel's letter).

Was there a lot of homesickness?

That was bad. I don't care if those crystal glasses, antiques, and other possessions disappear. But those letters, I really must have them.

What did Olga think the experience was like for Marcel as a child—the bits that he can't really remember. Some people, of course, have kept letters and documents and have recollections of conversations about what the adults felt like when they were hiding children.

I'm going to see Olga in the near future. She's not that pushy at the moment because she is eighty-six. She's got all her marbles. But as she's got older she is very conscious of her age, and she is afraid that I'm going to see her as an old woman.

No longer this glamorous woman at the Folies Bergères?

There was a time when it was, "when are you coming, when are you coming?" and I'll say, "Oh, well I'll probably come," but then she'll say, "Ah, you've got to remember that I'm looking a lot older now, and I'm a lot shorter." She would spend easily two hours a day doing her makeup. Sometimes I think to myself, how many years has she wasted on her makeup? What a life this is.

Yet I was there when she would entertain a man in the bathroom! Really! It's only more recently that I understand the significance of it all. You know, they didn't go to the bathroom to go brush their teeth!

In many ways she is a bit prudish, oddly enough.

Since we first met, Marcel has been able to visit Olga more often. He travels from London every month to visit her.

Marcel has been very frank about the little things that worry him. On the whole he enjoys life and is definitely looking forward to retirement.

How does he feel he is functioning? In general terms, if it were a jigsaw puzzle, what he is saying is that there are a few bits around the margins that don't fit exactly but, on the whole, is he relatively happy and optimistic.

I would say that. I would certainly say that. But the word "anxiety," I've never really thought until you said anxiety. That is exactly right. I'm not depressed or miserable or manic depressive. But anxiety is really the right word that would describe me fully. And yet, as I say, I certainly don't find it stops me from being basically a happy person.

Without minimizing it, does he overcome the anxiety every day?

You are not minimizing, you know, you are explaining it.

I must say, because my problem was one of security, when I reached about fifty my life improved quite considerably. There came a point in my life when I realized I had achieved the goal that was most important to me. Does that sound logical?

All of a sudden I realized that I had enough money in the bank, I had a pension fund, my kids were all right and, I realized that I had achieved the goal that I had been striving for for fifty years. Up to then there were three kids that had to be fed and nurtured, and I didn't know whether I was going to keep my job.

NOTES

1. Marcel was in hiding and visible (see Dwork, 1991).
2. *Fils et Filles des Déportés Juifs: militants à la memoire.*
3. *Frum* in Yiddish means observant.
4. Since we first met, Olga lives in a well-run rest home in Paris, and Marcel now has copies of the precious letters.

PART II

Part II

CHAPTER 7

The Role of Oral History

History is the passage of memory.
—*Simon Schama, observing the lying-in-state*
of Her Majesty Queen Elizabeth the Queen Mother, 2002

History is also about interpretation of evidence; the view of events is dependent on identifying the bias in records. There is often no way of checking or of identifying the source of a written account. With oral history the person providing the evidence sits in front of you.

There is also the issue of the child as witness and "historical fact." Debórah Dwork, in *Children with a Star* (1991), did meticulous research and, based on many interviews, discusses the consistency of people's stories, the nature of oral history as "emplotment," that is, the way people shape their narratives as "romance, comedies, tragedies, satire" (see also Henry Greenspan 1998).

Depending on a variety of factors, such as age, emotional arousal, and other variables, children's ability like, or even more than, other "witnesses" may be more or less reliable. Adult narrative may block childhood feeling, and an affective vocabulary may be inadequate.

Which of us has not experienced some confusion on discovering that an often recited memory is an overrehearsed composite, collage, or palimpsest derived from a photograph we have seen or events that have been described to us.

Some Hidden Children, Irena for example, are perfectly aware and acknowledge that an event may be a "screen memory" or cannot be attributed to a particular time or may even be an amalgamation of events experienced or told by others.

There is usually sufficient verifiable fact from external and objective facts to link these young children to the time and place of their hiding experience. One is not, after all, trying to validate the chronology of World War II or counter the Holocaust deniers. It is the emotion, feeling, and perception unique to the individual that is captured here.

An interesting example of events experienced as an adult arose sometime after I had interviewed Wlodka (Chapter 3), hidden as a child with her twin, Nelly. She could describe the outline of events in her hiding experience, but much of the detail and affective feeling was missing, because she had been very young. The older she was, during her years in hiding, the more detailed were the perceptions that she recalled.

When I was researching aspects of the Resistance in the Warsaw ghetto uprising, I came upon an objective account of the circumstances of her rescue. She had told me that she and her twin had been concealed by Michal Klepfisz, the renowned ghetto fighter.

Vladka Meed (Feigele Peltel-Miedzyrecki), a young woman Resistance courier, describes in her book *On Both Sides of the Wall: Memoirs from the Warsaw Ghetto* (1987) how the Blit twins, Nelly and Wlodka, were affected by the separation from their parents and how eagerly they asked her for news of their mother when she visited to bring food and funds for them. As an adult observer she could describe events and emotions objectively; they could not or, perhaps mercifully, they had suppressed them.

There is, of course, a problem in searching for feelings and emotions experienced by children because of limited childhood awareness, perception, and language—unlike those of adult survivors.

It is hard to have to ask people to "provide evidence" of their endurance of these events, as highlighted by the concerns arising from the Wilkomirski text.

For some people there are also independent witnesses, surviving siblings and other family members, friends, and their foster hiding families who can cross-check their recollections. To obtain Yad Vashem awards as Righteous Gentiles for the rescuers, substantial documentary evidence is required. Many of the survivors have had to provide dossiers of their experiences in the long weary struggle to qualify for restitution and pensions.

The latter has raised difficult issues for some, new areas of potential injustice. Suppose, for example, that an individual injured in a man-made or medical disaster seeks and eventually, after long civil litigation, receives appropriate compensation. Although assessing the risk of future deterioration of symptoms is part of the evaluation, it is usually accepted that the injured person may also improve, if not actually recover. Assuming that the injuries and the claim for compensation are genuine, there is no legal justification for later reversal or withdrawal of compensation if improvement or adaptation takes place.

Yet despite the great difficulty in qualification for compensation (see Chapter 2 for discussion about *Wiedergutmachen,* reparations), for those Hidden Children who have been successful (and one has only recently received compensation in April 2000 and December 2001), some are understandably reluctant to declare themselves "well-adjusted" individuals fifty years later lest they risk compromising their hard-won pensions.

It is true that the professional historian has to evaluate the validity of oral evidence (Faris, 1980; Dwork, 1991; Portelli, in Perks and Thompson, 1998). Is there a difference between the interpretation of narratives and information recorded spontaneously during interviews with survivors and those with patients or clients carried out by professionals from psychosocial disciplines, namely physicians, psychiatrists, and psychologists (Greenspan, 1998)?[1] The latter are trained to evaluate the relevance of verbal and nonverbal, behaviors, evasion, elision, anxiety, embarrassment, and the effects of other emotional states on accuracy. They are also expected to pick up subtle nuances of memory or information failure, conscious or unconscious.

Furthermore (perhaps professional historians are more fortunate here), physicians have a wide experience with individuals adept at self-promotion and deception for pathological or maladaptive reasons, people who habitually embroider the truth and who usually have other detectable abnormal or unhealthy traits of personality (Ford, 1996).

In the series of encounters in this book, although the aim was to allow the individual an opportunity for spontaneous recall of his or her childhood and subsequent experiences, it was also different from over-rehearsed "testimony" to the extent that it was always a dialogue with clarifying, or more probing open, not closed, questions.

However, the lives considered here are not merely the more or less accurate recollections of childhood under Nazi Occupation (the eldest was no more than twelve; many were much younger and several only infants). We have tried to explore together their feelings and perceptions about their subsequent development. In considering positive outcomes the latter are of equal importance to easily verified facts to the historian of personality and individual competence.

It is a sad reflection of the times we live in that an early proposal for this work raised questions relating to the controversy surrounding Wilkomirski's book *Fragments* (1996), originally published as an autobiography but later believed to be fictitious. Heated press debates followed this allegation, which included the questions about the extent to which this "mattered" or whether it was to be considered as "testimony" or as "literature."

Historians, whether scholars in the field or those trained in medical and scientific traditions, understand the intrinsic importance of drama and literature.

They are aware that they do not necessarily represent objective truth, that perception, feeling, and emotion have to be distinguished from verifiable documentary fact (and, of course, also, from deliberate falsification).[2]

This is even more important when events may be subjected to fanatical revisionist activity (recent Irving Judgment, 2000).

NOTES

1. This is apparent from the full, unedited text of the interviews, which inevitably had to be reduced for publication but will be deposited with the original tapes as an oral history archive.

2. There is, of course, also a difference between the interpretation of written and oral narratives; see Portelli, in Perks and Thompson, 1998. Written reports of events may also be subject to reporting bias or propaganda, and the writer's identity may be concealed or distanced from the document.

CHAPTER 8

The Care of Separated Children

To what extent are the experiences of these children comparable to other forms of separation of bonds, such as fostering and adoption? Jewish children were rescued from deportation by placement in families and institutions. Such fostering experience was sometimes followed by the return of one or both parents and often resulted in temporary or permanent loss of identity. The social conditions then prevailing—war, danger, and the threat of deportation—compounded these disruptions.

When we first read about the most well-known experience of hiding, the diary of Anne Frank, the impact was so forceful and the images conjured up were so strong and poignant that for many they came to represent the archetype of the Hidden Child.

ASSUMPTIONS AND STEREOTYPES

Because direct knowledge of surviving Hidden Children was limited for so long by the apparent marginalization of their experience by their elders (Krell, 2001), we had relatively little to improve our understanding for many years. Some personal accounts began to emerge, for example, those of Claudine Vegh (1979) and Janina David (1981). Debórah Dwork in 1991 surveyed the whole canvas of Jewish Youth during Nazi domination of Europe.

Many now attribute the time of taking stock and reflection to their attendance at the New York International Survivor Gathering in 1991, referred to in earlier chapters. Their ability to consider their perceptions and feelings about their lives, in and out of hiding and afterward, has enabled them to speak out. Collections of autobiographical accounts, for example, Jane Marks (1994) and Paul Valent (1994), were also illuminating. More personal autobiographies followed, for example, Larissa Cain (1997) and Janina Fischler-Martinho (1998). Other collections of childhood memories recorded soon after the war in Poland were reissued in translation (Wiktoria Śliwowska, 1998; Maria Hochberg-Mariańska and Noe Grüss, 1996).

The possibility of studying the period before it is too late to glean the grains of experience is now diminishing. Children old enough to have a reasonable recall of contemporary events are now nearing seventy; those who were infants can only talk of their later childhood.

Listening to the recovered voices of other Hidden Children, some recorded in these pages, one hears of the diversity of hiding experiences, ranging from the relatively secure, warm, and nurturing, sometimes efficient and dutifully protective but distant, to the frankly neglectful and commercial.

With the exception of Janina (Chapter 3), who was exposed to the rudimentary conditions of life in the Polish countryside, Léa Pesok was probably the most badly treated and exploited of the Hidden Children who talked to me.

What saved her psychologically was not the hiding experience but the friendship of the kind Madame Maus, who came to give her Catholic instruction in secret.

LEA PESSOK

Lea Pesok was hidden in a basement launderette in Brussels by a woman who accepted payment for concealing her. She was harshly treated and deprived of any education. She led a miserable and malnourished life until she was moved to an apartment where she could see daylight, even if she could not go out.

Eventually she was befriended by an aristocratic Belgian lady working for the Resistance who visited her in her solitary confinement, originally to give her Catholic instruction. She helped her a little educationally and with moral support, almost certainly contributing to her remarkably successful personal survival. Because her own mother did not survive, she regarded this kind visitor as a mother substitute with whom she kept contact for the remainder of her life.

After my parents were deported the concierge said that I mustn't worry and that I could stay with them until my parents returned. They were very kind but they were very elderly, perhaps in their late seventies or so. Because I was desperate, with no family and most of our friends already deported, the concierge got in touch with the Red Cross. Someone came to check me out and place me. The person who actually took me in did this for money. She said that she didn't mind because the money was good, and she got extra ration books.

I was just taken to this person, whom I had never seen before. She had a launderette in the cellar, and this is where she lived and sent the washing away for people. At the side of the shop was just one room with a tiny kitchen where she did everything, slept, and ate. I just had to bear with it because I thought that it wouldn't be too long. Everybody told me it was only for a little while, but I was very unhappy. Eventually she made me sort out the dirty washing and clean, and I never had enough food. My periods stopped because I was anemic, and I also had dental problems because I was so malnourished.

She didn't eat much herself. She was a peculiar person and just didn't understand how to treat a child. Sometimes when I would tell her that I didn't feel well enough to work, she would say, "I'll tell the Gestapo to come and collect you!" She used to listen to the English radio broadcast at night and say, "You will never see your family again, they are all burnt!" She used to give me a hell of a life.

A lady, Mademoiselle Maus, came to give me private lessons in religion (Catholic instruction). She also helped me along with some grammar and so on. She was very sweet, and she could see I was very unhappy. So whenever she saw me she would bring me a sandwich or some food. She said she would like to take me away but she was frightened that Mademoiselle Canclaire might possibly turn nasty.

Lea Pessok today—sadly no childhood images survive. Courtesy of Lea Pessok.

I am surprised, when I think about it now, how I coped. It was very hard at the time, but when I think about it now I wonder, was it really me who was in that situation?

After the Liberation I had to learn how to walk in the street again! I was frightened, I wasn't used to it. And after the war, my health was poor; I kind of couldn't eat much, my stomach was like shrunk, so whatever I ate, I seem to have gone big (distended). I used to get faint, and I couldn't function properly. But, you know, I soon picked up on that and when I met my husband, I was very happy; I thought I was very, very lucky, and I never had problems, when I had the children.

(Even though she had been so malnourished.)

It wasn't like today. Like every couple starting off married life, things were difficult, but we were a very happy family, and I kept on saying how lucky I was because I was free. Of course, I didn't have much of a family life— but there's also instinct; I was happy with my husband, and I put my whole life into it. I think when you are happy in a situation, you do the job properly. Like I say, I was a strong person.

When I took the babies to be weighed at the baby clinic, I used to ask whomever I met there if they would come back for a cup of tea. I used to encourage them to visit me, even eight years later after we moved to Pinner, where I am now. We used to have a little Jewish shop, a little delicatessen where I bought the *challa*. If I saw a Yiddisher woman with children, I used to invite her, and I got lots of friends all around me.

It was remarkable that after such deprivation of social contact during the war, when she was not allowed to go out, not allowed to be seen in daylight, that she kept the capacity to make friends.

After she was married and living in Britain, Lea feels she responded positively to everything. She was determined to give her children what she had never had.

Like other Hidden Children described here, her recent years have not been without sadness and loss: her husband's death after many years of illness and her own ill health.

Coming to Britain happily reestablished her Jewish identity, although her affectionate mentor, the devout Mademoiselle Maus, would have preferred her to stay in Belgium and marry "a nice Catholic young man."

She was a model for me. I wish I could have had the opportunity to have her recognized (by Yad Vashem), to nominate her, in front of people, but it's hard to get recognition.

As for the strange Mademoiselle Canclaire, who treated her so unkindly behind the closed shutters of the launderette. . . .

I felt sorry for her afterward. I used to go and take her flowers, and I went to her funeral. She died a lonely person. Although she was educated she didn't know how to handle the situation. She used to sell the ration books, and she fed her dog more than she fed me, but at least she didn't betray me; she did save my life, that's the way I see it now. And it was very difficult to place children then.

Despite Lea's own serious illness she remains strong and feels that Mademoiselle Maus fostered her inner strengths.

Other experiences of Hidden Children were malign and abusive, like those described by some who talked to Paul Valent and by Mira Reym Binford in her film *Diamonds in the Snow*.[1] Yet those who were treated like Mira and Lea can say "but our lives were saved. . . ."

It may seem superfluous, therefore, to consider whether the best of these placements and their effects on the children had anything in common with the fostering and adoption of young people, either then (1939–45) or now. Yet the question is occasionally asked, usually by those unfamiliar with the literature or history of those times. Significant changes have taken place in the care of children in most European countries since then. We need to try to understand why protection of these children (an especially threatened group) was so potentially damaging over and above the known effects of separation and, yet, on the whole has yielded more success stories than expected.

EVACUATION AND DISPLACEMENT

Contemporary fostering aims to protect children from physically, emotionally, or sexually abusive family situations. In Britain childcare and protection was somewhat differently organized at the outbreak of World War II. The evacuation of city children, usually without their families, to an ostensibly safer area of England is one example.

Jack Rosenthal's television drama *The Evacuees* (1975) reflects his own experience.

Certainly there was fear for the safety of British children in the anticipated bombardment of cities and ports, and hurriedly organized mass placements were arranged in rural areas. Despite good intentions these arrangements were sometimes wildly inappropriate and ill-considered; children were often accommodated with an ill grace "for the war effort"; the habits, manners, and behavior, to say nothing of the frequent bedwetting and infestation by head lice, of these unhappy urban children were not always welcome. This story is only now being told in detail (Brown, 2000). Yet some inner city children blossomed in the country, used the opportunity to expand their interests and skills, and look back on those times with nostalgia.

Their new placements had to be arranged in haste, sometimes without careful attention to detail. The children were usually rapidly removed from their parents in threatened cities and ports but, of course, although the country was at war there was no need to hide them. The identities and religion of Jewish evacuees were not changed, although they were often placed with naive rural hosts who were sometimes poorly equipped to deal with their dietary and other needs. Most returned to their parents, sooner or later. So there are many ways in which this experience was, even if traumatic, different from separations associated with concealment, fear of denunciation, and discovery and with all the associated threats of deportation and annihilation. It was also completely unlike the experience of the earlier *Kindertransporte* where rapid evacuation not only involved hurried separation and dislocation, but also loss of country, culture, and language in a climate of fear and foreboding (Leapman, 1998).

Some British children were also displaced abroad for their safety, for example, to Canada and the United States, often by private initiatives, including some ultimately distinguished public figures such as the politician Shirley Williams, the historian Sir Martin Gilbert, and the actress Claire Bloom.

Another possible comparison is with standard fostering and adoption into the care system and away from failing parenting or maltreatment. Standards have steadily improved in the United Kingdom, and there has been a strong movement away from institutional placement of children in orphanages and children's homes and toward family or small group placements. There is no doubt, however, that we may still learn that some people with a duty to care for badly treated, vulnerable, and needy children have neglected and even abused them. Young people, already emotionally or physically damaged, usually reach the care system more vulnerable and in need of help than normal children. Their outcome, too, has been variable despite much professional input invested in their care.

Evidence of other damage has emerged in the accounts of the later difficulties experienced by children forcibly exported from Britain to Australia (Humphreys, 1994).

The care of vulnerable and damaged children in Britain has improved more recently with the passing of The Children Act 1989.[2]

Yet because of the trauma that some such children have already experienced, it is clear that the outcome of contemporary fostering and adoption is not always ideal. The decision to adopt may be so long delayed that the children are ultimately hard to place (Clarke and Clarke, 2000, quoting Tizard, 1999).

In contrast, children who had to be concealed for reasons of race and religion who were at risk from the Nazi threat, whose parents made desperate efforts to save them even when they could not save themselves, were previously cherished and well cared for. They parted from their parents with great mutual anguish. They were usually from stable, if not always materially comfortable, backgrounds (in Poland, particularly, Meed [1987] points out that, as a rule, only children from reasonably affluent families could be hidden—poor and large families had little chance). Nechama Tec suggests that they were usually from secular or at least somewhat assimilated backgrounds, since "few Orthodox children made it into Christian families."[3]

Of course affluence was a relative concept once the Nazi regime had restricted Jewish occupations and professions, banned people from running their own businesses, and confiscated property and possessions.

Separation from their families was accompanied by such understanding they might have of the risks (of hiding or not hiding), if they were old enough, and by inexplicable disruption of family attachments if they were too young to comprehend. Children who are fostered or adopted today because of poor parenting differ from children hidden to protect them from Nazi persecution.

They do not discover that the separation from parents resulted from criminal sociopolitical acts involving murder and extermination by the invader or controlling regime. So direct comparisons with peacetime fostering and childcare are probably unproductive.

Not all hidden children were equipped, either by age or temperament, such as Janek (Chapter 3) or by previous experience, such as Janina in the Kraków ghetto (Fischler-Martinho, 1998), for the difficulties and deprivations in store. Very small children or infants may have been absorbed relatively effortlessly into large families, for example, in Holland (Dwork, 1991) and the accounts of Anita, Basia, and Bert (Chapter 5), but repeatedly one hears, in the accounts of those like Nicole and Sophie, the fear implicit in the efforts of these little children to be good, compliant, and obedient, to a worrying extent. Often these constraints emanated as much from the child as from harsh exhortation or admonition from the hiding parents.

Such repression of natural childish exuberance is likely to give rise to a range of traits in adulthood, such as overconformity, inability to set limits, excessive need to please others, and other limitations to the development of self-confidence and self-worth. These characteristics, in turn, if not resolved may produce an unhappy adult who lacks confidence, and they may impair healthy relationships, including marital and parental ones.

Unresolved separation and losses (Brown, Harris, and Coupland, 1977; Brown and Harris, 1978; Brown, Harris, and Bifulco, 1986) have been shown to predispose people to depressive illnesses or to other difficulties of attachment and "letting go," which may be rekindled by the occurrence of other losses throughout the life span.

The point here is not to deny that these may occur, to a greater or lesser extent, to individuals who have faced such experiences. However, some, including those who reflect on their early experience in this book, neither perceive themselves as seriously troubled people nor appear so objectively to the clinician. Just as important, and possibly contributory to their successful mastery of their experiences, is their attitude to their childhood trauma.

Of course Hidden Children are not alone in successfully overcoming separated and traumatic childhoods to achieve a reasonable balance and adjustment in adult life. As always in clinical practice we hear much more about pathology than success (Vanderpol, 2002); bad news sells more newspapers than good news.

This brings us to the question of resilience, what it is and how it comes about.

The notion of promoting and encouraging healthy survival is now attracting increasing attention with a contemporary shift away from an exclusive interest in pathology and damage.

The first half of the twentieth century has seen many tragic events involving large populations resulting in racial prejudice and genocidal acts, including those against children (Charny, 1999).

Since the end of World War II, conflicts in Africa and Asia, as well as the more recent interracial wars in the Balkans and the conflicts in Afghanistan and the Middle East, remind us that events affecting large populations and their children continue to challenge their emotional and physical safety and well-being. While working to promote the optimum care for vulnerable children, we can learn from the experience of the adults here being described. Even in the face of apparently insurmountable hazards, many more young people than may have been realized do have a chance to master separation, deprivation, and fear.

With this knowledge we can balance the original negative assumptions pointing to poor outcomes and do what we can to promote, encourage, and believe in the real existence of successful survival for the many.

THE PLACE OF ATTACHMENT IN HIDDEN CHILDREN

Children who become securely attached to a parental figure early in life have considerable advantages. Although it might seem strange at first sight, such children cope better with the disruption of a close bond than others who have had variable experiences from poor caregivers. The latter promote a kind of attachment characterized as "insecure," which can create problems in their own future lives as parents.

There can be little doubt that the adults who describe their early experiences in this book had many varieties of disruption from their primary caregivers.

Whenever opportunity presented itself, however, most of the children described here were able to reattach themselves to a new caregiver, and for some (such as Anita, Sophie, and Marcel, for example) to form a satisfactory attachment that lasted for the rest of their lives, even when one or even both parents survived. Contrary to what might be supposed, there is nothing wrong in having multiple (satisfactory) attachments—the literature confirming the protective qualities of this situation is now of long standing and began to assuage the guilt of working mothers as long ago as the 1960s. It is when children are exposed to multiple caretakers *without* first establishing a good, secure attachment that, although they may appear to be relatively indifferent to changes of primary caregiver, they are in fact quite indiscriminate in their relationships, seeking affection and nurturance from anyone who appears—the archetype of the very institutionalized child.

Without very careful management, and often despite this, such children often have significant behavioral problems and difficulty in making and sustaining relationships in later life. Problems in prioritizing the needs of their own infants and young children, and establishing appropriate affectional relationships with others are explicable, then, in disrupted, dismissive attachments in their own early lives.

Although the real camera lens, as well as the metaphorical, retrospective one, can be deceptive, it is interesting now to look back at some of the early pictures, both photographic and in words, of this group of Hidden Children.

Their photographs as small children show them to be well cared for. They appear confident, lively, and outgoing.

The expression on the face of the merry little boy hopping over the fence (see illustration, Janek) conveys the confidence derived from his early loving relationships.

Remarkably, even the isolation of his years in solitary confinement did not destroy his spirit. Something very powerful must have sustained him. As we saw earlier, the fact that most of these children, Janek included, happened to find themselves in their predicament in the latency period (see Chapter 2) was probably a significant piece of the resilience jigsaw puzzle.

Photographed during the hiding period we see another appealing and lively little boy, Marcel, clearly thriving in his new and rather unusual household, despite early deportation of his father and his mother's mental illness. Of course, on the whole, attachment works both ways; attractive children with easy temperaments are more appealing to caretakers.

But in the end, although we can speculate about the intrinsic features of the children themselves, the most plausible explanations seem to lie in their early start in life and in the security of their attachments to their parents, which enabled them to withstand the deprivations of the next few years, as well as their own personalities and inherited characteristics.

Surviving children who initially criticized their parents for having parted with them, believing that they did not care, have come to appreciate the courage and pain involved (Dwork, 1991).

Jane Marks (1994) quotes such a revelation at a workshop for Hidden Children: "Don't you believe it, your mother *was* maternal—she saved your life!"

And when Irena was young and learned of her origins, it took years before she could see her mother's parting with her for the painful sacrifice it was.

Robert Frank,[4] separated abruptly from his parents and siblings in Angoulême, suffered terribly from what he saw for many years as abandonment. In fact it was one of the situations described by Lawrence Langer (1991) as "choiceless choices."

ISOLATION AND SENSORY DEPRIVATION

The subject of isolated, abandoned, feral children found in forests, sometimes alleged to have been nurtured by wild animals, has continued to excite interest, from the tale of Romulus and Remus, Kaspar Hauser, the "Wild boy of Aveyron" described by Itard, "Genie," and others. In the psychological literature, however, one of the best known examples of concealed children is that of twins first described and followed up by Koluchová (1991).[5] The extraordinary ill treatment of these twins and the condition in which they were found, severely retarded physically, verbally, and intellectually, were believed to herald irreparable damage. The process of their care and outcome, followed over twenty years after their rescue, makes for fascinating reading. This has allowed a somewhat optimistic reappraisal of extreme isolation effects in children (Clarke and Clarke, 2000).

Those children were probably preverbal when they were concealed, so the "catch-up" in their verbal ability was remarkable and has challenged the debate about critical developmental periods.

However, this does not imply that concealing children with little or no external stimulation is in any way beneficial.

The most extreme example of a comparable situation demonstrated in this book is that of Janek (Chapter 3). However, although he was hardly able to speak on his release, he had fortunately learned to read before his confinement in the locked room and was of an age when escape into fantasy was both possible and comforting.

Other Hidden Children, if not concealed with adults, have described various means of passing the time. Paul Valent (1994, 1998) and Ehud Loeb (2001) cite instances of children comforting themselves with transitional objects[6] or thoughts, memories, and fantasies of family life in the past and the hoped for life to come after the war.

NOTES

1. *Diamonds in the Snow,* 1994, a documentary film made by Dr. Mira Reym Binford, filmmaker and Holocaust survivor, is about three Hidden Children in Będzin, Poland, and explores ambivalence and "trying to make sense of a time that made no sense" (www.jewishfilm.com).

2. The Children Act 1989.

3. Nechama Tec, "Conflicts of Identity," *The Hidden Children Newsletter,* Fall/Winter 1997, 1.

4. Robert Frank, a French Hidden Child, now a dentist in Paris, whom I met too late to include in detail in this book, kindly provided me with the text of an earlier interview, recorded for the CDJC (*Centre Documentation Juive Contemporaine*) in 1993.

5. Twins, rejected by their stepmother, were isolated and enclosed in a cellar. Their physical and emotional and intellectual development was severely affected. Little improvement was expected. Skilled intervention including devoted foster care, described in the psychological literature over a twenty year follow up, resulted in remarkable recovery and integration.

6. Transitional object: one that "takes the place of" that from which the child is learning to separate, which the child associates with maternal comfort, for example a soft toy or a "comfort blanket." See also Winnicottt, *Transitional Phenomena*, 1953.

CHAPTER 9

❧

Understanding Resilience

On s'est toujours émerveillé devant ces enfants qui ont su triompher d'épreuves immenses et se faire une vie d'homme malgré tout. Le malheur n'est jamais pur, pas plus que le bonheur.
(We are always astonished by children who have overcome adversity, rebuilding their lives in spite of everything. Unhappiness is never complete, any more than happiness.)
—Boris Cyrulnik, *Un Merveilleux Malheur*, 1999

The concept of resilience as it applies to children has attracted increasing interest in the English-speaking world during the past few decades, less so in mainland Europe. Recently, however, the highly popular work of psychiatrist Boris Cyrulnik (1999, 2000) has brought the topic to professionals and the general public through writing and media exposure in France.

Interest in resilience has stemmed from attempts to understand stressful life events in children, repeatedly demonstrating strong links between such events and the risk of maladjustment and emotional disorders (Moskovitz and Krell, 2001). Early work focused on the relationship between resilience and the ability to withstand extremely adverse social, family, and educational disadvantage without delinquency. More recently this focus has also extended to the prevention or avoidance of depression and anxiety and resistance to or, better, coping with psychological injury following war and natural and man-made disasters. There is now an extremely large and complex scientific literature concerning the prevention of difficulties in later life following adverse events. Much of the literature relates to the capacity to overcome posttraumatic stress disorder in adults or adolescents rather than small children.

An appreciation of the concepts as well as the scope of the research evidence may be helpful in understanding and balancing positive or negative outcomes for children at risk. What follows is a brief, simplified overview of contemporary research.

RELEVANCE TO HIDDEN CHILDREN OF THE HOLOCAUST

One of the problems in discussing successful adaptation over a lifetime in Hidden Children involves the difficulty of applying scientific methods to a small group of individuals, but some broad principles merit consideration.

Comparisons of the experiences recounted in this book by the Hidden Children in Chapters 3 to 6, with large numbers of other self-reports and interviews—for example, in Dwork (1991), personal accounts in Hochberg-Mariańska and Grüss (1996), and Śliwowska (1998)—suggest some common themes.

The subject has been studied extensively by the distinguished child psychiatrist Michael Rutter:

> The related notion of "resilience," the term used to describe the positive pole . . . of individual difference in people's responses to stress and adversity. For many years the phenomenon had been put aside as largely inexplicable and therefore of little interest (Ainsworth, 1962). However, the issue of individual differences would not go away, and there came a growing appreciation that it was a key topic in risk research and that understanding the mechanisms involved should throw crucial light on the processes involved in risk itself, as well as having implications for prevention and intervention. (Rutter, 1990)

COMMON THEMES

Here we are considering positive adaptation in people who were children fifty or more years ago. To what extent can one extrapolate from what is known of resistance to adverse circumstances? The late twentieth and early twenty-first centuries are surely not comparable to the period when children in most European countries were to a greater or lesser extent affected by war. Jewish children, especially, were threatened, abused, and annihilated in vast numbers. The coping skills of the survivors, who reflect on their life experience in this book, apply to a period when personal trauma, poverty, and deprivation were overlaid by prevalent sociopolitical events (Krell, 2001). Such survivors may stimulate reflection, enabling us to follow a thread out of the labyrinth of misunderstanding and misconception of inevitable damage; they also allow us, perhaps, to consider that such positive survival may yet be possible and is probably more common than hitherto supposed (Hemmendinger and Krell 2000; Valent, 1998). Studying strength and achievement can also confirm that the outcome after an emotional insult is not inevitably or uniformly hopeless. The Remembering for the Future Holocaust 2000 Conference (Roth and Maxwell, 2001; Bluglass, 2001) encouraged the application of scholarship to other past, present, and future genocides.

Consequently, information or explanation about the non-inevitability of damage following severe childhood trauma may prevent universal pessimism in those who care for damaged children. Of course, most authors cited here focus on aspects of resilience in domestic and environmental hazards, not exposure to conditions in Europe in World War II.

Michael Rutter has also suggested that:

> resilience could not be thought of as an attribute born into children or even acquired during development. It is the indication of a process which characterizes a complex social system at a moment in time. . . . Resilience cannot be seen as anything other than a series of social and intrapsychic processes which take place across time given felicitous combinations of child attributes, family, social and cultural environments. In principle all the psychosocial processes which underpin healthy development may be involved. (Rutter 1990)

So while well-adjusted, successful, emotionally healthy survivors, enjoying reasonably healthy living, do not claim any "virtue" for their present state other than, possibly, chance and personality characteristics inherited from their own parents, we must not denigrate or marginalize other survivors who have been less fortunate. Their more troubled and difficult lives, their need for psychological support or interpersonal therapies, are not the result of lack of any effort of will, motivation, or moral fiber. They are just different, as are we all one from another.

Is "resilience" the right word anyway? It has come into our present usage from the study of physics, signifying "springiness"—the ability to reform after bending, stretching, or compression. It has come into the psychosocial vocabulary meaning a similar "springing back after severe stresses" (Valent, 1998). "Resistance to adversity" is a useful concept, although that might suggest an active process exercised from choice, carried out with will, deliberation, and intent and, thus, possibly imputing *relative* weakness to those who are less able to do so. That is not intended here.

It was not uncommon for camp survivors to encounter praise for the bravery of those who came out alive, sometimes imputing lack of will, initiative, or courage to those who had succumbed.

Worse, survivors were sometimes assumed to have acted at the expense of others in order to stay alive (Des Pres, 1976).

Yet many acknowledge that survival in such conditions depended on many factors, often chance or luck.

The variability of factors, circumstances, inconsistencies, and enigmas surrounding the characteristics of children or other "well-adjusted" survivors may be similar: a jigsaw puzzle or amalgam of events, inherited genetic characteristics, a conjunction of favorable (or relatively less unfavorable) circumstances. Lest this view seem negative, dismissive, or over simplistic, we should remind ourselves of the positive value of learning optimistic lessons from the past to illuminate the detail of some of the dark corners of our history.

Of those favorable or less unfavorable circumstances referred to above, George Vaillant (1993) suggests:

- Cognitive strategies
- Attributional style
- Temperament
- Social supports
- Ability to internalize social supports
- Psychosocial maturity
- Hope and faith
- Social attractiveness
- Ego mechanisms of defense
- Absence of risk factors and presence of protective factors
- Luck, timing, and/or context
- Self-esteem and self-efficacy

To the "strategies" in the previous list one should add "intellectual abilities," as this almost always features in resilience.

The above list includes "defense mechanisms." Vaillant's attribution of resilience in successful adults to the existence of "mature defense mechanisms" is an attractive and persuasive way of understanding their resilience following difficult childhood experiences (Vaillant, 1993).

Defense mechanisms were described by Sigmund Freud as a means of understanding or explaining human behavior in response to personal conflicts. In traditional psychoanalytical work they are challenged and confronted and, if not actually relinquished, the individual is expected to become at least insightful, less in conflict with himself or herself and significant others. Some of these mechanisms are perfectly normal ways of functioning at certain developmental stages but may be counterproductive or even pathological at others.

Mature coping mechanisms are common in healthy individuals between the ages of twelve to ninety and include:

- *Altruism*: vicarious but constructive and productive service to others.
- *Humor*: overt expression of ideas and feelings without individual discomfort and without unpleasant effect upon others.
- *Suppression*: the conscious or semiconscious decision to postpone paying attention to a conscious impulse or conflict.
- *Sublimation:* indirect or attenuated expression of instincts without either adverse consequences or marked loss of pleasure.

It is the "mature defenses" that concern us here as we consider adjustment in the group of former Hidden Children discussed in this book. As Vaillant says:

> Defenses are healthy. However disordered, sick, sinful, or unreasonable defenses may appear to the observer, they reflect an adaptive response and an intact working brain. By themselves defenses are not evidence of illness. As in the case of immune mechanisms, however maladaptive the results, defenses are deployed in the service of coping. The distinction between "defending" and "coping" are quite as arbitrary as the distinction between the unhealthy pus of acne and the healthy ingestion by our white corpuscles of intruding bacteria. The situations that call forth defenses and those which call forth white corpuscles are perilous; we cope as best we can. The distinction between adaptive and maladaptive is often in the eyes of the beholder. (Vaillant, 1993)

Vaillant advocates demonstrating the "wisdom of the ego" in those successfully overcoming adversity by trying to use biography to demonstrate that defenses reflect health and creativity and not illness, by the use of vignettes from the lives of potentially disadvantaged people. He points out that longitudinal studies of normal adult development showed that defenses are as important to well-being as immune mechanisms; that human creativity that transmits pain can also restore the self; and that as the physical body grows during childhood, the human ego is capable of maturation during adulthood.

While defenses can be viewed as compromise, some writers see resilience as a balance sheet of relative absence of *risk factors* and the relative presence of *protective factors*.

In other words, if the "load" of disadvantage and deprivation is too heavy, hardly any child will succeed. But with a balance of positive circumstances, few fail completely.

These circumstances include good intellectual ability, attractive appearance, and easy temperament. One can see how important these attributes would have been in bonding Hidden Children to their new caregivers.

Rutter (1990) has cautioned, however, that it is not a matter of a simple equation, that if some succumb to the "sum of accumulated risk factors minus the sum of accumulated positive experiences . . . it appears inadequate to account for the phenomena."

More recently Rutter has favored the notion of interactive *processes* rather than *factors* in the lives of resilient people.

Paul Valent has reviewed the relevant literature in detail, adding reflections based on his own experience and group work with child survivors. Importantly, he examines the evidence from a developmental as well as a historical perspective. Thus, the way in which a child conceptualizes and responds to adversity is mediated by his or her developmental stage and capacity for understanding, thinking, and behaving:

> Early notions that to have survived the Holocaust showed tremendous resilience, and to have done well showed that at least some humans could take anything, were parallel to early notions of invulnerability (Anthony and Koupernik, 1974). To some extent, as Wolff (1995) suggested, this was wishful thinking. On the whole, bad things produce bad effects, and child survivors of the Holocaust on the whole did worse than the general population . . . outward appearances may well conceal inner unhappiness and vulnerabilities which may come of age even after many decades. (Valent, 1998)

He emphasizes the complexity of interacting vulnerability and resilience, the relative weights of these depending on the prevailing circumstances, modifying the adaptive child's response, such as passive compliance or assertiveness.

> And while cutting off emotions and memories was adaptive . . . later it was their processing which was adaptive . . . resilience was not a simple concept like a tennis ball springing back, but like vulnerability it was part of a complex system. Although a simplified image, perhaps humans may be more realistically pictured as complex balloons with biological, psychological and social features . . . affected by life stresses. When the stresses are over, the balloon may spring back to its previous shape, and may even be "steeled" or be springier next time. On the other hand, it may be worn thin and more vulnerable or "sensitized" by the experience. Traumas puncture the balloon. The leak may be dealt with by patching the leak, creating knots in the balloon, or standing on the puncture. Multiple distensions, compressions, knots and patches are the result of complex traumas. (Valent, 1998)

He compared these "worn parts" around damaged or weakened areas of the balloon to the vulnerability of the survivor, resilience being the springiness that allows repair and disentangling of long hidden knots of earlier traumas and vulnerabilities accomplished through new insight and understanding.

   Resilient children generally are known to be bright, competent, and to have high self-esteem. Surviving children had to readjust earlier coping mechanisms to understand, reframe, and reconcile their past responses to themselves and others in the postwar context.

   Children who coped positively have also shown how traumatic situations may foster creativity and how they come to think about identity and meaning, which includes trying to make sense of past trauma and prevent others from future suffering. Professionals who work with vulnerable children echo Valent's admiration of the personal and psychological success of persecuted children.

> That many fell by the way is also the nature of vulnerability of the human condition in the face of trauma. But that it could be done at all, and that the majority struggled toward it, is a reflection of human resilience.

We may learn lessons from the past for the prevention of trauma in the future in today's genocides But one should not take apparent absence of trauma at face value, either. Preventive work, exploring a child's feelings to minimize isolation, and the provision of appropriate "attachment figures" are vital. Valent urges professionals to use the knowledge gained from children's responses to adversity to plan active intervention for children at future risk.

   Thus, knowledge derived from resilient child survivors may be used to help children in current conflicts.

   These sentiments were similarly articulated by Peter Fonagy:[1]

> It is striking that although resilience must be specific to particular circumstances which may seem to have little in common (economic deprivation, parental divorce, nuclear disasters, maltreatment, forest fires, parental delinquency or psychopathology, institutionalization), the indicators of resilience which emerge from the studies have a reassuring predictability about them.
>
> In the current social and economic climate, it is hard to envisage a mental health service with the capacity to meet the demand for help (let alone the underlying need) at the same time as being equitable, accessible and acceptable to all those who need it. The current interest in resilient children is part of a shift of focus to primary prevention, driven by economic necessity as well as by desire for social justice. (Fonagy, 1994)

Resilience, Fonagy believes, is normal development under difficult conditions. Studying, as he does, the quality of attachment in infancy, he also notes the current evidence for the prognostic nature of security in the first two years predicting many of the attributes in preschool and subsequent stages of development, characteristic of a resilient child.

In other words, children who are securely attached to their parents are less vulnerable to the effects of separation and deprivation. He also reminds us of the work of Donald Winnicott (1965) on the benefits of fantasy in childhood, that phase of development "when feelings, thoughts and objects may be played with and when pretend worlds may be created and inhabited. The capacity to suspend the demands of immediate physical reality and contemplate alternative perceptions yet retaining the distinction between what is fantasized and what is real must offer a tremendous advantage to the individual in dealing with life's adversities."

This is precisely what is described by many children in hiding (Dwork, 1991) and, in particular, by Janek in his "solitary confinement" (Chapter 3).

Sula Wolff, also a distinguished child psychiatrist, in "The Concept of Resilience" (1995), highlighted the complexity of psychopathology in possible prevention and maintaining therapeutic optimism. She reviewed definitions of resilience, the nature of risk factors, and the processes that modify them. She too makes a strong case for exploring resilience so as to maximize it in the face of adversity and stress, social and economic deprivation, family discord, divorce, and maternal depression. As she remarks, the current focus might be "a self-comforting device, because the consequences of childhood adversity can be so devastating. And moreover, many of the features of resilient children such as high intelligence seem to be largely God-given, hardly open to intervention."

Notions of resilience and vulnerability, risk, and protective factors indicate the complexity of psychiatric disorders and their causes:

> The need to go beyond simple associations between antecedents and consequences, always (looking for) exceptions to the rule.
>
> The discovery of why some children in adversity nevertheless do well helps to identify previously undetected possibilities for preventive action. The idea of resilience keeps hope alive in clinical practice: however much the dice are loaded against a good outcome, we know that many children escape their ill fate and that a remote possibility for the individual child may well succeed. (Wolff, 1995)

She favors the wider definition of Masten et al. (1988), that is, resilience as *the process of, capacity for, or outcome of successful adaptation despite challenging or threatening circumstances.*

As suggested earlier, an easy temperament evoking maternal affection in early life is favorable to resilient children. Smaller families and later family disruption allow them to form closer bonds to primary caregivers.

Some of the circumstances of Hidden Children who consider themselves to be resilient, enjoying a good quality of emotional and social life, apply here, for example, their secure early attachments in small nuclear families.

Given such limited numbers of survivors described here, even with numerous examples quoted in *The Children Accuse* (Hochberg-Mariańska, and Grüss, 1996) and Śliwowska, *The Last Eye Witnesses* (1998), collections of personal accounts of children surviving in Poland, many with very good outcomes), we do not really know enough about these people in depth. It is difficult to "cherry pick" attributes and circumstances applicable to all in this sample.

Wolff (ibid.), quoting from a study by Felsman and Vaillant (1987), observes the influence of political and socioeconomic climate. She comments, "Young men from a deprived and delinquent background attempting to make their way in the present world are much less fortunate than the vulnerable group in the study who benefited from education and training in the Army." She points out that the evolution of most delinquent teenagers during times of full employment into responsible adults contrasts with studies of delinquency during periods of unemployment. Thus, variations of social and economic circumstances from decade to decade do to some extent influence outcome. "The notion of resilience has opened many doors to effective public action . . . for clinicians it is vital to know that, however ominous the prognosis for an individual child, escape into health is an ever present possibility" (Wolff, ibid.).

SUMMARY

In summary, what are we to make of "resilience" as it applies to some Hidden Children? As scholars of the Holocaust and many survivors themselves are aware, we do not know the proportions of those people who have survived well and those who are struggling. As long ago as 1984 Gaby Glassman, reviewing the literature, noted serious flaws in the early studies of the Second Generation. She too urged balanced recognition of adaptation and resilience as opposed to assumptions of pathology (Glassman, 1984).

Of course, some survivors have indeed required psychological help over time (Bloomfield, 1997), and not all of those who might benefit from intervention request it. Possibly some of the most damaged suffer in silence.[2] Yet others, like those described in this book, function well and have managed to integrate their life experiences into their present-day lives—not always easily, not without pain, but effectively.

In the final section of this book I will reflect on the accounts of individuals of their wartime and postwar late-twentieth century lives in the light of the "mature" defense mechanisms described by George Vaillant. To what extent do any or all of these coping mechanisms figure in their lives? Can we now begin to discuss shared characteristics and better understand how they have mastered adversity?

In his lecture "Genocidal Mentalities,"[3] Professor Ian Kershaw acknowledged that the prognosis for the future in terms of repeated genocides is a gloomy one. Yet only now are we beginning to learn, half a century after the end of World War II, that despite the efforts of those with "genocidal mentalities" Hidden Children "surviving well" can give us cause for some cautious optimism for themselves and for children in other contemporary sources of conflict. This should not, however, be interpreted as a license to dismiss the real needs of children and to assume that, because some overcome adversity remarkably well, we can ignore the risks and dangers.

> *The meaning of things is not in things themselves,*
> *but in our attitudes to them.*
>
> —Antoine de St. Exupéry

NOTES

1. The Emanuel Miller Memorial Lecture was given by Professor Peter Fonagy in 1992 and published in 1994.

2. P. Valent, personal communication with author, January 2002.

3. "Genocidal Mentalities," the Inaugural Lecture at the Remembering for the Future Conference, London, January 2002.

Conclusion

As we saw in the earlier overview of contemporary resilience research, one explanation for surviving well may be in the use of mature-coping psychological defenses. Vaillant lists, for instance, humor, altruism, suppression, and sublimation, and the reader may see numerous examples in the surviving Hidden Children's reflections on their lives in Chapters 3 through 6.

A sense of humor, wit, and high intelligence are evident on meeting them. The capacity to find humor in past and present events is perhaps among the most important keys to living positively. A great deal of what they had to tell me about their past was sad, solemn, and tragic, and they did not dismiss or deny these aspects nor avoid the emotions they evoked.

Altruism can take many forms. Many successful survivors have become educators, doctors, therapists, and social workers. Although some writers such as Langer (1991) dispute the possibility of finding any meaning after the Holocaust, some survivors do cite it as a powerful driving force. For others, helping and healing may be a practical contribution to *tikkun olam* (healing the world).

Suppression or sublimation is self-explanatory; the key is in the proportionality. The capacity to live well, with mature coping mechanisms despite repeated adversity, demonstrates their use, even as adults, of these patterns suggested by Vaillant, in measures neither too much, too little, but "just right."

Although necessarily abridged for publication, these conversations are as complete and representative of each individual as possible.

As an objective observer, a clinician who works with sick and damaged people, I have to reiterate, however, that although they may have their daily ups and downs like most people, the survivors who talked to me are most emphatically not clinical cases.

Those included here are but a handful of a very much larger number of resilient Hidden Children I have encountered, and it is encouraging to find that there are many others. Some are still evolving personally. The opportunities provided by the 1991 reunion in New York, the solidarity derived from group discussions in Europe, the United States, Canada, Australia, Israel, and elsewhere have opened the door for more and more who felt for so long unheard and marginalized.

They have been able to leave their cellars, cupboards, and other metaphorical hiding places and to recover their voices. As Nicole David says, there is a "certain urgency" for them to do so. Fortunately, they are mostly in good health, but it is still timely to record their optimistic reflections for the future. It is also a reminder of the need for the best quality of care for all children at risk, while still also believing in their innately positive abilities.

THE LIVES OF HIDDEN CHILDREN

From their firsthand description of various forms of hiding, dislocation, fear, and privation and disguised under the cover of false identities, we have the chance to enter partially into their young lives. The impact of war and genocide on the lives of hunted children cannot be dismissed. The fact that this small number who have shared their experiences with me are able to enjoy the present with such zest is still surprising and humbling to the onlooker.

The reader can appreciate the litany of adverse experiences described: separation, loss, poverty and malnutrition, loyalty and ambivalence, but also recognition of selfless care and concern from most rescuers.

To all those Hidden Children who were willing to talk patiently to me over several years, answer questions, check details, and lend me precious photographs and documents, I give my very grateful thanks. Listening to them and learning from them has been a personally enriching experience and a great privilege.

> It is perfectly true, as the philosophers say . . .
> "Life can only be understood by looking backwards, but they forget to add that it also has to be lived forwards."
> —Søren Kierkegaard, *Journals* (1843)

Appendix A: Sprich, Auch Du

SPRICH, AUCH DU

Sprich, auch du,
sprich als letzter,
sag deinen Spruch.

Sprich—
Doch scheide das Nein nicht vom Ja.
Gib deinem Spruch auch den Sinn:
gib ihm den Schatten.

Gib ihm Schatten genug,
gib ihm so viel
also du um dich verteilt weißt zwischen
Mittnacht und Mittag und Mittnacht.

Blicke umher:
sieh, wie's lebendig wird rings—
Beim Tode! Lebendig!
Wahr spricht wer Schatten spricht.

Nun aber schrumpft der Ort, wo du stehst:
Wohin jetzt, Schattenentblößter, wohin?
Steige. Taste empor.
Dünner wirst du, unkenntlicher, feiner.
Feiner: ein Faden
an dem er herabwill, der Stern:
um unten zu schwimmen, unten
wo er sich schimmern sieht: in der Dünung
wandernder Worte.

From the collection: *Von Schwelle zu Schwelle* (1955) © Paul Celan (1920–1970)

Appendix B: Rescuers

RESCUERS

CHILDREN	RESCUERS*
POLAND	
Irena Milewska (née Grasberg)	Tadeusz and Halina Paszkowski, Tamara Assorodobraj, Nina Assorodobraj-Kula.
Janek Weber	Ludwig and Aniela Nowak, Michal and Anna Wierzbicki and their children.
Wlodka Robertson (neé Blit)	The "courier" Vladka (Feigele Peltel- Miedkowska), now Vladka Meed, Michal Klepfisz, the ghetto fighter, Mrs. Stanislaw Dubiel and their adult children, Henryk, Stasiek, and Halina, Jan and Krystyna Serafin of Warsaw, The Serafin family of Fatiny village, The village of Wilcza Wólka, near Gruszec.
Janina Fischler-Martinho	Josef Fischler (her brother), The "Simple Man" of Olsza, a poor suburb of Kraków, Madame Henia Wiktor, a family friend.

*Some, but not all, of the rescuers of the Hidden Children cited here have been recognized by awards from Yad Vashem as Righteous among the Nations.

CHILDREN	RESCUERS

BELGIUM

Henry Birnbaum and Charlotte Weber (neé Birnbaum)	Joseph and Léonie Morand.
Nicole David (née Schneider)	Gaston and Josephine Champagne and their children, especially Paulette who later became a nun (Soeur Yvan Marie).
Lea Pessok	Madame Maus.
Sophie Rechtman (née Granosc)	Monsieur and Madame Grassard.
Ruth Eisenfeld (née Hochhauser)	Madame Yvonne Verly, and Monsieur and Madame Secret and their daughter.

HOLLAND

Milly Horowitz (nee Steinberg)	Marie and Wim Hofstee.
Bert Woudstra	Pastor Leendert Overduijn, Dr. André and Mrs. Geertrui Noordenboos and their family, Mrs. Nel Huber and her family, Berend Miggels.
Anita Waisvisz	Hermina Hendrika Heinen and her family, of Aalten village.
Basia Bonnewit	Truus and Hermann van Oosten.

FRANCE

Marcel Ladenheim	Olga and Esther Masoli.
Bettine Le Beau (Michaels) (née Fallek)	"Tante Marthe" and "Tonton Abel" Marre.

Bibliography

Ainsworth, Mary D. "The Effects of Maternal Deprivation: A Review of Findings and Controversy in the Context of Research Strategy." In *Deprivation of Maternal Care: A Reassessment of Its Effects.* Geneva: World Health Organisation, 1962.

Anissimov, Myriam. *Primo Levi, ou la tragédie d'un Optimiste.* Paris: J. C. Lattès, 1996. Translated by Steve Cox. *Primo Levi, or the Tragedy of an Optimist.* New York: Woodstock, 1999.

Anthony, James E., and Cyril Koupernik, eds., *The Child in His Family Vol 111: Children at Psychiatric Risk.* New York: Wiley, 1974.

Armstrong, Diane. *The Voyage of Their Life: The Story of the SS Derna and Its Passengers.* Sydney, Australia: Flamingo/Harper Collins, 2001.

Ballard, James G. *The Empire of the Sun.* London: Flamingo, 1994.

Bastiaans, Jan. *Psychosomatische gevolgen van onderdrukking in verzet (Psycho-somatic Sequelae of Persecution and Resistance).* Amsterdam: Noord-Hollandsche Uitgevers Maatschappij, 1957.

Berghahn, Marion. *Continental Britons: German-Jewish Refugees from Nazi Germany.* Oxford, Hamburg, and New York: Berg, 1988.

Bergman, Martin S., and Milton E. Jucovy. *Generations of the Holocaust.* New York: Columbia University, 1982.

Bettelheim, Bruno. "Individual and Mass Behaviour in Extreme Situations." *Journal of Abnormal and Social Psychology* 38 (1943): 417–52.

———. *Surviving and Other Essays.* New York: Knopf, 1979.

Bloch, Gay, and Malka Drucker. *Rescuers: Portraits of Moral Courage in the Holocaust.* New York and London: Holmes and Meier, 1992.

Bloomfield, Irene. "Counselling Holocaust Survivors." *Counselling* 59 (February 1997): 42–47.

Bluglass, Kerry. "Surviving Well: Resistance to Adversity." In Vol. 3 of *Remembering for the Future: The Holocaust in an Age of Genocide,* edited by John

K. Roth and Elisabeth Maxwell, 47–62. Hampshire, England, and New York: Palgrave/Macmillan, 2001.

Bok, Sissela. *Lying: Moral Choice in Public and Private Life*. London, Melbourne, and New York: Quartet, 1980.

Bowlby, John. "Separation Anxiety: A Critical Review of the Literature." *Journal of Child Psychology and Psychiatry* (1960): 251–69.

Brown, George W., and Tyrrell Harris. *Social Origins of Depression*. New York: Free Press, 1978.

Brown, George W., Tyrrell Harris, and Antonia Bifulco. "Long-term Effects of Early Loss of Parent." In *Depression in Young People*, edited by M. Rutter et al., 251–98. New York: Guilford Press, 1986.

Brown, George W., Tyrrell Harris, and John Coupland. "Depression and Loss." *British Journal of Psychiatry* 130 (1977): 1–18.

Brown, Mike. *Evacuees*. Stroud: Sutton Publishing, 2000.

Cain, Larissa. *Une enfance au Ghetto de Varsovie*. Paris: Éditions L'Harmattan, 1997.

Celan, Paul. *Selected Poems: Twentieth Century Classics*. Translated by Michael Hamburger. Anvil Press Poetry, 1988; rev. ed. 1995; London: Penguin, 1990, 1996.

Charny, Israel W., ed. *Encyclopedia of Genocide*, 3 vols. Santa Barbara, Calif., Denver, and Oxford, England: ABC Clio, Inc., 1999.

Chevalier, Tracy. *Girl with a Pearl Earring*. London: Harper Collins, 2000.

The Children Act 1989. Her Majesty's Stationery Office, London, 1989.

Clarke, Ann M., and Allan D. B. Clarke. *Early Experience and the Life Path*. London and Philadelphia: Jessica Kingsley, 2000.

Cohen, Maurits. "My War Began in 1945." In *Children with a Star: Jewish Youth in Nazi Europe*. New Haven and London: Yale University Press, 1991.

Cyrulnik, Boris. *Un merveilleux malheur*. Paris: Editions Odile Jacob, 1999.

———. *Les Vilains petits canards*. Paris: Editions Odile Jacob, 2000.

David, Janina. *A Square of Sky/A Touch of Earth: A Wartime Childhood in Poland*. New York: Penguin, 1981

Davidson, Shamai. "The Treatment of Holocaust Survivors." In *Spheres of Psychotherapeutic Activity*, edited by Shamai Davidson. Jerusalem: Medical Department, Kupat Cholim Center, 1972.

de Mause, Lloyd, ed. *The History of Childhood*. London: Souvenir Press, 1974, 1976.

Des Pres, Terrence. *The Survivor*. New York: Oxford University Press, 1976.

Dwork, Debórah. *Children with a Star: Jewish Youth in Nazi Europe*. New Haven and London: Yale University Press, 1991.

Eitinger, Leo. "Concentration Camp Survivors in the Postwar World." *American Journal of Orthopsychiatry* 32 (1961): 367–75.

Eitinger, Leo, and Robert Krell. *The Psychological and Medical Effects of Concentration Camps on Survivors of the Holocaust: A Research Bibliography*. Vancouver: University of British Columbia Press, 1985.

Epstein, Helen. *Children of the Holocaust*. New York: Penguin, 1988.

Faris, David. "Narrative Form and Oral History: Some Problems and Possibilities." *International Journal of History* 1 (November 1980): 159–70.

Felsman, J. K., and George E. Vaillant. "Resilient Children as Adults." In *The Invulnerable Child*, edited by E. J. Anthony and B. T. Kohler. New York: Guilford, 1987.

Fischler-Martinho, Janina. *Have You Seen My Little Sister?* London: Valentine Mitchell, 1998.

Fogelman, Eva. "A Bibliography: Psychosocial Impact of the Holocaust on Second Generation of Survivors." In *Children of the Holocaust*, edited by Helen Epstein. New York: Penguin, 1988.

Fogelman, Eva, and Bela Savran. "Brief Group Therapy with Offspring of Holocaust Survivors: Leaders' Reactions." *American Journal of Orthopsychiatry* 50 (1) (1980): 96–108.

Fonagy, Peter, M. Steele, H. Steele, A. Higgett, and M. Target. "The Theory and Practice of Resilience." *Journal of Child Psychology and Psychiatry* 35 (2) (1994): 231–57. (The Emanuel Miller Memorial Lecture, 1992.)

Ford, Charles. *Lies, Lies, Lies!!!: The Psychology of Deceit*. Washington, D.C., and London, England: American Psychiatric Press, Inc., 1996.

Frank, Anne. *The Diary of Anne Frank*. The Critical Edition, prepared by the Netherlands State Institute for War Documentation; English translation by A. J. Pomerans. First published in the USA by Doubleday, New York, and in Great Britain by Viking, London, 1989.

Frankl, Viktor E. *Man's Search for Meaning: An Introduction to Logotherapy*. New York: Washington Square Press, 1989.

Freud, Anna, and Sophie Dann. "An Experiment in Group Upbringing." In *Psychoanalytic Study of the Child*, edited by R. Eissler, 1945–79, 6: 12–69, 1951.

Gies, Miep. *Anne Frank Remembered: The Story of the Woman Who Helped to Hide the Frank Family*. New York: Simon and Schuster, 1987.

Gilbert, Martin. *The Holocaust: The Jewish Tragedy*. London: Fontana/Collins, 1987.

———. *The Boys: Triumph over Adversity*. London: Phoenix, 1997.

———. *Holocaust Journey: Travelling in Search of the Past*. London: Phoenix, 1998.

———. *The Righteous: The Unsung Heroes of the Holocaust*. New York: Henry Holt, 2003.

Gill, Anton. *The Journey Back from Hell: Conversations with Concentration Camp Survivors*. London: Grafton, 1988.

Glassman, Gaby. "The Child of Survivors." Master's thesis, University of Amsterdam, 1984.

Greenspan, Henry. *On Listening to Holocaust Survivors: Recounting and Life History*. Westport, Conn.: Praeger, 1998.

Harrington, Richard, and Lucy Harrison. "Unproven Assumptions about the Impact of Bereavement on Children." *Journal of the Royal Society of Medicine* 92 (1999): 230–33.

Hass, Aaron. *Aftermath: Living with the Holocaust*. Cambridge: Cambridge University Press, 1995.

Hassan, Judith. "The Survivor as Witness." In *Remembering for the Future* (Conference Proceedings), edited by Yehuda Bauer, 1093–95. Oxford: Pergamon, 1989.

Hemmendinger, Judith, and Robert Krell. *The Children of Buchenwald; Child Survivors of The Holocaust and Their Post-War Lives*. Jerusalem: Gefen, 2000.

Hilberg, Raoul. *The Destruction of the European Jews*. 3 vols. New York: Holmes and Meier, 1985.

Hochberg-Mariańska, Maria, and Noe Grüss. *The Children Accuse*. London: Valentine Mitchell, 1996.

Hoffman, Eva. *Shtetl: The History of a Small Town in a Vanished World*. London: Vintage, 1999.

Humphreys, Margaret. *Empty Cradles*. London: Doubleday, 1994.

The Irving Judgment. *David Irving v. Penguin Books and Professor Deborah Lipstadt*. London: Penguin Books, 2000.

Karpf, Anne. *The War After*. London: Heinemann, 1996.

Karski, Jan. *Story of a Secret State*. Boston: Houghton Mifflin, 1944.

Keilson, Hans. *Sequentielle Traumatisierung bei Kindern*. Stuttgart: Ferdinand Enke, 1979. (*Sequential Traumatisation of Children*. Jerusalem: The Magnes Press, 1979.)

Kestenberg, Judith S., and Ira Brenner. *The Last Witness: The Child Survivor of the Holocaust*. Washington, D.C.: American Psychiatric Press, 1996.

Kestenberg, Milton. In *Generations of the Holocaust*, edited by Martin S. Bergmann and Milton E. Jucovy. New York: Columbia University Press, 1982.

Kisker, Karl P. "Die Psychiatrische Begutachtung der Opfer Nationalsozialistischer Verfolgung." In *Psychiatria et Neurologia*. Dresden: Geselloch, 1961.

Klarsfeld, Serge. *Memorial to the Jews Deported from France, 1942–1944*. Documentation of the deportation of the victims of the Final Solution in France. New York: The Beate Klarsfeld Foundation, 1983.

Koluchová, Jarmila. "Severely Deprived Twins after 22 Years' Observation." *Studia Psychologica* 33 (1991): 23–28.

Kolvin, Israel, Frederick Miller, Michael Fleeting, and Philip Kolvin. "Risk/Protective Factors for Offending with Particular Reference to Deprivation." In *Studies of Psychosocial Risk*, edited by Michael Rutter, 77–95. Cambridge: Cambridge University Press, 1988.

Krell, Robert. "Therapeutic Value of Documenting Child Survivors." *Journal of the American Academy of Child Psychiatry* 24 (4) (1985): 397–400.

———. "The Mystery and Dignity of Very Young Survivors." In *The Hidden Child Newsletter*. New York: The Hidden Child Foundation/ADL (winter 1998/1999): 1, 7.

Krell, Robert, ed. *Messages and Memories: Reflections on Child Survivors of the Holocaust*. 2nd ed. Vancouver: Memory Press, 2001. Distributed by B. Shert Ltd 6435 West Blvd, Vancouver BCM 3 K6, Canada.

Krell, Robert, and Marc Sherman, eds. *Medical and Psychological Effects of Concentration Camps on Holocaust Survivors; Genocide: A Critical Bibliographic Review*, vol. 4. New Brunswick: Transaction Publishers, 1997.

Krystal, Henry, ed. *Massive Psychic Trauma*. New York: International Universities Press, 1968.

Kushner, Harold S. *When Bad Things Happen to Good People*, Twentieth Anniversary ed. New York: Schocken Books, 2001.

Langer, Lawrence L. *Holocaust Testimonies: The Ruins of Memory*. New Haven: Yale University Press, 1991.

Leapman, Michael. *Witnesses to War*. London: Penguin, 1998.

Levi, Primo. *If This Be a Man*. London: Penguin, 1979.

Lipstadt, Deborah. *Denying the Holocaust: The Growing Assault on Truth and Memory*. London: Penguin, 1994.

Loeb, Ehud. "Expressing Childhood Experience: A Writing Workshop." In Vol. 3 of *Remembering for the Future: The Holocaust in an Age of Genocide,* edited by John Roth and Elisabeth Maxwell, 150–66. London: Palgrave/ Macmillan Reference, 2001.

Marks, Jane. *The Hidden Children: Secret Survivors of the Holocaust*. London: Piatkus, 1994.

Masten, Ann S., N. Garmezy, A. Tellegen, D. S. Pellegrini, K. Carlin, and A. Larsen. "Competence and Stress in Schoolchildren: The Modifying Effects of Individual and Family Qualities." *Journal of Child Psychology and Psychiatry* 29 (1988): 745–64.

Meed, Vladka. *On Both Sides of the Wall: Memoirs from the Warsaw Ghetto*. Translated from the Polish by Dr. Steven Meed. New York: Holocaust Library, 1987.

Minty, Brian. "Annotation: Outcomes in Long-term Foster Family Care." *Journal of Child Psychology and Child Psychiatry* 40 (1999): 991–99.

Montaigne, Michel de. *The Complete Essays*. Translated by M. A. Screech. London: Penguin, 1993.

Moskovitz, S., and R. Krell. "The Struggle for Justice: A Survey of Child Holocaust Survivors' Experience with Restitution." In Vol. 2 of *Remembering for the Future: The Holocaust in an Age of Genocide,* edited by John K. Roth and Elisabeth Maxwell, 923–65. Hampshire, England, and New York: Palgrave/Macmillan, 2001.

Moskovitz, Sarah. *Love Despite Hate*. New York: Schocken Books, 1988.

———. "Barriers to Gratitude." In Vol. 2 of *Remembering for The Future* (Conference Proceedings), edited by Yehuda Bauer, 494–505. Oxford: Pergamon, 1989.

Oliner, Samuel, and Pearl Oliner. *The Altruistic Personality: Rescuers of Jews in Nazi Europe*. New York: Free Press, 1988.

Paldiel, Mordecai. "The Altruism of the Righteous Gentiles." In *Remembering for the Future: The Holocaust in an Age of Genocide,* edited by Yehuda Bauer et al. Oxford: Pergamon, 1989.

Parker, Tony. *The Frying Pan: A Prison and Its Prisoners*. London: Hutchinson, 1970.

————. *The People of Providence: A Housing Estate and Some of Its Inhabitants.* London: Hutchinson, 1983.

Parkes, Colin M. *Bereavement: Studies of Grief in Adult Life.* London: Penguin, 1972.

Perks, Robert, and Alistair Thompson. *The Oral History Reader.* London: Routledge, 1998.

Porter, Jack N. "Social Psychological Aspects of the Holocaust." In *Encountering the Holocaust,* edited by B. L. Sherwin and G. S. Ament, 189–222. Chicago: Impact Press, 1979.

Rakoff, Vivian. "Children and Families of Concentration Camp Survivors." *Canada's Mental Health* 14 (1969): 24–26.

Reicher, Edward. *Une vie de juif: L'odyssée d'un médecin juif en Pologne.* Translated from the Polish by Jacques Greif and Élisabeth Bizouard Reicher. Paris: Éditions L'Harmattan, 1996.

Ribière, Germaine. *L'affaire Finaly: Ce que j'ai vécu.* Paris: Centre de Documentation Juive Contemporaine, 1998.

Ringelblum, Emmanuel. *Notes from the Warsaw Ghetto: The Journal of Emmanuel Ringelblum.* Edited and translated from the Polish by Jacob Sloan. New York: Schocken Books, 1974.

Robinson, Shalom. "Late Effects of Persecution in Persons Who as Children or Young Adolescents Survived Nazi Occupation in Europe." *Israel Annals of Psychiatry and Related Disciplines* 17 (3) (1979): 209–14.

Rosenthal, Jack. *The Evacuees.* Television drama. Producer Mark Shivas/Director Alan Parker. *Period Drama: Evacuation of Jewish Schoolboys to the Country in World War II,* BBC, 1975.

Roth, John K., and Elisabeth Maxwell, eds. *Remembering for the Future: The Holocaust in an Age of Genocide.* Hampshire, England, and New York: Palgrave/Macmillan, 2001.

Rutter, Michael. "Psychosocial Resilience and Protective Mechanisms." In *Risk and Protective Factors in the Development of Psychopathology,* edited by J. Rolf, A. S. Masten, D. Cicchetti, K. Nuechterlein, and S. Weintraub. Cambridge: Cambridge University Press, 1990.

Sigal, John J. "Second Generation Effects of Massive Trauma." *International Psychiatry Clinics* 8: 55–65. Reprinted in H. Krystal, and W. G., Niederland. *Psychic Traumatization.* Boston: Little and Brown, 1971.

————. "Hypotheses and Methodology in the Study of Families of Holocaust Survivors." In *The Child in His Family,* edited by James Anthony and Cyril Koupernik, 411–18. New York: Wiley, 1974.

Śliwowska, Wiktoria, ed. *The Last Eye-witnesses: Children of the Holocaust Speak.* Translated by J. Bussgang and F. Bussgang. Illinois: Northwestern University Press, 1998. (Originally published as *Dzieci Holocaustu Mowi.* Warsaw, Stowarzyszenie Dzieci Holocaustu w Polsce [Association of Children of the Holocaust in Poland], 1993.)

Smith, Stephen. "The Trajectory of Memory: Transgeneration and the Pitfalls of Narrative Closure." In Vol. 3 of *Remembering for the Future: The Holocaust in An Age of Genocide,* edited by John K. Roth and Elisabeth Maxwell, 437–

51. Hampshire, England, and New York: Palgrave/Macmillan, 2001.

Spitz, Réné. *The First Year of Life: The Psychoanalytic Study of Normal and Deviant Object Relations.* New York: International Universities Press, 1965.

Stille, Alexander. *Benevolence and Betrayal: Five Italian Jewish Families Under Fascism.* New York: Summit, 1991.

Terkel, Studs. *Hard Times: An Oral History of the Great Depression.* New York: Pantheon, 1970.

Trossman, Bernard. "Adolescent Children of Concentration Camp Survivors." *Canadian Psychiatric Journal* 12 (1968): 121–23.

Vaillant, George E. *The Wisdom of the Ego: Sources of Resilience in Adult Life.* Cambridge, Mass.: Harvard University Press, 1993.

Valent, Paul. *Child Survivors: Adults Living with Childhood Trauma.* Port Melbourne, Victoria: William Heinemann Australia, 1994.

———. "Resilience in Child Survivors of the Holocaust: Toward a Concept of Resilience." *Psychoanalytic Review* 85 (4) (1998): 517–35.

Vanderpol, Maurice. "Resilience: The Missing Link in Our Understanding of Survival." *Harvard Psychiatric Review* 10 (2002): 302–6.

Vegh, Claudine. *Je ne lui ai pas dit "Au revoir."* Paris: Éditions Gallimard, 1979. (English translation by E. P. Dutton, 1984.)

Wangh, Martin. *"Die Beurteilung von Wiedergutmachungsanspruchen der während der nationalsozialistischen Verfolgung geborenen Kinder."* In *Spätschäden nach Extrembelastungen,* 270–74. Herberg, 1971.

Wiesel, Elie. *Tous les Fleuves Vont a la Mer (All Rivers Run to the Sea: Memoirs).* New York: Knopf, 1995.

Wijsenbeek, Henricus. Lecture held at Netherlands-Israel Symposium on the impact of Persecution. Jerusalem. October, 1977.

Wilkomirski, Binjamin. *Fragments: Memories of a Childhood 1939–48.* Translated from the German by Carol Brown Janeway. New York: Schocken, 1996.

Winnicott, Donald W. "Transitional Objects and Transitional Phenomena." *International Journal of Psychoanalysis* 34 (1953): 89–97.

———. *The Maturational Process and the Facilitating Environment.* London: Hogarth Press, 1965.

Wolff, Sula. "The Concept of Resilience." *Australian and New Zealand Journal of Psychiatry* 29 (1995): 556–74.

Wolffheim, Nelly. *Psychoanalyse und Kindergarten und andere Arbeiten zur Kinderpsychologie.* Munich: Ernst Reinhardt, 1966.

Ziemian, Joseph. *The Cigarette Sellers of Three Crosses Square.* Translated from the Polish by Janina David. London: Valentine Mitchell, 1970.

Zucotti, Susan. *The Italians and the Holocaust: Persecution, Rescue and Survival.* New York: Basic Books, 1987.

———. *The Holocaust, the French and the Jews.* New York: Basic Books, 1993.

Index

About the Author

KERRY BLUGLASS is a Consultant Psychiatrist and Senior Clinical Lecturer in the Department of Psychiatry at the University of Birmingham, United Kingdom.